Time Out SHORTLIST

Cyprus

WHAT'S NEW | WHAT'S ON | WHAT'S BEST

www.timeout.com/cyprus

Contents

Don't Miss

Itineraries

Cyrus by Area

Essentials

Published by Time Out Guides Ltd
Universal House
251 Tottenham Court Road
London W1T 7AB
Tel: + 44 (0)20 7813 3000
Fax: + 44 (0)20 7813 6001
Email: guides@timeout.com
www.timeout.com

Managing Director Peter Fiennes
Editorial Director Ruth Jarvis
Business Manager Dan Allen
Editorial Manager Holly Pick
Assistant Management Accountant Ija Krasnikova

Time Out Guides is a wholly owned subsidiary of Time Out Group Ltd.

Chairman Tony Elliott
Chief Executive Officer David King
Group General Manager/Director Nichola Coulthard
Time Out Communications Ltd MD David Pepper
Time Out International Ltd MD Cathy Runciman
Time Out Magazine Ltd Publisher/Managing Director Mark Elliott
Production Director Mark Lamond
Group IT Director Simon Chappell
Marketing & Circulation Director Catherine Demajo

This edition first published in Great Britain in 2009 by Ebury Publishing
A Random House Group Company
Company information can be found on www.randomhouse.co.uk
Random House UK Limited Reg. No. 954009
10 9 8 7 6 5 4 3 2 1

Distributed in the US by Publishers Group West
Distributed in Canada by Publishers Group Canada

For further distribution details, see www.timeout.com

ISBN: 978-1-84670-094-1

A CIP catalogue record for this book is available from the British Library.

Printed and bound in Germany by Appl.

Cyprus Shortlist

The **Time Out Cyprus Shortlist 2009** is one of a new series of guides that draws on Time Out's background as a magazine publisher to keep you current with everything that's going on in your destination. As well as **Cyprus**'s key sights and the best of its eating, drinking and leisure options, it picks out the most exciting venues to have opened recently and gives a full calendar of annual events. It also includes features on the important news, trends and openings, all compiled by locally based editors and writers. Whether you're visiting for the first time in your life or the first time this year, you'll find the *Time Out Cyprus Shortlist* contains all you need to know, in a portable and easy-to-use format.

The guide divides Cyprus into seven areas (the five main towns and their environs, the Troodos Mountains and North Cyprus), each containing listings for Sights & Museums, Eating & Drinking, Shopping, Nightlife and Arts & Leisure, and maps pinpointing their locations. At the front of the book are chapters rounding up these scenes within the Republic of Cyprus, and giving a shortlist of our overall picks. We also include itineraries for days out, plus essentials such as transport information and hotels.

Our listings give phone numbers as dialled within Cyprus. From abroad, use your country's exit code followed by 357 (the country code for Cyprus) and the number given. To call North Cyprus, see the information in 'Resources A-Z'.

We have noted price categories by using one to four € signs (€-€€€€), representing budget, moderate, expensive and luxury. Major credit cards are accepted unless otherwise stated. We also indicate when a venue is NEW.

All our listings are double-checked, but places do sometimes close or change their hours or prices, so it's a good idea to call a venue before visiting. While every effort has been made to ensure accuracy, the publishers cannot accept responsibility for any errors that this guide may contain.

Venues are marked on the maps using symbols numbered according to their order within the chapter and colour-coded as follows:

- 1 Sights & Museums
- 1 Eating & Drinking
- 1 Shopping
- 1 Nightlife
- 1 Arts & Leisure

Map key

Major sight or landmark	
Railway station	
Park	
College/hospital	
Neighbourhood	PAFOS
Pedestrian street	
Main road	
Church	
Mosque	
Airport	

Time Out Cyprus Shortlist

EDITORIAL
Editor Natasha Polyviou
Copy Editor Tanya Sassoon, Elizabeth Winding
Proofreader Mandy Martinez

DESIGN
Art Director Scott Moore
Art Editor Pinelope Kourmouzoglou
Senior Designer Henry Elphick
Graphic Designers Kei Ishimaru,Nicola Wilson
Advertising Designer Jodi Sher

Picture Editor Jael Marschner
Deputy Picture Editor Lynn Chambers
Picture Researcher Gemma Walters
Picture Desk Assistant Marzena Zoladz
Picture Librarian Christina Theisen

ADVERTISING
Commercial Director Mark Phillips
International Advertising Manager Kasimir Berger
International Sales Executive Charlie Sokol
Advertising Sales (Cyprus) Georgia Toutouzian, Dias Media Group

MARKETING
Marketing Manager Yvonne Poon
Sales & Marketing Director, North America & Latin America Lisa Levinson
Senior Publishing Brand Manager Luthfa Begum
Marketing Designers Anthony Huggins

PRODUCTION
Production Manager Brendan McKeown
Production Controller Damian Bennett
Production Co-ordinator Kelly Fenlon

CONTRIBUTORS
This guide was researched and written by Nicos Andreou, Simon Bahceli, Rosemarie Malaos, Shona Muir, Theoni Panayi, Toby Pearce, Sophie Polyviou, Xenia Tsiamanta and the writers of *Time Out Cyprus for Visitors*. The editor would like to thank Simon Coppock, Guy Dimond, Alex Rhys-Taylor, Constantinos Sarkas and Cyrus Shahrad.

PHOTOGRAPHY
Photography: pages 7, 22, 27, 37, 38, 39, 41, 52, 53, 55, 56, 58, 60, 62, 64, 112, 113, 116, 117, 126, 130, 132, 133, 135, 136, 137, 138, 139, 140, 142, Louisa Nikolaidou; pages 8, 10, 49, 77, 79, 82, 85, 86, 89, 90, 91, 92, 93, 96, 148, 149, 152, 153, 155, 156, 157, 158, 160, 161 Duncan Cox; pages 11, 50, 73, 74, 78, 98, 109 George Ierodiakonou; page 12 Michalis Kyprianou; pages 15, 18, 45 Eirini Theodorou; page 28 Savas Demitriou; page 32 Cyprus Tourism Organisation; pages 36, 42, 43, 120 courtesy of Time Out Cyprus; page 59 Sotiroula Tsirponouri; page 95 Yannis Hatzigeorgiou; page 169 Michalis Michaelides; page 179 Androulla Christou.

The following images were provided by the featured establishments/artists: pages 23, 46, 47, 65, 68, 94, 107, 110, 119, 123, 145, 163, 164, 166, 167, 171, 172, 173, 176, 177, 178.

Cover image: chapel at the Anassa Hotel © Chris Parker/Axiom

MAPS
Maps by JS Graphics Ltd (john@jsgraphics.co.uk) based on material supplied by Netmaps, S.A.

About Time Out

Founded in 1968, Time Out has expanded from humble London beginnings into the leading resource for those wanting to know what's happening in the world's greatest cities. As well as our influential what's-on weeklies in London, New York and Chicago, we publish more than a dozen other listings magazines in cities as varied as Beijing and Mumbai. The magazines established Time Out's trademark style: sharp writing, informed reviewing and bang up-to-date inside knowledge of every scene.

Time Out made the natural leap into travel guides in the 1980s with the City Guide series, which now extends to over 50 destinations around the world. Written and researched by expert local writers and generously illustrated with original photography, the full-size guides cover a larger area than our Shortlist guides and include many more venue reviews, along with additional background features and a full set of maps.

Throughout this rapid growth, the company has remained proudly independent, still owned by Tony Elliott four decades after he started Time Out London as a single fold-out sheet of A5 paper. This independence extends to the editorial content of all our publications, this Shortlist included. No establishment has been featured because it has advertised, and no payment has influenced any of our reviews. And, for our critics, there's definitely no such thing as a free lunch: all restaurants and bars are visited and reviewed anonymously, and Time Out always picks up the bill.
For more about the company, see www.timeout.com.

Don't Miss

A mosaic at Kourion p111

WHAT'S BEST

Sights & Museums

History buffs will have a field day with Cyprus's abundance of ancient monuments, while those planning to visit just a handful of archaeological sites have a choice pick of classical remains. From the Tombs of the Kings (p117) and the Pafos mosaics in the west, to Ancient Kourion (p111) and Amathus (p109) around Lemesos, Larnaka's Choirokitia (p76) and Nicosia's astonishingly well-preserved 16th-century city walls, the island's past is evident at every turn. A host of archaeological and Byzantine museums with hordes of antiquities can be found in most towns, housing collections of pottery, statuary, coins, tools and weaponry.

Folkloric museums are another common theme, exploring everyday Cypriot life through the ages via displays of clothing and household items – examples can be found in the Folk Art Museums of Lemesos (p99) and Dherynia (p63), the Ethnographic Museums of Nicosia (p83) and Pafos (p116) and the Pilavakion Museum (p131). Larnaka and Lemesos both have medieval museums housed in the atmospheric setting of their seafront fort or castle.

More unusual repositories of exhibits include the Fatsa Wax Museum (p76), the Classic Motorcycle Museum (p82) and the Postal Museum (p85). In the villages of the Troodos mountains, tiny showrooms are often built around a single significant artefact, such as the Old Olive Mill (p144).

Unfortunately, the scars of the island's recent past are even more clear to see. Cyprus has been a divided country since the Turkish invasion of 1974, which came in response to a Greek-instigated coup. No country apart from Turkey recognises the occupied areas (as they are known in the Republic) as a legitimate state. Since Cyprus was admitted to the EU in 2004, the Turkish-Cypriot-termed Turkish Republic of North Cyprus (TRNC) is considered EU territory with a disputed foreign presence. Therefore, the *acquis communautaire* – the body of EU laws and regulations – does not apply there.

In both halves of the country, churches and mosques are scattered around towns made up of streets with a mixture of Greek and Turkish names – testament to a unified past that it is hoped regular reconciliation talks between the governments of both sides will restore.

Name games

Place names are more complicated than they need be in Cyprus. Once upon a time, Larnaka was the more aesthetically pleasing Larnaca, Pafos was Paphos and Lemesos was Limassol. The end result of a seemingly logical method of transliterating Greek names into English has resulted in traditional spellings, which have been used both locally and internationally for centuries, being thrown out of the window.

In this guide, we have included both versions of the most potentially head-scratching cases in order to reduce confusion (see Cape Greco/Kavo Gkreko). For the majority of places, though, we have gone with the new spelling, which will allow you to get your bearings when consulting street signs (Ayia Napa is now Agia Napa, for

SHORTLIST

Best for antiquities
- Cyprus Archaeological Museum (p83)

Top archaeological wonders
- Ancient Kourion (p111)
- Pafos Mosaics (p117)
- Ancient Salamis (p161)

Nature at its best
- Cape Greco (p55)
- Cedar Valley (p140)

Most unusual museums
- Classical Motorcycle Museum (p82)
- Natural Sea Sponge Exhibition Centre (p99)

Best Byzantine treasures
- Archbishop's Palace & Makarios III Cultural Foundation (p82)
- Panagia tou Araka (p144)

Regal castles
- Kolossi Castle (p11)
- Buffavento Castle (p154)

Best for panoramic views
- Agios Neophytos Monastery (p125)
- Bellapais Abbey (p157)

Most enchanting churches
- Panagia Forviotissa (Asinou) (p141)
- Agios Nikolaos tis Stegis (p141)

Best folk art collections
- Ethnographic Museum, Pafos (p116)
- Ethnographic Museum/ Pierides Foundation (p62)

Best for natural history buffs
- Museum of Marine Life (p52)
- Larnaka Municipal Museum of Natural History (p66)

Ancient Kourion p111

instance). The exception is the capital city. Although its official new name is Lefkosia (which you'll see on road signs), most people still use the old name, Nicosia, when referring to the town in English. As a result, we've stuck with the more commonly used Nicosia when referring to the capital in reviews.

Do bear in mind that other places have been transformed into utterly misguided versions of their former incarnations, even when they have Latin characters as their roots (skewing Goethe Street into Gkaite, Yuri Gagarin to Gioury Gkangarin and Shakespeare to the wincingly painful Saixpir, for example). The Cypriot government has never made an official statement to the international community about the changes, so while Bombay and Peking have smoothly made the transition to Mumbai and Beijing, visitors to Cyprus could find themselves booking a holiday to Limassol and no trace of it when they get there. Look out for Lemesos, be aware that people might call it Limassol, and you'll be fine.

The lay of the land

The most up-and-coming destination on the island is the capital (p79), which until recently barely registered on the tourist map. Since the opening of several checkpoints on the Green Line (the UN buffer zone separating the Republic of Cyprus from the Turkish-occupied north), interest has increased and visitors are trickling in with increasing regularity. Even if you're staying in one of the coastal resorts, Nicosia is a charming and happening city that merits exploration over a couple of days. If you're based in the south but are curious to see North Cyprus, it's perfectly feasible to cross over for a day trip, either by car or on foot.

The second largest urban conurbation after Nicosia, Lemesos (p98) offers such pleasant diversions as a seafront sculpture park and a small medieval castle – as long as you steer clear of the high rise hotel-dominated tourist area to the east of town. Larnaka (p65) is arranged in a similar manner, with the town built right up to the famous Phinikoudes seafront promenade. It's less obviously a tourist destination, despite being the site of the island's main international airport. That said, its quaint backstreets in the old Turkish quarter, prettily set fort and bars filled mostly with locals make for a quietly atmospheric stop-over.

Further east from here, Agia Napa (p50) and its less brash neighbour, Protaras, boast the most stereotypically stunning beaches on the island – sugary sands, warm waters and plenty of pedalo and banana boat action to punctuate those languid stints soaking up some rays. One of the best cultural openings in recent years is the Thalassa Municipal Museum of the Sea (p53), whose shiny attractions include a full-size replica of the *Kyrenia II*, one of the most famous shipwrecks in the region. At the northern end of the Protaras strip, the Magic Dancing Waters show (pxx) is good fun for children, with its flash lasers and smoke effects.

The chief treasures of the Pafos region (p112) are its plethora of ancient monuments and the natural wonder of the Akamas peninsula, which can transform a city-based holiday into a memorable activity break tackled in a four-wheel drive, on a mountain bike or in a pair of sturdy walking shoes.

To truly get away from it all, however, the gentle charms of the Troodos mountains (p130) are sure to create a trip to remember. To get a true feeling for the fantastic scenery, sleepy villages and touchingly hospitable people, it's best to dedicate several days to driving around the winding roads. Their location in the middle of the island makes the mountains easily accessible from any point in the country. You could, in theory, spend a day at the beach then drive into the mountains for some cool air in the evening.

Attractions in these rural communities are usually limited to hiking trails, good honest food and local churches, often overflowing with ornate Byzantine icons. The lifestyle is laid-back and unhurried, so don't expect things to run in the regimented way they do in cities – if the church you want to see is closed, you may have to fetch the keeper of the keys from the village coffee shop. Just ask around and you'll be pointed in the right direction. A small donation will be much appreciated. You will also find that museums and restaurants don't operate like clockwork, but open according to demand and won't rush you to finish your meal just because it's getting late. As long as you're aware that this is the chilled-out pace of life in Troodos, it's a thoroughly good choice for a relaxing break.

Seasonality

Choosing when to visit largely depends on where in Cyprus you're heading. The urban centres of Nicosia, Larnaka and Lemesos are alive year-round, but tourism-centred Pafos is much quieter in the winter. Agia Napa is mainly a summer-only destination – the large hotels operate year-round but many smaller ones, as well as eating and drinking venues, are only open in the peak season of April to October.

Aphrodite

Ioannis Yiakoumides's molecular cooking p17

WHAT'S BEST

Eating & Drinking

If you thought Cypriot cuisine was all about tavernas, you're in for something of a surprise – the island's culinary evolution has come on in leaps and bounds in recent years. Of course, if you're crazy about meze, Cyprus is the perfect place to indulge your passion, but there are so many more dining experiences to choose from. You need to know which lazy tourist trap establishments to dodge, but showing them up are a slew of chefs and restaurateurs doing great things with Cypriot grub.

Like many in the Mediterranean, this is a country which cares fervently about food. Cypriots will hungrily discuss food for hours, from the latest hot restaurant opening to mama's home-cooked masterpieces. Here, people subscribe to the local, organic and seasonal mantras not because they're fashionable, but because that's how things have been done since time immemorial. If you come across a market (the CTO has a list), then make sure you grab the chance to sample some incredibly flavoursome fruit or vegetables – the speedily grown produce back home will taste lucklustre once a ruby red watermelon from these shores has reawakened your tastebuds.

However, things on the food produce scene have changed quite a bit since EU accession, as the opening of new trade opportunities has brought a dizzying array of imported produce to grocery shelves.

Culinary hotspots

Vying for the crown of the island's foremost foodie destination are Lefkosia and Lemesos. The latter has the edge, with the capital not too far behind. Lemesos locals are very serious about their food, and with a restaurant round almost every corner there's something for every taste and wallet, from charming village tavernas to gastronomic temples in five-star hotels. Like any self-respecting 21st-century capital city, Lefkosia offers an astounding choice of comestibles, from raw Japanese to slow-cooked local.

Larnaka used to be a culinary desert but a lot has changed lately in both mentality and standards, with several dependable options now available. Agia Napa obliges with style and, in most cases, at a fairly reasonable price. Without a doubt, the best places to eat in Pafos are local, Cypriot-owned tavernas, as scores of so-so global eateries mean this is not one of the island's finest destinations for eating out.

Tavernas

Cypriots have a horror of there being too little food on the table, so get ready for a seemingly endless parade of delicious small dishes, along with a genuinely warm welcome. It would definitely be a huge mistake to visit the island without tasting the Cypriot and Greek meze.

Aigaio (p86), with its picturesque seasonal courtyard and cosy indoor area, has been impressing its patrons since the 1980s and is considered one of the best tavernas in the capital. You certainly shouldn't leave without ordering the heavenly *sheftalies* (grilled meat sausages), and vegetarians will be delighted by specialities like aromatic okra simmered in an intense tomato sauce.

It's not straightforward to find by yourself, but any taxi driver will take you to Zanettos (p92),

SHORTLIST

Best new openings
- Vasiliskos (p63)
- Oinohoos (p88)
- Sushi La (p90)

Trendiest bars
- Breeze (p108)
- Domus Lounge Bar (p87)
- Scarabeo (p89)

Top tavernas
- Voreas (p76)
- Aigaio (p86)
- Seven St Georges (p129)

Stand-out design
- Bottle House Club (p144)
- Sushi La (p90)

Most spectacular views
- Umi (p61)
- Marco Polo (p88)

Most romantic venues
- Love Bites (p53)
- Oinohoos (p88)

Fabulous fusion
- Beige (p103)
- Mavromatis (p108)

Best wine list
- Risto la Piazza (p120)

Best for fish lovers
- Spartiatis (p61)
- Ta Psarakia tou Nikou (p104)
- Pyxida (p89)

Veggie heaven
- Coffee Nest (p38)
- Syrian Arab Friendship Club (p90)

Best value for money
- Dino Art Café (p103)
- Ta Piatakia (p104)
- Il Forno (p88)

Eastern promise
- Zen Room (p109)
- Nippon (p68)
- Pagoda (p120)

ΧΑΙΡΕ ΚΑΙ ΠΙΕΙ ΕΥ
KEO
The Taste of Cyprus
KEO
KEO
PREMIUM BEER

one of Cyprus's oldest tavernas. It's been around since 1938, serving a succession of more than 20 dishes that will have you planning a return visit before you leave. The excellent pork kebab and snails with *pourgouri* (bulgur wheat) are a must.

Voreas (p76) near Larnaka was voted by *Time Out Cyprus* as the best restaurant of its kind on the island in 2008. Order the meze and you'll discover flavours for the first time. The traditional village bread, old recipes from Rizocarpaso, the chicken and pork kebab and the dessert *pitta tis satzis* are unforgettable. The beautifully presented dishes at Koutsonikolias (p76) come from the owner's granny's notebook, so do try the meltingly tender *ofto* and *kerpasto*, both lamb dishes. Baked asparagus, deer and wild boar are also not to be missed.

Fettas Corner (p118) in Pafos is also respected for the authenticity of its recipes. Leave room for the honey-drizzled doughnuts (*lokmades*). Seven St Georges (p129) and Araouzos (p127) are worth a visit for their finger-licking food and traditional surroundings. Xylino (another *Time Out* award winner, p63) offers regional dishes, wild vegetables and game, along with superb fish – the fresh squid melts in the mouth.

Fish restaurants and tavernas take pride in offering the day's catch, while others import fresh oysters, prawns and lobsters two or three times a week from around the world. Pyxida (p89) in Lefkosia is overbooked seven days a week. The full meze offers the chance to try a huge variety of fish at keen prices. For meze with a twist, point your belly in the direction of Middle Eastern joints: the Syrian Arab Friendship Club (p90) never fails to please.

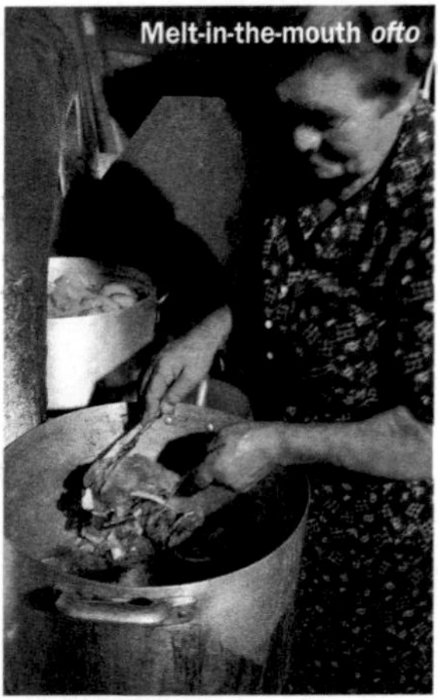

Melt-in-the-mouth *ofto*

Restaurants

Promising young cooks and dynamic executive chefs, along with the personal touch of the restaurateurs, are key to the success of well-regarded Cypriot restaurants. Excellent restaurants are legion in the gastronomic capital of the island, Lemesos. Mavromatis (p108), in the super-swanky Four Seasons hotel, combines elements from Greek and French cuisine, resulting in such marvels as lamb chops with hummus and manouri cheese.

Beige (p103), on the other side of town, has been voted the best international restaurant in Cyprus for three years running. Owner Louis Pierides has put his personal stamp on the renovated old mansion, while chef Nelson Reposo cultivates the kind of haute cuisine where every extravagant detail makes you feel like a king. The Japanese Zen Room (p109) is always busy with both locals and visitors – try the black cod teriyaki, the Chilean bream with lemongrass and the devine tempura ice cream. For imaginatively

presented hearty Mediterranean meals, head to Artima (p103), housed in the atmospherically renovated Lanitis Carob Mills, which contains a number of dining options. At the Columbia Beach Resort near Lemesos (p175), chef Ioannis Yiakoumides specialises in intricate and highly creative molecular cooking.

In Lefkosia, Cos'altro (p87) in the centre of town is a trendy place, emphasising pastas (try the lobster one) and assorted Med delicacies. Although it's not open all year round, alfresco Marco Polo (p88) offers fusion cuisine with excellent views of the city from its seventh-floor vantage point. Nearby, Polynesian Pago Pago (p89), the only place of its kind in Cyprus, cherry-picks from Thai, Japanese and Chinese influences to transport you to the South Pacific with the musical accompaniment of its resident band.

Domus Lounge Bar (p87) is considered one of the most stylish and atmospheric restaurants in the capital. You could just go for drinks, but that would mean missing out on stunningly executed dishes such as octopus flavoured with orange, so be smart and book a table several days in advance. On chic Stasikratous street, Seiko (p90) has a menu with more than a hundred choices of freshly prepared and prettily presented sushi and sashimi.

In Larnaka, Japanese bistro Nippon (p68) is one of the most reputable restaurants around. Gil Panayiotou, who cut his teeth in London, pays special attention to fresh and pure ingredients, aiming to prepare a new dish every day. Try the indulgent king-size crab or the sesame salmon.

For excellent sushi in Pafos, Asiachi (p118) is a good bet. Its minimalist decor, friendly staff and vast array of dishes score big points. In the same area, there are two reasons for choosing Risto La Piazza (p120): it serves authentic Italian cuisine and has won awards for two consecutive years for its peerless selection of wines. Sommelier Vasos Manoli will gladly guide you in matching your food and wine.

Bars

Whether you're fond of summery cocktails, a glass of heady red wine or a simple beer, you'll have no trouble finding a suitable watering hole. New openings with a buzz include Taj Mahal (p90) and mini chain the Brewery (p87), which recently opened a branch in the capital.

Lemesos has a reputation for fun, trendy after-hours beach bars (see box p107). Alternatively, Draught Microbrewery (p103), serves the best beer in town. While you sample the dips, the DJ mixes songs from the 1970s and '80s. One of the most popular venues in Larnaka is cocktail bar/chillout lounge Times Music Bar (p69), but for a fabulous location, Ammos (p76) is right on the beach. It serves a great selection of food and drinks in outstandingly realised, all-white surrounds.

In Agia Napa, a sense of style is being cultivated and the vibe is finally about offering a good time rather than just pocketing the tourist euro. Love Bites (p53) is wonderfully atmospheric, as is the Cliff Bar (p56) at the Grecian Park Hotel. The incredible sea views and soulful music will keep you up all night.

Dos and don'ts

Cypriots tend to eat late: it's common to make restaurant bookings from 9pm onwards. That said, in tourist areas many places start to get busy much earlier.

This has a knock-on effect on bars, where most of the action doesn't start until at least 11pm. If you're driving, note that the police are out in force 24 hours a day and a zero-tolerance alcohol policy.

Moufflon Bookshop p95, 122

WHAT'S BEST

Shopping

Despite its relatively small size (the entire population could fit into London seven times over), Cyprus is becoming a hotbed of up-and-coming fashion talent and style. With its urban centres spreading and growing, the demand for fashionable shops, bars and restaurants is multiplying rapidly; and that demand is being met enthusiastically. Each major city is developing its own unique style, with the action concentrated in the dominant shopping capitals of Nicosia (Lefkosia) and Lemesos.

Each city boasts a distinctive array of shops that define its style, although popular shops such as Debenhams, Marks & Spencer, Topshop and Zara do pop up repeatedly. The discerning Cypriot shopper blends a mix of high street and high-end fashion, often sporting designs from the island's cutting-edge designers: Flexi (p93) in Nicosia is a fantastic first stop for those after a unique piece of clothing from the likes of Joanna Louca or Dora Schabel. Image is everything here, and key staples among the overly trend-conscious run along the lines of a Louis Vuitton bag, oversized sunglasses (Tom Ford is popular) and the latest BMW.

To cater to this seemingly insatiable desire for designer goods, designer shops have sprung up all over the island in the last few years. Nicosia alone brims with Gucci, Dolce & Gabbana, Longchamp, Louis Vuitton and

Balenciaga, among countless boutiques that stock world famous brands. For those who don't lust after the latest it-bag, options for splashing the cash range from high street chains to local designers, jewellers, bookshops and music stores.

Opening hours

Most shops follow similar hours, from nine in the morning till eight at night, with the majority closing for a couple of hours for lunch and a siesta (generally 1-3pm in winter and 1-4.30pm in summer).

On Wednesdays and Saturdays all shops take a half-day, closing at around 2pm, and on Sundays everything is shut. In high season in tourist resorts, however, some shops (especially supermarkets) keep longer hours to meet demand.

Designer must-haves

For high-end shopping in Nicosia, your first port of call should be ritzy Stasikratous street in the centre of town. Home to a dense cluster of designer shops, it offers consumer opportunities aplenty. Jostling for space are countless boutiques, stocking designers from Alexander McQueen to Miu Miu, as well as outposts of Dolce & Gabbana, Fendi, Louis Vuitton, Burberry, Max Mara and Longchamp. Within the surrounding streets look out for Cara, Matita, Equinox, MBLE, ADD+, and Timinis – all of which stock high-end designer fashion and accessories.

All of these boutiques are within walking distance of each other, making for a pleasant stroll around the centre of Nicosia. With new shops constantly opening (and less successful ones dropping off the map without warning), you never know what fresh gems you'll stumble across.

SHORTLIST

Best for beauty buys
- Mastic Spa (p95)
- Korres (p94)
- MAC (p105)

Cutting-edge designer gear
- Boukla Boukla (p105)
- Flexi (p93)
- Vitrine Designer Boutique (p96)

Best local designers
- Stalo Markides (p40)
- Kyriaki Costa (p40)
- Krama by Skevi Afantiti (p94)

Excellent accessories
- Kristina P (p40)
- Joanna Louca (p18)
- Dora Schabel (p93)

Sterling jewellers
- Motivo Gallery (p121)
- G Stephanides Son & Co (p93)

Fab for foodies
- Oak Tree Wine Cellar (p72)
- Niki Agathokleous Traditional Sweets (p146)

Best homegrown crafts
- Phini Pottery (p132)
- Cyprus Handicraft Centre (p71, 105, 121)
- Gatapou (p93)

Best for kids
- Bear Factory (p104)

Best for interior design
- Thesis (p106)
- Mobhaus (p38)

Best bargains
- Calzedonia (p71)
- Zara (p73)

Best for bookworms
- Ant Comics (p40)
- Moufflon Bookshop (p95, 122)

With branches in Nicosia, Pafos and Lemesos, 34 The Shop (p104) is one of the most practical upmarket stores, stocking Paul Smith, Pepe Jeans, Nolita and Replay among other hip brands. With clothes for men, women, and children it's a one-stop shop for the fashionable family. Jeans lovers of both genders should set their radars to Calvin Klein Jeans (p105) in Lemesos. On the fashionable Agiou Andreou street in the same town, razor-sharp fashion boutique Boukla Boukla (p105) stocks clothes and accessories by three Greek fashion designers, and is definitely the place to go for lovers of unconventional garments. One of the most on-the-pulse and well-stocked boutiques in Lemesos is the newly opened Splash by the Beach (Georgiou I 129, 25 318 803). With designers ranging from Hoss Intropia to Givenchy and Giambattista Valli, whatever your taste is you're guaranteed to find something that takes your breath away.

High street sweep

Walking around the centre of each town gives you a real feel for the city and its inhabitants. The pace of life is slower in Cyprus, and most people intersperse their shopping with regular coffee breaks. As a result, the shopping streets are dotted with cafés – perfect for taking a break and people watching. For a great view of Nicosia and its surroundings, the Debenhams (p92) department store on Ledras has an observation point on the 11th floor. From here you get a bird's eye view of most of the town and the Occupied Territories.

Over the past few years, Ledra Street and the surrounding area have been rejuvenated, with new shops and restaurants breathing fresh life into the oldest, most historical part of the city.

The majority of mainstream shops can be found in the three largest cities (Nicosia, Lemesos and Larnaka) giving the shopping districts a unified feel. Zara (p73), Topshop, Bershka (p92) , Stradivarious and Pull and Bear can be found in all three cities and are perfect places to seek out reasonably priced everyday wear.

Department stores such as Debenhams (p92) and Marks & Spencer (p72), as well as local department stores Pissarides and Mavros, are also prevalent – handy when time is of the essence. Calzedonia (p71), Damart (p105), Intimissimi and Yamamay are the best places for essentials like pyjamas, leisurewear, lingerie, socks and tights – all carry cheerfully coloured items in a multitude of hues and prices are very affordable.

Area watch

The capital's shopping areas are vast and varied, with Archiepiskopou Makariou III avenue the focal point. Boutique-rich Lemesos rewards a (long) stroll along its own Makariou and into the Old Town via Anexartisias, with excellent window-shopping and tons of temptation to flex the plastic. Larnaka's main drags are around Ermou and Zinonos Kitieos.

Agia Napa is better known for clubbing than shopping, and the short tourist season means many shops double up on services (it's not unusual to come across a café renting cars, for instance). A handful of stylish shops cater for fashion addicts: the best two are Maze (p54) and the London Clothing Co (p54). The latter has a branch in Nicosia, too, and carries brands such as French Connection, Versace and Bench for men and women.

Pafos has grown rapidly in the last few years. While it boasts a new shopping centre on the outskirts of town and an array of tourist-orientated shops, particularly along the seafront, it lacks some of the popular chains found in other cities. There's still scope for shoe-shopping, leather goods, silver, gold, pottery and (available island-wide) bottles of locally-made *zivania*, the traditional firewater. That, and its grapey cousin, the sherry-like Commandaria, make excellent presents.

Natural beauty

For those in search of the next hot beauty trend, the Mastic Spa (p95) in Nicosia shouldn't be missed. Its face, body and hair products contain a unique ingredient: mastic from the Greek island of Chios. You can also book in for beauty treatments here.

Another name to look out for is that of cult Greek brand Korres (p94), which has just opened a compact boutique in Nicosia. For everyday grooming, Beauty Line obliges with several shops in each main city, carrying a vast range of perfumes, make-up and lotions for face and body. If you want expert advice on make-up, then MAC's stores in Nicosia and Lemesos (p105) are the only place to go, with clued-up staff and eyeshadows and lipsticks in every shade imaginable.

Cyprus Handicraft Centre

Local talent

Since the rejuvenation of Nicosia's old town, many young designers and artists have chosen to base their studios within the city walls. It's worth exploring the streets surrounding Ledras, as you'll find the ateliers of hot designers such as Kyriaki Costa (p40), Stalo Markides (p40), Sofia Alexander and Etherial, as well as the studios of various artists at the Chrysaliniotissa Crafts Centre (p38). Internationally successful designer Joanna Louca has her showroom and workshop in the new part of town (Medontos 5C, off Stasinou, 22 452 702), as does Erotokritos, who has just opened his first shop on the island (Mykinon 10, off Mnasiadou).

If you're on the hunt for locally produced, hand-made gifts, then the Cyprus Handicraft Centre should be your first and only stop. Based in Nicosia, Larnaka (p71), Limassol (p105) and Pafos (p121), this organisation is sponsored by the Ministry of Commerce in order to preserve traditional craftsmanship. It proffers quality objects, from pottery and dolls to lacework and woven baskets – first-class options for souvenirs that last.

Breeze p108

WHAT'S BEST

Nightlife

Gone are the days when planeloads of clubbers touched down in Agia Napa for a week of partying till the sun came up, waking mid-afternoon, baking in the sun for a while and then hitting the clubs again in one debauched cycle. The nightlife scene has been downsized, and rather than the garage of those heady years at the beginning of the millennium, the main sounds you're likely to hear in the old haunts are pop, R&B and commercial dance.

Now that the scene has lost some of its focus, most visitors no longer come here specifically for clubbing. Familiar names like Castle Club (p54) and Black & White (p54) still pack the punters in, but going out is more likely to involve pubs and bars. In Cyprus, many bars stay open until 2-3am, functioning as clubs in everything but name – so look in the 'Eating & drinking' sections of this guide as well as 'Nightlife' for tips.

Clubs generally open at 11pm or midnight, and keep going until 3-4am. In venues which charge an entry fee, your first drink is usually included in the price of admission.

Beach parties

One well-received trend that looks set to last is beach bars, where you can kick your shoes off and let loose till the wee hours. Guaba (p108) is hugely popular, and deservedly so. It opens in the summer months, like most beach bars, and attracts around 3,000 revellers to its idyllic seaside setting. DJs spin an eclectic mix of house, progressive and electronica as a Ray-Ban wearing crowd moves to the beat on the hot sand, partying

ACADEMY
RESTAURANT
For reservations 22762816, 41 Klimentos str., Nicosia

from the afternoon until the early hours of the next day. Breeze (p108), also in Lemesos, is another stylish spot that draws queues of well-dressed revellers. Note that many of these beach bars only finalise their opening plans in April, when licences are up for renewal, and may change name or even location year on year. The fluidity of the scene is partly what keeps it vital.

Bikini Bar (p58) is Agia Napa's prime waterside party spot. It's mainly frequented by Cypriots, who come to dance to chart tunes spun by various DJs until 4am every Saturday in the summer. Pafos gets in on the trend with Bario del Mar (p129) on Geroskipou beach. Not too far from the centre, the beach is set east along the coast from Poseidonos avenue.

Clubbing central

The predominant sounds in Nicosia are decent house and progressive. Trance is also still going strong in the city's clubs, thanks to chief proponents Versus (p96) and the newly opened, much hyped and extremely popular Klubd (p96). For clubbing with a sophisticated edge, Zoo (p96) is the place to be. It plays Greek and international pop music, offering fantastic views of the walled city from its elevated position. If you like to be squeezed like a lemon while you try not to spill your drink, you could always try Sfinakia (p96), which is perenially overcrowded but fails to live up to its own hype. Club-hopping is a favourite activity in the capital, which explains all those traffic jams at ungodly hours, especially at weekends.

Once upon a time, Lemesos's tourist strip was alight with the neon signs of back-to-back nightclubs swarming with tourists. Today, only a handful of clubs remains, the emphasis having shifted to upbeat Greek and English bars complete with funky music and trendy decor. On a more unfortunate note, however, the town has earned notoriety for hosting the most cabarets on the island; in this context, a cabaret is not a establishment proffering post-modern burlesque entertainment, but an unreconstructed strip joint. Beware the devious tactics these establishments use to get unsuspecting (and usually drunk) patrons to pay for drinks they never ordered.

Lemesos's chief club is the mainstream Sesto Senso (p106). Metropole Retro Music Club (p106) is an alternative for those who like their hits a little more vintage, and new arrival 7 Seas Music Bar (p99),

SHORTLIST

Best new
- Klubd (p96)

Best for stylish clubbing
- Plin 2 at the Grecian Park Hotel (p165)
- Zoo (p96)

Best megaclubs
- Black & White (p54)
- Castle Club (p54)

Best for serious music fans
- Klubd (p96)
- Versus (p96)

Best for outdoor partying
- Bikini Bar (p58)
- Drops (p108)
- Guaba Beach Bar (p108)

Best for retro tunes
- Metropole Retro Music Club (p106)
- Loop (p96)

Best for live music
- Enallax (p96)

Best gay venue
- Secrets Freedom Club (p78)

Much of the action in Larnaka is aimed at residents rather than visitors, but if you want to party alongside the locals then this is an ideal place to do it; try the newly-opened Geometry (p73), which pumps out the latest hits to shake your booty to. The Larnaka-Dhekelia Road is also a hotspot, although it's more touristy. The strip is several miles long, and hence a bit of a trek to attempt on foot.

Agia Napa has fewer clubs than in years gone by, and the hottest places are no longer the cluster around the central square. Instead, head for the crossroads of Agias Mavris and Loucas Louca streets for the trendier venues. A little-known pointer is to try Plin 2 (see Grecian Park Hotel, p165), tucked away beneath a chic hotel at Cape Greco, just outside the centre of Agia Napa. A favourite insider hangout for Cypriots holidaying in the area, it's definitely one where you need to dress smartly.

As in many other countries, male-only groups may well get turned away at the door – you're more likely to get in if you arrive in a mixed group. A Cypriot quirk is making reservations for clubs. Similar to ringing ahead and putting yourself and your mates on the guestlist, making a reservation is a way of ensuring you get a sofa or seated area where you won't be squashed. There's a minimum spend clause attached to this, usually a bottle of spirits at around €100. This version of clubbing is for those for whom going out is all about being seen (and being seen to have cash to spend), rather than the music.

Places like Versus (p96) and Klubd (p96) are more like London clubs, where you can show up in smart-casual attire (cool trainers are fine), and lose yourself in the music. Sporadically, well-known DJs arrive on the island for one-off events – nothing like the heyday of Agia Napa, when summer-long residences were the norm. Recent visiting DJs include Ferry Corsten, Lange and Martin Schultz.

Nightlife in Pafos is pretty disappointing, and mainly limited to bland, rowdy venues around the epicentre of Agiou Antoniou street that cater mostly to booze-fuelled tourists. If a night out listening to Abba and trawling karaoke bars is your thing, then you'll be in your element here, but do exercise a bit of caution as you're likely to come across many a drunk and disorderly character. One venue that stands out amid the sea of uninspiring clubs is Cartel (p122), which attracts a good mix of locals and visitors. There's a great rooftop area in the warmer months to boot.

The gay scene in Cyprus is fairly quiet, but two good choices include Secrets Freedom Club (p78), near Larnaka airport and Different (p122) in Pafos. Secrets is the biggest gay club on the island, featuring a happening dance floor, a chillout lounge and regular special events.

Live music

Most music events held throughout the year are concerts by popular Greek artists. However, there has been an influx of international talent of late, and in the past few years the island has hosted high-profile gigs by Sting, Bryan Adams and Simply Red.

More reliable, however, are the plethora of bars where you can soak up a bit of authentic atmosphere by listening to bands playing Greek music. Basement bar Enallax (p96) is a good bet if you want a taste of local rock and blues. If Latin beats are more your thing, Marco Polo (p88) lends itself to rooftop dancing with twinkly views over Nicosia.

Kourion Amphitheatre p111

WHAT'S BEST

Arts & Leisure

The local arts scene can never be on the scale of those in the great European metropoleis, but for its size, Cyprus has a busy cultural schedule. The art scene is blossoming, the concert calendar is getting busier, contemporary dance festivals and performances by visiting ballet companies are happening with increasing regularity, and there are numerous theatre productions and a thriving film scene. Much of this activity, however, is concentrated in the spring, autumn and winter months, so visitors may find things relatively quiet in the blazing height of summer.

Nonetheless, an undisputed highlight of the long, hot summer months is the trend for bringing magnificent ancient monuments into service as stages for a variety of festivals. Cyprus's strategic position at the crossroads of three continents proved irresistibly attractive to everyone from the Myceaneans to the Romans, and a 10,000-year-long succession of conquerors left a legacy of stately sites that survive to this day. Monuments such as Kourion Amphitheatre in Lemesos, Pafos's waterfront castle and Famagusta Gate on Nicosia's Venetian Walls are all still in use for events that range from concerts to theatre seasons.

Festival fever

One of the most outstanding and important festivals of the year is Kypria (p35) , which is celebrated in almost every town during September. Its name comes from the word *Kypros*, the Greek name for

Cyprus, and it means 'of Cyprus'. Organised by the Ministry of Education and Culture, its programme includes ballet, opera, cinema, art, theatre and music, performed by distinguished artists from Cyprus and different parts of the world. Illustrious past participants include Béjart Ballet Lausanne and Moscow's Helikon-Opera.

Classical music & opera

In late summer (at the end of August or the beginning of September), another event grabs the attention of culture vultures. The Pafos Aphrodite Festival (p35, www.pafc.com.cy) presents a classic opera at the old harbour, just outside the walls of the Medieval Fort (p116). Recently the honours went to Trieste's Teatro Lirico Giuseppe Verdi, who performed Puccini's *Madama Butterfly*. Listening to the love, passion and tragedy of opera under the stars, mingled with the scent of the salty sea air, is a magical experience.

Classical music concerts usually take place at venues in Nicosia and Lemesos, including Strovolos Municipal Theatre (Strovolou 100, Nicosia, 22 313 010), Pasydy Auditorium (Demostheni Severi 3, Nicosia, 22 662 278), the Makarios III Amphitheatre at the School for the Blind (Oktovriou 28, Nicosia, 22 31 45 07) and the extremely active Rialto Theatre in Lemesos (p106).

The apex of the classical calendar is the Pharos Chamber Music Festival (p32), which takes place in the atmospheric Kouklia Royal Manor House in Pafos. The Pharos Arts Foundation has a busy programme of concerts throughout the year; it's worth checking the website to see what's on when you visit (www.thepharostrust.org).

Nicosia Municipal Theatre

Theatre

The show goes on for the island's main festival of the dramatic arts, which awakens antiquity with an alternative approach. Usually held in August, the Festival of Ancient Greek Drama (p35) takes place at Cyprus's most prestigious stages (Pafos Ancient Odeon, Makarios III Amphitheatre and Kourion). The plays are performed in a range of languages by Cypriot and Greek actors, but also by foreign theatre companies. Some are given a modern twist, highlighting the meaning of the story rather than presenting a conventional ancient tragedy. One notable production saw Aeschylus's *The Persians* staged by Astragali Teatro with actors from Italy, Malta, France, Greece, Albania and Cyprus.

There is a thriving theatre scene in Nicosia, with quality shows regularly staged by the state-maintained Cyprus Theatre Organisation (THOK), Nicosia Municipal Theatre (opposite the Cyprus Arcgaeologiacl Museum) and smaller companies. Plays are almost always performed in Greek, though you will sometimes come across a production in English or with English surtitles. If you get the chance, you should also try to catch a traditional shadow puppet theatre performance featuring wily folk hero Karagiozis.

Lemesos has its own theatre company, ETHAL, although most

productions are in Greek. However, some excellent and very active English-speaking amateur theatre groups have emerged in the past decade. In March, look out for the non-profit Premiere Group (www.pg.cyisp.com) performing drama and musicals. For atmosphere, it's hard to beat the Shakespeare Festival, usually performed in late June at Kourion (p111).

Dance

An annual highlight takes place in spring, when 16 European countries unite for the European Dance Festival (p34). Performances take place at the Rialto Theatre (p106); aspiring dancers should look out for accompanying workshops.

Indeed, Lemesos is something of a dance hub, with the Rialto also hosting the Dance Platform (p33) of new contemporary works, and the Summer Dance Festival (p35). The latter brings guerilla performances to unexpected locations like the seafront promenade, to engage audiences not usually drawn to dance.

Film

Cinema is well loved in Cyprus, and fans of art house and indie movies can look forward to a week's worth of films during Cyprus Film Days (p33) in March. This non-competitive festival, held at Pantheon Art Cinema (p97) in Nicosia and the Rialto Theatre in Lemesos (p106), is open to all and presents the best of world cinema. The www.filmfestival.com.cy site has up-to-date info on Cypriot film fests, including Lemesos International Documentary Festival (p35) and Images and Views of Alternative Cinema (p34).

In between festival periods, audiences can watch the most recent global releases in cinemas such as the island-wide K Cineplex chain and the Rio (p106) in Lemesos, which has a seasonal outdoor screen.

SHORTLIST

Most anticipated events
- Carnival (p32)
- Lemesos Wine Festival (p35)

Best multi-arts festival
- Kypria (p35)

Best for highbrow music
- Pafos Aphrodite Festival (p35)
- Pharos Chamber Music Festival (p32)

Best for theatre buffs
- Ancient Kourion (p111)
- Festival of Ancient Greek Drama (p35)
- Rialto Theatre (p106)

Best for cinephiles
- Cyprus Film Days (p33)
- Rio (p106)
- Weaving Mill (p97)

Best for dance
- Rialto Theatre (p106)

Best for relaxation
- Omeriye Hamam (p97)

Handily for visitors, the vast majority of films shown in Cyprus are screened in their original language, with Greek subtitles. The exceptions are animated children's films, which are screened for two different audiences – one version in the original language, and the other dubbed into Greek.

Film clubs are popular among local and foreign intellectuals. Fans of alternative cinema and European films should try Cine Studio at the University of Nicosia (Makedonitissis 46, Engomi, 22 358 662), the Artos Foundation (p97), Pantheon Art Cinema (p97), the Rialto and the Weaving Mill (p97).

Street parties

The biggest street events in Cyprus are the carnival celebrations, which last for almost two weeks. Although

While in Cyprus share your moments.
Roam with MTN.
Your mobile phone network in Cyprus!
For more information please call our MTN Call Centre at 136.
www.mtn.com.cy
MTN
OFFICIAL SPONSOR
SOUTH AFRICA 2010
FIFA

festivities take place in towns all over the island, Lemesos hosts the most famous merrymaking (p32). Carnival begins 50 days before Easter, on the second Thursday before Lent. On Green Monday (p33), after the last day of Carnival, it's customary for Cypriots to head to the fields to begin the 40-day countdown to Easter, when tasty vegetarian food is on the picnic menu to mark the first day of fasting.

Another street event that sees the streets filled with every kind of blossom is Anthestiria (p34), which celebrates spring and nature's reawakening. It derives its name from the word 'anthos', which means flower. Two parades of flower floats and people carrying beautiful fresh blooms take over the main avenues of Larnaka and Pafos. The revelry dates back to ancient Greek times, when feasts were organised in Athens every four years to honour Dionysus, the god of theatre and excess.

Also celebrating the island's natural produce is the Lemesos Wine Festival (p35). Wine making has an extremely long history on the island: in fact, Italian archaeologists recently discovered that the production of wine dates back almost 6,000 years in this part of the world. The island's oenological heritage, with museum artefacts of wine pots dating back to 3,500 BC, is one of the oldest in the entire Mediterranean basin, and leads to the assumption that Cyprus triggered the spread of winemaking to Greece, Italy, France and other Med regions. Wine making is toasted every September at Lemesos Wine Festival (p35), which takes place in the town's Municipal Gardens. The feast of tastings and buffets attracts over 100,000 people, accompanied by music and dancing at the gardens' open-air theatre.

Outdoor activities

An action-packed event that takes in some of the island's most picturesque scenery is the Cyprus Rally (p33), which starts in Lemesos and covers all of the free areas in the Republic of Cyprus. The route takes competing cars through some spectacular regions, past countless sites of cultural and historical interest.

If spectating isn't enough and you want to experience your own outdoor adventure, take a safari jeep ride into the Akamas Peninsula (p124). A number of tour companies can take you deep into this unspoilt natural terrain, bumping over rugged dirt tracks and past remote, rocky seashores.

If you prefer to use your own two feet to explore, the Cyprus Tourism Organisation (www.visitcyprus.com) can provide detailed routes for treks into Akamas, as well as along the cool mountain trails of the Troodos Mountains (p130).

Golf is another activity that's steadily growing in popularity on the island. Courses include the Aphrodite Hills resort (p177), and the Vikla Golf & Country Club (p111).

Indulgent pampering

To unwind from the stresses of everyday living, book yourself in for some serious holiday relaxation at any one of the slew of luxury spas found on the island. Most are set in upmarket hotels, including Thalassa (p178) and Le Meridien (p175).

Alternatively, sweat it all out the traditional way at the wonderfully renovated Turkish baths of the Omeriye Hamam (p97) in Nicosia. One good session of steam and pummelling and you'll be fully rejuvenated and ready to resume sightseeing.

WHAT'S ON

Calendar

The following are the pick of annual events that happen in Cyprus. Further information and exact dates can be found nearer the time from flyers and seasonal guides available from hotels and tourist offices (p187). Events listings can also be found in English-language newspapers (p187) and *Time Out Cyprus*.

Dates highlighted in **bold** are public holidays.

January

Ongoing **Agia Napa/Paralimni Cultural Winter** (see Nov); **European Cultural Winter** (see Nov)

Jan-Apr **Musical Sundays**
Larnaka Seafront Stage, Onisilos Seaside Theatre, Lemesos & Pafos Archaeological Park entrance
www.visitcyprus.com
Traditional, classical and contemporary songs and dances every Sunday.

Early Jan **New Year International Regatta**
Lemesos
www.cya.org.cy
Organised by the Cyprus Yachting Association.

6 Epiphany Celebration
Various venues
In coastal towns, following a ceremonial blessing of the waters, the Holy Cross is flung into the sea by a priest, and men dive in to recover it.

February

Ongoing **Agia Napa/Paralimni Cultural Winter** (see Nov); **European Cultural Winter** (see Nov); **Musical Sundays** (see Jan)

Late Feb-early Mar **Carnival**
Lemesos & Pafos
www.limassolmunicipal.com.cy
Lemesos is the main home of carnival, with 11 days of festivities ending with the final Grand Carnival Parade. Pafos hosts two smaller events.

Late Feb-Mar **Cyprus Sunshine Cup**
Tochni, Kalavasos & other venues
www.mtbcyprus.com
International mountain bike race series.

March

Ongoing **Agia Napa/Paralimni Cultural Winter** (see Nov); **European Cultural Winter** (see Nov); **Musical Sundays** (see Jan); **Cyprus Sunshine Cup** (see Feb)

Feb/Mar **Green Monday**
Throughout Cyprus
Public holiday marking the beginning of Lent. People take to the countryside to enjoy a veggie picnic and fly kites.

Early Mar **Dance Platform**
Rialto Theatre, Lemesos
www.rialto.com.cy
This three-day festival is the island's premier contemporary dance event.

Early Mar **Spring Historic Car Rally**
Lemesos to Agia Napa
www.fipa-cyprus.org.cy
A classic car event organised by the Friends of Historic & Old Cars.

Early Mar **Troodos International FIS Races**
Dias Slope, Troodos
www.cyprusski.com
Organised by the Cyprus Ski Federation.

Mid Mar **Cyprus Marathon**
Pafos
www.cyprusmarathon.com
Three different events: a marathon, half marathon and 10km road race.

Mid-late Mar **Cyprus Film Days**
Rialto Theatre, Lemesos, Pantheon Art Cinema, Nicosia & Cine Studio, Nicosia
www.filmfestival.com.cy
Presenting what's new on the international indie film scene, this week-long movie fest screens notable independent productions and recent releases.

Mid Mar **Cyprus Rally**
Various venues
www.cyprusrally.com.cy
The return of the Cyprus leg of the World Rally Championship means rally fans can once again watch fast cars tear through the island's countryside.

Late Mar **Cyprus Fashion Week**
Famagusta Gate, Nicosia
www.cyprusfashionweek.com
See box p36.

Late Mar **Nicosia International Documentary Film Festival**
Nicosia
www.cyprusdocfest.org
Five-day documentary film festival.

April

Ongoing **Musical Sundays** (see Jan)

Early Apr **Berengaria International Music Festival**
Rialto Theatre, Lemesos, p106
www.festivalberengaria.com
Chamber and solo music performances by international stars.

Mid Apr **Ledra Music Soloists International Festival**
PASYDY Auditorium, Nicosia
Two-week chamber music festival.

Apr/May **Easter Celebrations**
Throughout Cyprus
The most important Greek Orthodox religious feast is celebrated with evening processions on Good Friday, outdoor midnight mass on Easter Saturday and traditional games on Easter Sunday and Monday.

Late Apr/early May **Cyprus Amateur Open**
Secret Valley Golf Club/Aphrodite Hills Golf Club, Pafos
www.cgf.org.cy
A Cyprus Golf Federation event.

May

Ongoing **Cyprus Amateur Open** (see Apr)

May-June **European Dance Festival**
Rialto Theatre, Lemesos, p106
www.rialto.com.cy
Contemporary dance companies from a dozen or so countries around Europe send teams to compete with Cypriot dance troupes.

Mid-late May **Anthestiria Flower Festival**
Larnaka, Lemesos & Pafos
www.limassolmunicipal.com.cy
Featuring exhibitions, flower markets and shows, the festival culminates in a colourful flower parade.

Late May **Aphrodite Rally**
Lemesos to Pafos
www.fipa-cyprus.org.cy
Classic car rally.

Late May-June **Pharos International Chamber Music Festival**
PASYDY Auditorium, Nicosia & Royal Manor House, Kouklia, Pafos
www.thepharostrust.org
A week of chamber concerts, recitals and lectures.

June

Ongoing **European Dance Festival** (see May); **Pharos International Chamber Music Festival** (see June)

Early June **Pentecost (Kataklysmos)**
Throughout Cyprus
50 days after Greek Orthodox Easter, the Festival of the Flood features waterfights, swimming and boat races.

Mid June **Images and Views of Alternative Cinema**
Theatro Ena, Nicosia
www.filmfestival.com.cy
Events and film screenings celebrating experimental and avant-garde films.

Mid-late June **Shakespeare Festival**
Kourion Amphitheatre, Lemesos, p111
The stunning setting of the ancient amphitheatre (also known as Curium) is used to stage plays by the Bard.

July

Early July **Larnaka Summer Festival**
Larnaka Fort & Pattichion Amphitheatre
Outdoor concerts; past shows include *Grease*, the West End musical.

Mid July **Ethnic Festival**
Behind Plateia Iroon, Lemesos
Global music performances.

Mid July **The Great Ballet Companies**
Municipal Garden Theatre, Lemesos
Weekend dance festival.

Mid July **International Music Festival at the Kourion Theatre**
Kourion Amphitheatre, Lemesos
www.kourionfestival.com
Covering a variety of styles.

July-Aug **International Festival of Ancient Greek Drama**
Kourion Amphitheatre, Makarios III Amphitheatre, Lekosia & Pafos Ancient Odeon
www.cyprus-theatre-iti.org
Epic adventures and heroism from the great dramatists are conjured up by companies from around the world, performing in various languages in three magnificent ancient theatres.

Late July **Commandaria Festival**
Alassa, Agios Georgios, Doros, Laneia, Monagri & Silikou
The villages of the Kourris Valley hold the annual festival dedicated to the delicious dessert wine.

Late July-early Aug **Summer Dance Festival**
Lemesos
Performances are held in unusual, public spaces in this week-long dance festival, aimed at engaging non-theatre-going audiences.

August

Ongoing **International Festival of Ancient Greek Drama** (see July); **Summer Dance Festival** (see July)

Early Aug **Lemesos International Documentary Festival**
B Municipal Market (Theatro Ena), Lemesos
www.filmfestival.com.cy
The main platform for projecting contemporary, creative documentary in Cyprus with screenings, talks and workshops organised by non-profit body Brave New Culture.

Late Aug-Sept **Wine Festival**
Municipal Gardens, Lemesos
www.limassolmunicipal.com.cy
12 days of Dionysian celebrations at this hugely popular event that has taken place annually since 1961, with casks of free wine from the local wine industries, as well as live music, theatre performances, traditional dances and food.

Late Aug-Sept **Pafos Aphrodite Festival**
Medieval Fort, Pafos, p116
www.pafc.com.cy
Three-day open-air opera festival staged against the picturesque backdrop of Pafos Harbour.

September

Ongoing **Wine Festival** (see Aug)

Sept-Oct **Kypria**
Various venues
This international multi-arts festival is one of the most significant cultural events in Cyprus. Established in 1991 by the Ministry of Education and Culture, its previous participants include Martha Graham Dance Company, Ute Lemper and Tap Dogs.

Late Sept **Urban Soul Festival**
Tripoli Park, Nicosia Moat
www.urbansoulfestival.com
The park fills with art for this one-day event, brimming with work from graphic designers, sculptors, multimedia artists and independent publishers, all swaying to an eclectic soundtrack (hip hop, reggae, fusion, electronic).

Late Sept **Agia Napa Festival**
Agia Napa Harbour
Three-day event including traditional food, arts, crafts, music and dances.

October

Ongoing **Kypria** (see Sept)

1 **Independence Day Celebrations**
Throughout Cyprus
The main event of this public holiday is a big military parade which takes place in the centre of the capital.

Mid-late Oct **Lemesia**
Lemesia
www.limassolmunicipal.com.cy
One of the biggest annual international sporting events in Cyprus. During the ten days, athletes from several countries compete in boxing, karate, triathlon, marathon, shooting, rhythmic gymnastics, cycling and more.

Late Mar **Cyprus Fashion Week**
Famagusta Gate, Nicosia
www.cyprusfashionweek.com
Second outing of the year for the designers. See box p36.

November

Nov-Mar **European Cultural Winter**
Larnaka Municipal Theatre
www.larnaka.com
Annual arts festival which in the past has included ballet, classical music, jazz and cinema from local and international performers.

Nov-Mar **Agia Napa/Paralimni Cultural Winter**
Agia Napa, Paralimni
Dance and music every Thursday in Agia Napa and every Friday in neighbouring Paralimni.

Late Nov **Cyprus International 4-Day Challenge**
Akamas, Pafos
www.cypruschallenge.com
Scenic marathon in Akamas.

Late Nov **Forest Park Rally**
Platres, Troodos
www.fipa-cyprus.org.cy
Classic car rally along winding mountain roads.

December

Ongoing **Agia Napa/Paralimni Cultural Winter** (see Nov); **European Cultural Winter** (see Nov)

31 **New Year's Eve**
Plateia Eleftherias, Nicosia
Music and foreworks see in the New Year. There are similar celebrations across the island.

Cyprus Fashion Week

Fashion fever sweeps the capital.

Cypriots adore designer labels as much as they love supporting a local name made good, so the only surprising thing about Cyprus Fashion Week (CFW) (p33) is that it took so long to arrive. Then again, everything in Cyprus happens *siga siga* – 'slowly slowly'.

CFW made its grand entrance in March 2008, and after a rapturous reception returned to the runway in October of the same year. It's now due to become a permanent, twice-yearly fixture. The Cypriot dispensation for latching on to anything new made the event an instant success, and the society pages were filled with photos of sharply dressed fashion industry insiders, editors and pop stars out in force. Organised by the local edition of Harper's Bazaar magazine and the Cyprus Fashion Designers' Association, the only part of the event open to the public is the exhibition space in the atmospheric Famagusta Gate Cultural Centre (p97), where the catwalk shows also take place.

The event is a huge boost to local designers, whose sterling work takes centre stage. Internationally known Erotokritos presented his collection in the first ever runway show. Soon after, in February 2009, he opened his first boutique in Cyprus, to go with his two Paris stores and his concession in Selfridges. Karl Lagerfeld muse and French supermodel-turned-designer Inès de la Fressange was another notable presence.

Cypriot names to watch include Sofia Alexander, whose intricate pleats and folds create garments that are visually stunning and suit any body shape. Natar/Yastrobnik are a hot male design duo (of both men's and womenswear), whose stunning knitted creations earned them plaudits at CFW. Also making waves on the scene is Pantelis Panteli, a Lemesos-based designer whose fantastical creations and over the top style has gained him notoriety in the Cyprus fashion world.

Inspired to get the look? Several of the designers have their workshops in Nicosia, and many are also stocked in Flexi boutique (p93). You can also hang with the glam set at Zoo (p96), host of the official fashion week after-party. Fabulous, dahling.

Itineraries

Nicosia Old & New

Within the sun-baked, sandstone Venetian Walls of Nicosia lies the heart of the old city, where medieval buildings, museums and historical churches stand (or crumble under) the weight of time. Yet there is still a lively pulse in the capital's core, where young designers set up shop, arty crowds convene for coffee and new communities of migrants make their homes and stomping grounds.

Acquaint yourself with the wonders within the walls with this stroll through the ancient alleyways, studded with inviting shopfronts and historic monuments. The route takes around two-and-a-half hours; allow more time if the heat persuades you to make frequent stops for refreshments.

Start at Chrysaliniotissa Street, just north of the Caraffa bastion of the city walls. **Panagia Chrysaliniotissa Church** (p85), set on this street, is believed to be the oldest Byzantine church in Nicosia. From here, follow Odysseos south and take a left at the T-junction to the **Chrysaliniotissa Crafts Centre** on Dimonaktos, where eight workshops and studios around a central courtyard display delicate jewellery, woodwork, glasswork, hand-made toys and other creations by Cypriot artists. It's a cool spot to pick up an original present, or just enjoy browsing.

If you're feeling peckish, the **Coffee Nest** café serves homely and innovative dishes, most of them vegetarian and deliciously healthy, like the sugar-free avocado and berry ice-cream. The maze of streets around the craft centre is an up-and-coming area, and many of the houses have been carefully restored to their former glory with

The wall of Nicosia

government assistance. As a result, it's in a much more polished state than many of the neighbourhoods within the walls.

From Dimonaktos, take a right on to Ipponaktos Street and another right to behold the uncanny sight of floating tables in the window of **Mobhaus** design store on Ektoros (Ektoros 18, http://mobdesign studio.com). This cutting-edge shop styles itself as a purveyor of 'interior architecture'. Heading back up the street towards the outskirts of the walls, turn left and walk past the landmark wooden doors of **Famagusta Gate** (p97) on Athinon. Originally known as Porta Giuliana after Giulio Savorgnano, the engineer who designed Nicosia's characteristic snowflake-shaped city walls, Famagusta Gate is one of three surviving entries to the city. The Porta Domenica (now Pafos Gate) is in the east, and the Porta del Provveditore (Kyrenia Gate) is in north Nicosia. Famagusta Gate has been stylishly renovated and now functions as a multi-space arts centre, hosting exhibitions and events such as Cyprus Fashion Week.

Head right on Thiseos and then left on Agiou Ioannou, towards the densely clustered sights around the square of Plateia Archiepiskopou Kyprianou. To your right are the **Museum of the National Struggle** (p84) and the **Ethnographic Museum** (p83), housed in the 18th-century Archbishopric. Next door, the newer and impossibly opulent **Archbishop's Palace** (p82) contains the Byzantine Museum and four art galleries. What looks more like a fortress further down the street is in fact **Agios Ioannis** (St John's) cathedral (p85), which is home to some stunning murals.

On the left of this street, the **Pancyprian Gymnasium** (p84) is the oldest secondary school still functioning on the island, and has its own wealth of museum treasures to be explored. If you follow the brown signs that point westwards behind the Archbishop's Palace, you'll reach the **Municipal Arts Centre**, set inside a beautifully renovated old power station on Apostolou Varnava. **Palia Electriki** (p89), a stylish restaurant, is also on-site.

Head back to Plateia Archiepiskopu Kyprinou, and at the bottom of the street bear right as Zinonos Kiteos curves around and delivers you to the door of the **House of Hadjigeorgakis Kornesios** (p83), a restored manor house of Ottoman splendour. Keep strolling right up Patriarchou Grigoriou towards the Turkish attractions in the square of Plateia Tillirias. The **Omeriye Hamam** (p97) and **Mosque** (p84) provide the old-time wonder, while **Hamam Pre-Club** (p87) adds glamour and liveliness to the scene at night. Cross the square and wander left up

ITINERARIES

Trikoupi; just off here, on Achilleos, you will find the workshop where **Kristina P** (Achilleos 5C, 22 460 080, www.kristinap.com) creates her whimsical hot-air balloon brooches and hand-woven leather bags.

Retrace your steps down to the other end of Trikoupi to find **db:Fly** (Trikoupi 91). Nestling between new Halal supermarkets, ad hoc parking lots and dusty bric-a-brac shops, it stocks sleek design gifts and little gadgets. You are now on the edge of the UN buffer zone (as the subtly named café Berlin No2 suggests), so it's time to round the corner and move south once more, past derelict houses and near-forgotten shoe makers to Lefkonos Street.

Behind the imposing school and **Faneromeni Church** (p83) is the hidden cultural gem of the **Weaving Mill** (p97). The unassuming facade of this old building shelters a haven for film enthusiasts, who regularly hold screenings and events here. Squatting behind the larger church is **Stavros tou Missirikou Church**, a medieval Orthodox affair converted into a mosque in 1571. Its odd amalgamation of Byzantine, Gothic and Italian renaissance styles is worth a look.

Wander across the yard to Stoa Papadopoulou on the other side of Faneromeni Church, where you will find the shop of acclaimed Cypriot artist and fashion designer **Kyriaki Costa** (Plateia tou Manoli 70, 99 471 107, http://kyriakicosta.net), whose sleek and flattering cuts have caused a buzz internationally as well as on the local scene. If you'd like to do more than window shop, it's advisable to call in advance to make an appointment at the boutique. Opposite the shop, take a much-needed rest at the well-kept secret of **Kala Kathoumena** café (p88), where the more bohemian elements of Cyprus society catch up over cool frappes. Once refreshed, don't miss the independent **Ant Comics** (22 660 384) bookstore on the same street, whose dedicated owners have also started up a club for graphic novel aficionados. It's the only place that stocks complete series from Marvel and DC Comics, as well as cult board games such as Warhammer and Warcraft.

Pass through the archway where the patrons of Kala Kathoumena idle, and emerge on Nikokleous Street, where you'll find the legendary **Hurricane Confectionery** (Nikokleous 7, 22 663 284). This pâtisserie has been open since 1942 – plenty of time to perfect that Cypriot classic, the hot cheese pie wrapped in layer upon layer of delicate, buttery filo pastry. The place has recently been polished up too, so it is a little more conspicuous in its back-street locale.

Follow the narrow road as it snakes past the bottom of busy Ledras Street and heads west to become Pygmalion Street, to the workshop of another hotly-tipped designer of the moment: **Stalo Markides** (4 Pygmalionos, www.stalo-markides.com). Markides puts her name to burlesque-inspired handbags and clutches, embellished with bold colours and leather pieces exquisitely cut to resemble feathers.

Moving away from the Green Line which divides the city in two, head south down Pericles, a quiet street lent a retro air by remnants of the recent past – peeling 7 Up adverts and daubed graffiti. The spruced-up **Shiantris** taverna (p90) is a little further along, recently expanded and relocated from a couple of doors down thanks to its well-executed and highly popular meze.

For an alternative lunch-time option, join the crowds on the

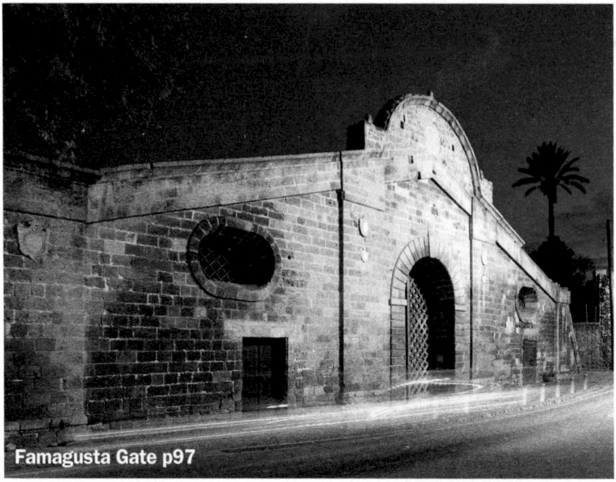

Famagusta Gate p97

well-trodden thoroughfare of Ledras and make a beeline to **Il Forno** (p88), for supremely tasty pizzas and pastas. For fresh, cheap eats it's hard to beat, and you can dine outdoors on the bustling shopping street. Those with a sweet tooth are spoilt for choice, as a number of ice-cream parlours vie for your change, but **Heraklis Garden Café** (p88), established in 1939 at the north end of Ledras, is a firm family favourite, thanks in no small part to the resident talking parrot.

Walk off your sugary sins by rambling under the wrought-iron balconies adorned with hanging flower baskets that line Ledras. Halfway along, on the corner of Ledras and Arsinoes, is the Debenhams department store. Ignore the wares on sale and make your way to the **Shacolas Tower Museum and Observatory** (p85) at the top of the street, which affords panoramic views of the city, the quarter just explored and the Turkish-occupied north.

Time for a sit-down? Families with young children might like to catch the old train that chugs at a stately pace along the cobbled streets from the south end of Ledras at Plateia Eleftherias, which spills out into the newer parts of Nicosia. Soak up the scene while you can, as plans are underway for a modernised square that will soon make this area unrecognisable.

North-east from here, off Onasagorou, lies the pedestrianised neighbourhood of **Laiki Geitonia**. Dodge the cheesy souvenirs and seek out delicate hand-embroidered lace made in the village of Lefkara (rumour has it the Queen (Elizabeth II) commissioned a piece of this dainty fabric for her own dining table). Here, older shopkeepers sit outside their stores and cafés, playing *tavli* (backgammon), swinging *kombologia* (worry beads) and catching up with the day's news – offering a glimpse of the languid pace life in Nicosia ticked at not so long ago.

Secret Beaches

Starting in Pafos, this road trip takes you on one of the island's most scenic drives, with stops for a splash or a snack at one of the many hidden coves where you'll likely have the shore to yourself.

The route is intended to fill a whole day, but the number of stops you make is entirely discretionary: you could choose to tick off each suggested point in a game of beach bingo, or take it easy, pause the game where it suits and chill out there until the sun goes down.

There's also the option of making a proper journey of it, by using this relatively short itinerary as a jumping-off point for a longer exploration from the west of the island into the Troodos mountains, or to keep on following the road as a roundabout route all the way to Nicosia – a much more pleasurable way to see the country than speeding straight through it along the highway.

First, you'll need to equip yourself with a road map of the island. The local **tourist office**, which has branches in Kato Pafos and Ktima (p187), produces a free visitor's map of the country, which should be sufficient for this trip. Alternatively, for those fussy about their cartography, **Moufflon Bookshop** (p122) in Ktima, the old part of Pafos, is a great place to procure books on all manner of Cypriot subjects, and stocks a variety of maps by different publishers.

A packed lunch is a good idea, especially if you're planning to go straight to the first destination, the remote **Lara Bay**. This section of the route is only possible with a four-wheel drive, as the far reaches involve

Paradise Place

navigating a loose-surface road that's unsuitable for cars not specifically designed for these conditions.

From Pafos, take the E701 road out of town, heading north-west. Follow signs for Agios Georgios on the F706. Just before the village, look out for a fork in the road and a sign pointing to Akamas on the right. Follow that road until you reach the mouth of the river Aspros with its small beach, and keep going to the mouth of the Avakas river at Toxeftra beach. Incidentally, walkers might like to take a break here and hike the three-kilometre trail of the **Avakas Gorge**. But if you're bound for the beach, keep going until you reach Lara. The journey should take around 20 minutes from the fork in the road.

It's imperative to stress that this is not an easy drive, as Akamas is made up of tough terrain – it's the undeveloped nature of the area that is its very attraction. Also, be especially environmentally conscientious here; this is a protected wildlife region, which blossoms with wildflowers in the more moderate months and provides sheltered nesting areas for Cyprus's endangered green turtles.

Turtle-watching and conservation trips are possible (see p125), but if you just want to share the habitat of these graceful animals for an hour or two, you can take in the charms of Lara Bay as long as you exercise due care and diligence. It's illegal to take any creature comforts such as umbrellas, beach beds or cars after a certain point – so park a respectful distance from the beach and make sure you don't leave any litter.

If you're in need of a sit-down meal after your stint soaking up the views at this expansive bay, then retrace your tracks back to Avakas, where you can make your way up to the spartan **Viklari Observation Point Restaurant** (p129). There is

ITINERARIES

also a restaurant at the Aspros river beach on the way back to the main road.

Those without a 4x4 can take the same initial route out of Pafos on the E701, but instead head in the direction of **Pegeia**. **La Frescoe** (p128) is a good spot in this village to pick up a supply of quality sandwiches. Past Pegeia, the E709 leads to the nearby village of **Kathikas**, home to **Araouzos Taverna** (p127), whose imaginative dishes are recommended if this is where you choose to break the journey.

If you've come directly from Pafos, you'll only be 25 minutes into the drive, so continue along the E709 towards Polis. When you reach the crossroads with a sign pointing left to **Latchi** (or **Latsi**) you can opt to take this route, especially if your vehicle did not allow for the earlier foray into Akamas. The alternative way to see the peninsula is to head for the harbour and either rent a self-sail motorboat for an expedition around Akamas (don't worry– you'll get a quick how-to lesson before being given the keys), or take the relaxed option and let the **Trident Boat Hire Company** (p129) do all the work for you on their waterborne tour. You may spot some signs to the **Baths of Aphrodite** just past Latchi harbour. Sheltered beneath some shady foliage, the pool where the goddess performed her ablutions and seduced the unsuspecting Adonis makes a pleasant enough diversion, but don't expect anything too spectacular.

If the sea air is whetting your appetite at this stage, the Polis-Latchi road features a good fish restaurant, **Psaropoulos** (p129). Bearing right at the crossroad at the end of the E709 will lead you to **Polis**, a small community whose chief attraction is a pleasant beachside campsite set in a eucalyptus wood. Accommodation in a higher price bracket is provided by the **Elia Latchi Holiday Village** (p177), with apartments dotted around lush green lawns. The **CTO** has a branch here (Vasileos Stasioikou, 26 322 468) for more local information. If you're staying in the area or passing by in the evening, the **Old Town** (p128) is a good destination for sampling well-made Mediterranean food in atmospheric surroundings.

After Polis, the road hugs the coast closely, and you'll need to make a conscious effort to keep your eyes straight ahead instead of gazing dreamily out to sea. Passengers, however, can sit back and enjoy the drive, which leads straight to Pomos and **Paradise Place** (p128). The 50-metre beach just before this café/bar, bears the same name. There are no other services on this out-of-the-way, pebbly shore, but you can always put up an umbrella and bask in the intense colours of Mediterranean blue set against the unusual orange hue of the surrounding rocks. Note that the water suddenly becomes very deep around three to four metres into the sea.

The veranda of the Paradise bar is wonderfully seductive, especially if the sun is setting, but if you're still up for adventure you can continue driving along the shore to **Pachyammos**. The beach is reached by an asphalted road just before the church of St Raphael the Miracle Maker. Time ticks by slowly in this tranquil spot, making its shallow waters the perfect place to turn your back on the world and commune with nature for a while.

The Wine Trail

A number of enterprising Cypriot winemakers have been causing a stir in the wine world in recent years, refining hundreds of years of local vine-growing history to produce more innovative and exciting offerings. Over 50 boutique wineries have cropped up along the slopes of the Troodos Mountains, where the combination of soil, sun and toil has sprung award-winning wines.

The belt is divided into four separate clusters of villages, each recognised by EU legislation as regions producing wine of 'controlled appellation' (from a specific area). This tour takes you around the Krassohoria region near Lemesos. It's perfectly possible to do it on a single day's road trip from Lemesos; alternatively, the itinerary can be taken at a more leisurely pace and extended over two days to include gloriously scenic drives past groves of knotted olive trees and quiet mountain villages.

In either case, some forethought is required. These regional producers are often small, family-run enterprises that will happily let you sample their wares as long as you give them a call a couple of days beforehand to make sure there is someone on hand to show you around. It's often hard to find stockists of the fruits of these small-scale wineries, so it's worth purchasing any wines you like on the spot. Most wines won't break the bank, as prices generally range from a modest €5 to €10 per bottle.

The journey starts with a bit of history, at the **Cyprus Wine Museum** (25 873 808/www.cypruswinemuseum.com), just

Cyprus Wine Museum

off the Kantou/Sotira exit of the old Lemesos to Pafos road. The museum (open 9am-5pm daily, admission €3-€5) traces the Dionysian legacy of wine making on the island back to 2500 BC. It illustrates the changing significance of the beverage (and its by-product, the firewater known as *zivania*) through the centuries with local artefacts such as goblets and enormous clay *pitharia*, traditionally used for storing wine. On the lower ground floor you can sample and buy a generous selection of Cyprus wines.

Not far from here is **Kolossi Castle** (p111), where the Knights Templar set up their headquarters in the late 12th century. They began exporting the island's rich dessert wine to Europe's royal courts, christening it Commandaria. This honey-hued beverage is considered the oldest named wine still in production today, and Richard the Lionheart declared it 'the wine of kings and the king of wines'. Its distinct flavour comes from indigenous grape varieties, mavro and xynisteri, that are laid out and left to dry in the sun after picking, a process that sweetens them. The wine is matured in old oak casks for a minimum of two years, with delicious results.

After this tantalising historical intro, it's time to try some of the good stuff. Head up into the mountains towards the **Krassohoria** or **Wine Villages**, where every house once had its own wine-making equipment. Along the Erimi-Omodos road E601, just outside the red-roofed village of Agios Amvrosios, lies the ecological winery of **Gaia Oinotechniki** (Agios Amvrosios, 25 943 981, www.gaia.com.cy),

which produced the first certified organically grown wines on the island. Tastings start from €2, and although some of the wines may seem old fashioned, their pioneering eco-credentials are what sets this place apart. In the neighbouring village of Pachna, **Yiaskouris Winery** (Pachna, 25 942 470, 99 633 730) has cemented a reputation for itself by making one of the best shiraz on the island. The Yiaskouris Dry White, made from local xynisteri grapes, is also a winner.

Assuming you've been making good use of the spittoon, it's time to get back into the car and, bearing right towards Vouni and Pera Pedi, climb to the village of **Kilani**. Sitting at an altitude of 1,100 metres, this little village is packed with wineries, but you can't miss the Austrian-style building of **Agia Mavri Winery** (Kilani, 25 470 225, 99 341 535, www.ayiamavri.com) that grandly overlooks the road. To reach it, take the second turning signposted to Kilani on the left.

The winery's friendly founder, Mrs Yiannoulla Ioannidou, can demonstrate the laborious methods which were originally used to plant, harvest and ferment the grapes, before taking you to see the modern steel tanks and pot-bellied French oak casks employed today. The winery produces a glut of wines, the most striking being the sweet white muscat, an aromatic and dense wine that has won international awards.

Also in Kilani you will find **Domaine Vlassides** (Kilani, 99 441 574). It's headed by Sophocles Vlassides, a qualified oenologist who blazed the way for modern winemakers in Cyprus. His forte is full-bodied reds, such as the cabernet sauvignon and the dry shiraz, which was awarded the Grand Gold medal at the Third Cyprus Wine Competition 2008.

By this time you might need to recharge with a bite to eat; fortunately, two fine establishments are within easy reach of the village. Heading back the way you came towards **Vouni** you will find **I Orea Ellas** (Ellados 3, Vouni, 25 944 328, open Fri-Sun 12-3.30pm, 7-11pm; reservations essential), where mouthwatering Greek specialities such as *tirokafteri* (spicy cheese dip), leek burgers and chicken in a rich mushroom sauce are served with panache, sometimes to the accompaniment of live music in the evenings. To keep things fresh, the specials menu changes to focus on the cuisine of different areas of the Greek mainland. For an interesting meaty alternative, head up towards the village of **Pera Pedi**, where the unusual **Taverna Neromilos** (Anexartisisas, Pera Pedi, 25 470 536, 99 304 595, open Tue-Sun from 12.30pm; reservations recommended at weekends) serves up deer and wild boar in a Czech-themed joint. In the same village, you can also buy bottles of local wine decorated with the paintings of acclaimed Cypriot artist Kikkos Lanitis from **Constantinou Winery** (Pera Pedi, 25 470 370), which is also famed for its orange liqueurs.

From Pera Pedi, cruise onwards and upwards, veering right towards Saittas and then following the E806 towards **Pelendri**, home to the idyllically-set **Tsiakkas Winery** (Georgou Sourri 2, just outside Pelendri, 25 991 080, 99 567 898, www.swaypage.com/tsiakkas, closed Sun). The winery turns out some really enjoyable classics like the toasty, oak-aged cabernet sauvignon. Look out, too, for the Vamvakada, a wine made from the Cypriot maratheftiko grape – considered the variety that will put Cyprus on the viniculture map, so long as farmers are encouraged to grow this low-yield wonder.

It should be time to head to base by now, but don't be tempted to take the B8 shortcut back to Lemesos; instead, hit the road you have come by, go past the turning to Pera Pedi and follow the signs to Mandria. The road then becomes the E601 towards Erimi; you should stop off at the picturesque village of **Omodos** for some less alcoholic (but just as delectable) traditional grape products.

In the cobblestoned streets you will find old ladies selling the naturally sweet *palouze* (a jelly-like dessert made from grape juice and flour), *epsima* (grape juice concentrated to the viscosity of honey) and *soujoukos* (threads of walnuts or almonds dipped in grape juice and sun-dried until a thick roll is formed). In Omodos, not far from Timios Stavros Monastery, you can also visit the restored *linos* or wine-press, which proudly testifies to the village's medieval wine-making history.

The surrounding villages have a fecund past intimately tied to the vine, and an even brighter future. The regional wineries springing up around the Lemesos and Pafos area are too numerous to mention here, but more information can be found at www.cypruswineries.org. If you would rather sample as much wine as possible in one spot, then the **Wine Festival** (p35) held in Lemesos every September features the products of the larger producers, as well as some intriguing independents.

Cyprus by Area

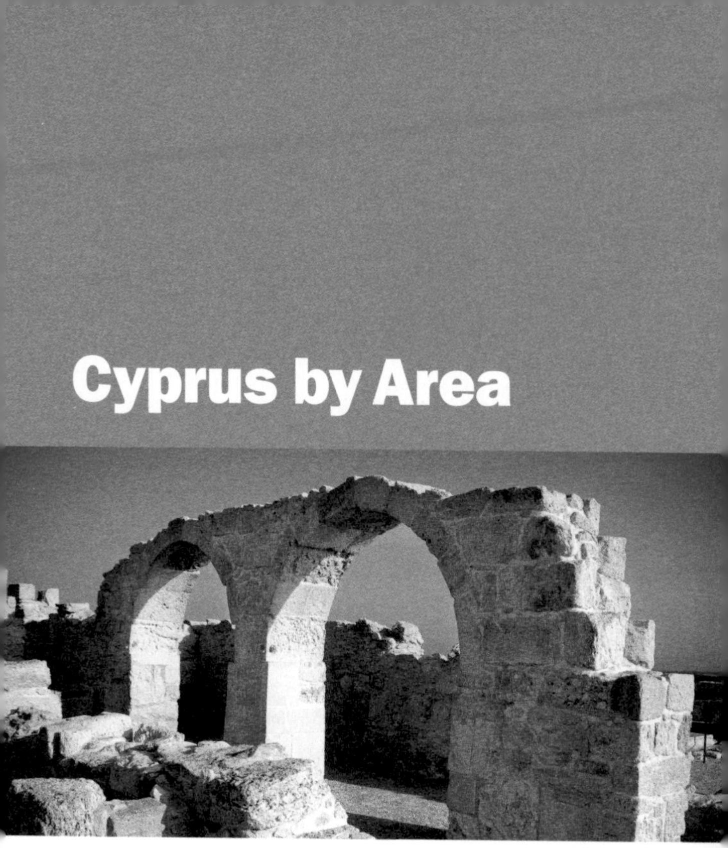

Agia Napa port

Agia Napa & Protaras

Agia Napa

The early noughties heyday of Agia Napa as the summer party centre of the UK Garage scene has all but fizzled out. By the middle of the decade, the clubbers and DJs had moved on and now the summer club scene in this tiny fishing village, which enjoyed a dizzying rise to fame, is in major decline. Even though Agia Napa is no longer a prime clubbing destination there are still more than a few good bars and clubs, some off the beaten tourist track, where you can have an enjoyable night out. Pop, R&B and commercial dance are now the predominant sounds.

The good news is that the area's natural assets, notably its beaches, which are among the best on the island, can now have their moment in the sun (see box p55). Noteworthy sights include **Agia Napa Monastery** in the central square, which dates back to the 16th century and offers a haven of tranquillity in this lively resort. Just up the road next to the town hall is the third-century **Church of Agia Mavri**, which previously housed the **Museum of Marine Life**, now incorporated into the **Thalassa Municipal Museum of the Sea** on Kryou Nerou street. The Cyprus Tourism Organisation (CTO) office is virtually next door.

Agia Napa

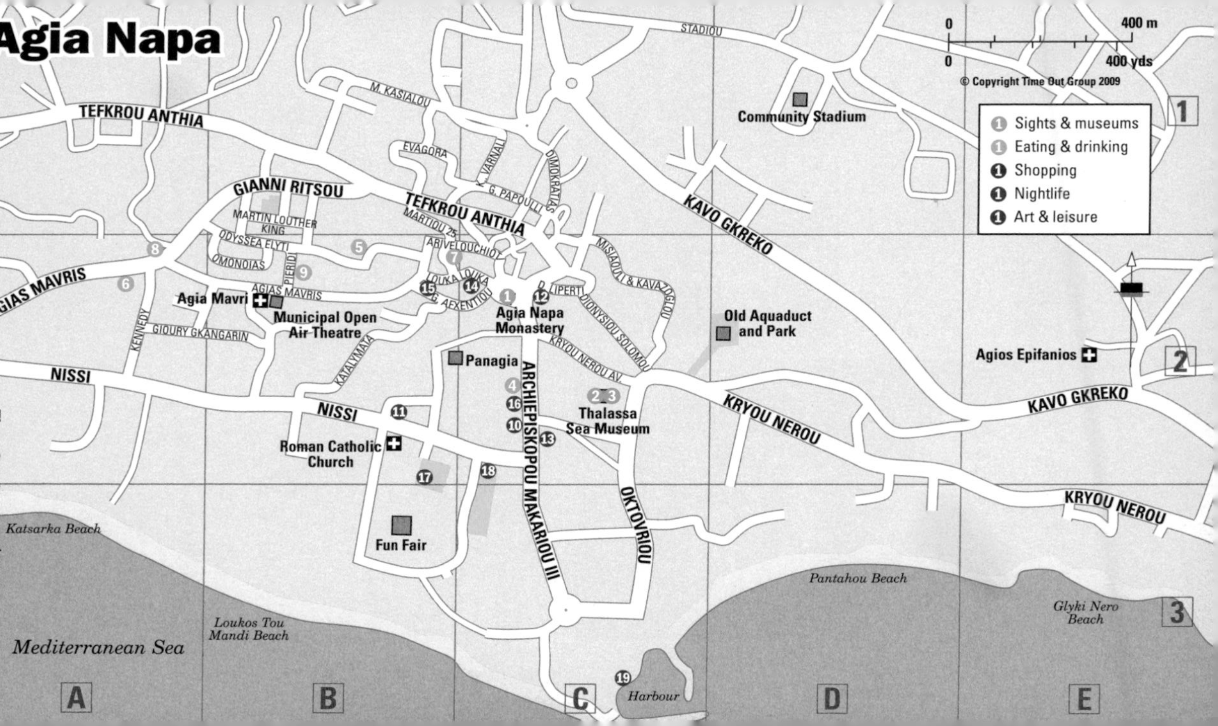

0
400 m
0
400 yds
© Copyright Time Out Group 2009
Sights & museums
Eating & drinking
Shopping
Nightlife
Art & leisure
1
2
3
A
B
C
D
E
TEFKROU ANTHIA
M. KASIALOU
STADIOU
Community Stadium
EVAGORA
K. VARNALI
DIMOKRATIAS
G. PAPOULLI
GIANNI RITSOU
MARTIN LOUTHER KING
ODYSSEA ELYTI
OMONOIAS
PIERIDI
MARTIOU 25
ARIVELOUCHIOT
KAVO GKREKO
MISIAOULI & KAVAZOGLOU
D. LIPERTI
DIONYSIOU SOLOMOU
KRYOU NEROU AV.
AGIAS MAVRIS
Agia Mavri
Municipal Open Air Theatre
LOUKA LOUKA
G. AFXENTIOU
Agia Napa Monastery
Old Aquaduct and Park
Agios Epifanios
KENNEDY
GIOURY GKANGARIN
KATALYMATA
Panagia
NISSI
ARCHIEPISKOPOU MAKARIOU III
Thalassa Sea Museum
KRYOU NEROU
OKTOVRIOU
Roman Catholic Church
Fun Fair
Katsarka Beach
Loukos Tou Mandi Beach
Mediterranean Sea
Harbour
Pantahou Beach
Glyki Nero Beach

Agia Napa's central square

CYPRUS BY AREA

Time to cool down, and the sandy beach at **Agia Napa Harbour** is less than 200 metres away. It's surrounded by a handful of pubs, cafés and souvenir shops, along with the fish restaurants for which this little town is famous. It's a short walk to Nissi Avenue, the best-known street in town, which leads to the white sands of **Nissi Beach**, from where you can see the island's only bungee jump. Not far from here is the adrenaline-soaked **Waterworld Waterpark**.

Sights & museums

Agia Napa Monastery

Plateia Seferi. **Open** 9am-6pm daily. **Admission** free. **Map** p51 C2 ❶

'Our Lady of the Forest' (the ancient Greek word 'Napa' means woodland) is one of the last monuments built by the Venetians before the Turkish occupation of 1570, and is quite well preserved. Once the focal point of the village, it looks a little out of place nowadays among the bars and souvenir shops, but it provides a cool and peaceful place to escape the crowds. It houses an Orthodox church, a pretty fountain, shade-giving trees and a handful of ageing nuns. The church, cut into the rock and partially underground, is entered down a flight of steps. To the east is a small Latin chapel, adjacent to which more steps lead down to a 600-year-old sycamore tree. Beside the monastery stands the lavish conference centre of the World Council of Churches.

Museum of Marine Life

Inside Thalassa Municipal Museum of the Sea, Kryou Nerou 14 (23 816 366). **Open** *June-Oct* 9am-1pm, 6-10pm Mon-Sat; 9am-1pm Sun; *Nov-May* 9am-2:30pm Mon; 9am-5pm Tue-Sat. **Admission** €3; €1 reductions; free with Thalassa Municipal Museum of the Sea ticket. **Map** p51 C2 ❷

Previously located in the Agia Napa Town Hall, this museum is now part of the Thalassa Municipal Museum of the Sea. It focuses on the different types of marine life that can be found locally and their effect on the island's history. Look out for the extensive fossil collection, as well as the careful reconstruction of the seabed.

Thalassa Municipal Museum of the Sea

Kryou Nerou 14 (23 816 366). **Open** *June-Oct* 9am-1pm, 6-10pm Mon-Sat; 9am-1pm Sun; *Nov-May* 9am-2.30pm Mon; 9am-5pm Tue-Sat. **Admission** €3; €1-€2 reductions. **Map** p51 C2 ❸

The only museum of its kind in the Mediterranean region links the sea to the history of the island. An audiovisual pleasure, this contemporary, interactive museum is spread out on six levels, housing several collections of artefacts, ceramics, sculptures, paintings and engravings. The highlight, though, is the life-size replica of the *Kyrenia II* – a 4th century BC merchant vessel and the oldest Greek ship ever found. It was discovered by chance off the coast of Kyrenia in 1967, at a depth of 30m.

Eating & drinking

Central

NEW *Archiepiskopou Makriou III (23 816 555).* **Open** 10am-midnight daily. €. **Café**. **Map** p51 C2 ❹

This new addition to the area can be found in front of the Napa Plaza hotel, serving salads, burgers and pasta with an Italian leaning in stylish surrounds. Breakfast and a rainbow selection of fresh fruit juices are also available.

Guru Bar/Love Bites

Odyssea Elyti 11 (23 721 838). **Open** *Restaurant* 7-11pm daily. *Bar* 6pm-2am daily. €€€. **Bar/restaurant**. **Map** p51 B2 ❺

Two atmospheric venues in one. The menu at Love Bites is packed with tempting options, including a new sushi bar, and the pre-club Guru Bar garden oozes romance. It's decorated with little buddhas and has a very welcoming vibe. The music policy covers everything you can stick a 'world' label on, from ethnic and progressive to Latin and oriental. Lounge back and relax with a nargileh (water pipe).

Hokkaido

Agia Mavris 35 (23 721 505/www.hokkaidocy.com). **Open** 6pm-midnight daily. €€. **Japanese**. **Map** p51 A2 ❻

This Japanese restaurant maintains very high standards as well as entertaining patrons with its chefs' nimble movements and elaborate cookery skills, demonstrated as they make a show of cooking your teppanyaki. It's fun for youngsters, and half-price kids' portions are available.

Los Bandidos

Ari Velouchioti 2 (23 723 258). **Open** 5.30-11pm daily. €€. **Mexican**. **Map** p51 B2 ❼

Possibly the best Mexican on the island, this restaurant has a fun rather than romantic vibe and offers excellent food at decent prices. The strawberry margarita is a must, preferably sipped in the pretty summer garden.

Mai Thai

NEW *Yianni Ritsou 1 (23 721 568/www.maithaicy.com).* **Open** 6pm-midnight daily. **€€. Thai. Map** p51 A2 ⑧
There's an inviting menu of tongue-tingling flavour combinations such as stir-fried duck with black peppercorns and oyster sauce at this new Thai restaurant. Staff are accommodating and prices very reasonable.

Potopoieion to Ellinikon

Theodosi Pieridi 2 (23 722 760). **Open** 11.30pm-late Sat. **€€. Taverna. Map** p51 A2 ⑨
This taverna's USP is its five-piece band, which on Saturday evenings serenades diners with folk music and *rembetika* – a Greek equivalent of the blues.

Shopping

Carats Jewellers

Archiepiskopou Makariou III 16 (23 721 226/www.caratsjewellers.com). **Open** 9am-11pm Mon-Fri; 11am-7pm Sun. **Map** p51 C2 ⑩
A well-respected jeweller offering a stunning range of contemporary and creative designs. Commissioned orders are welcomed.
Other locations *Kryou Nerou 11 (23 721 959); Kryou Nerou 22 (23 816 333).*

London Clothing Co

Nissi 12 (23 723 566). **Open** 9am-11pm Mon-Sat; 11am-7pm Sun. **Map** p51 B2 ⑪
Versace, Bench and French Connection are among the brand names stocked in this shop. A favourite among the locals.

Maze

Archiepiskopou Makariou III 9A (23 721 360). **Open** 8am-11pm Mon-Fri; 8am-7pm Sat. **Map** p51 C2 ⑫
If you visit no other shop in Agia Napa, pop into this one for a one-stop spree. On offer is a gorgeous selection of summer dresses, stylish shoes, bags and belts, plus a small range of men's styles.

Planet Sound and Vision

Archiepiskopou Makariou III 27 (23 724 010). **Open** 9.30am-10pm daily. **Map** p51 C2 ⑬
This CD shop is the only one in the area that stocks the Napa compilations. There's a variety of other music and an extensive range of DVDs and games.

Nightlife

Black & White

Louca Louca 6 (23 723 400). **Open** *Mar-Oct* 1.30am-4am daily. *Nov-Feb* 1.30am-4am Fri, Sat. **Map** p51 C2 ⑭
Being the oldest kid on the Napa block and maintaining a prestigious live link with the UK's Choice FM and Radio 1 gives Black & White a certain edge. A heady mix of R&B, reggae, jungle, swing, hip hop, soul and funk keeps the crowds happy. Escape to the cosy chill-out zone for a breath of fresh air.

Castle Club

Grigori Afxentiou 5 (www.thecastleclub.com). **Open** 1am-4.30am daily. **Map** p51 B2 ⑮
Shaped like a castle and with an excellent DJ line-up year after year, Castle Club is a Napa favourite. New features include a VIP room with its own bar and staff. The music policy is R&B, house, trance, disco, chart and '70s and '80s, played across three rooms. If the gyrating and vibrating get too much, take a break in the chillout space.

Piazza Club

Archiepiskopou Makariou III, next to Napa Plaza (www.clubpiazza.com). **Open** 11pm-4.15am Sat. **Map** p51 C2 ⑯
Recently renovated, this swish establishment concentrates on Greek music. Check the website for additional summer openings.

Arts & leisure

Parko Paliatso Fun Fair

Off Nissi, behind McDonald's (23 724 744/www.parkopaliatsocy.com). **Open** 4pm-midnight daily. **Map** p51 B2 ⑰
This funfair features the usual bumper cars as well as a ghost train; but adults

Beachy keen

White, sandy shores and clear waters abound on the island's south-eastern coast.

No doubt you'll be dying to dip a toe in the Med, and the beaches around Agia Napa and Protaras are among the best on the island. Starting a few kilometres west of Agia Napa town centre on Nissi Avenue is the fishtail-shaped **Makronissos Beach**. Its lack of currents and shallow waters make it perfect for small children. For history buffs, the nearby Makronissos Tombs, a Neolithic burial site of 19 tombs cut into the rocks, can be visited for free.

Also off Nissi Avenue, four kilometres from Agia Napa, are the white sands of **Nissi Beach**. For those who like a nice stroll or a long trek, a wooden walkway along the coast begins here and continues eastwards, turning into a paved area around **Kermia Beach** and then into a 'nature trail' (a clearly distinguishable dirt track) that leads all the way to **Cape Greco**. On the way to Protaras, at the island's south-easternmost tip, Cape Greco (spelled Kavo Gkreko on road signs) attracts nature-lovers with its vertiginous cliffs, eroded rocks, stunning sea caves and crystalline waters.

A sign-posted turn-off will take you to **Konnos Bay**, an intimate, protected cove favoured by locals. Water sports are available here.

Further up the coast, **Protaras** is famed for its seductive beaches which, though crowded in summer, are every visitor's dream come true: powder-soft white sand and sparkling, shallow turquoise water. **Fig Tree Bay** and the slightly smaller **Green Bay** are among the most popular stretches of sand here.

Halfway between Protaras and Paralimni is the **Kapparis Resort**, with a good selection of restaurants, friendly bars and a succession of secluded coves in the shadow of towering limestone cliffs. The area has only recently come under development and is still a work in progress; take care, as much of the road is little more than dirt track.

CYPRUS BY AREA

Agia Napa Monastery p52

CYPRUS BY AREA

who are after something a bit different can try the Free Fall, which involves being dropped from ever greater heights by a hydraulic lift. Also on-site is the Sling Shot, the last of the dare-devil rides to survive EU regulations, which uses air compression to catapult riders skywards faster than a speeding bullet (60km per hour, to be exact). Accelerating at 6Gs, it's only for the bravest of thrill-seekers; €60 gets you two rides, a DVD and two T-shirts.

Seasons

Nissi 3 (no phone). **Open** 10am-2am daily. No credit cards. **Map** p51 C2 ⓲
A large complex featuring a rather unexciting mini-golf course (€4.50 a game), a bungee trampoline for kids (€4.50 for 5 mins), go-karts (€11-€30 for 5-30 mins) and maxi quads (€4.50).

Yellow Submarine

Agia Napa Harbour, in front of Vassos Fish Harbour Restaurant (99 658 280/99 596 280). **Map** p51 C3 19
This €10 trip in a mini, semi-submersible vessel includes the option to swim or snorkel. It's excellent entertainment for children as it incorporates a fish-feeding show. Voyages depart daily at 10.30am, 12.15pm and 2.30pm.

Protaras

East from Agia Napa along the coast, the areas of **Protaras** and **Paralimni** join Agia Napa to form a small triangle that is quick and easy to navigate on whatever wheels you're using. Just outside Agia Napa, **Konnos Bay** boasts the spectacular natural wonder of the sea caves. A little further on, Protaras has seen a wave of recent development and is geared more towards families and couples than its more famous neighbour. It's still a bustling, popular resort, however, and its restaurants tend to be better than Agia Napa's. Its compact size means most of the venues listed here can be found on or around the main strip running alongside the coast.

Fit travellers can hike up the steep path to the Byzantine **Church of Profitis Elias** (the Prophet Elijah), easily spotted at night when it is beautifully illuminated. During the day it affords panoramic views of the area. A sturdy handrail and a bench halfway along ease the uphill trek. The **Church of Agioi Saranta** (the 40 Martyrs), built into a rocky ridge on the Phanos Plateau, is an additional challenge but well worth visiting.

Sights & museums

Magic Dancing Waters

Leoforos Protara, next to McDonald's (99 623 143). **Show starts** *May-Oct* 9pm daily. Closed Nov-Apr.
Admission €13; €7 reductions.
This one-hour show incorporates jets of water 'dancing' to modern and classic tunes. Using a computerised system that regulates 20,000 nozzles, lasers, lights, fire and smoke, the overall experience is a spectacle for adults and kids alike. It's hugely popular, so arrive early to make sure you get a seat.

Ocean Aquarium

Leoforos Protara (23 741 111/ www.protarasaquarium.com). **Open** 10am-6pm daily. **Admission** €11; free-€7 reductions.
Displaying over 1,000 species of marine life, including sharks, piranhas, stingrays, tortoises, turtles, eels and sea urchins, the Ocean Aquarium offers an interesting escape from the heat – although the cramped quarters of the penguins and crocodiles do make for a depressing sight. There is a large and somewhat overpriced café set within beautifully manicured gardens, as well as a small souvenir shop where the emphasis is on cheap trinkets rather than quality mementoes.

Eating & drinking

Anemos Beach Restaurant

Iasonos, next to Capo Bay Hotel (23 831 488). **Open** *Summer* 9am-11pm daily. Closed winter. **€€. Fish.**

A popular fish restaurant (though the menu does include other dishes too), which has an enormous outdoor terrace and fabulous views on to Fig Tree Bay. See box p55.

Bikini Bar

Amfitritis 9, between Odessa & Trizas hotels (23 833 650). **Open** *Bar* 9am-7pm daily. *Club* Mid June-Aug 11pm-6am Fri, Sat; 9pm-3am Sun-Thur. Closed Sept-mid June. **Bar/club.**

The resident DJ will keep you partying all day at this beautifully-set beach bar. During the winter it functions as a café/bar and on summer nights it transforms into a beachside club, with a great reputation for quality music and talented DJs spinning the wheels of steel.

Cliff Bar

Grecian Park Hotel, Konnou 81, Cape Greco (23 832 000). **Open** noon-3am daily. **Bar.**

Perched on the cliff edge, this spectacular bar boasts incredible sea views and luxurious surroundings. It opens up whenever the sun makes an appearance, even during the winter, if only for a couple of hours. Drinks are pricier than at other bars in the area, but you're paying for the incredible location.

Cultura Del Gusto

Ifestou 7 (23 833 860). **Open** 5pm-midnight daily. **€€€. Italian.**

Treat yourself to something different from a menu that includes suckling pig, duck and deer, alongside more standard fare. Booking is essential at weekends.

Molti Café

NEW *Xenodohion 61 (23 832 896).* **Open** noon-1am daily (food till 11pm). **€. Café/bar.**

Refreshingly, a café-bar that isn't themed. Instead, this new spot in

Nissi Beach p55

CYPRUS BY AREA

What lies beneath

Take the plunge at these great diving spots.

Zenobia

The warm, clear waters and lack of strong tides and currents around Cyprus make the island an ideal place to learn to dive. Scuba diving schools have surfaced in every coastal town; ask at your hotel for recommendations or try Dive-In (www.dive-in.com.cy), a company with centres in Larnaka, Lemesos and Pafos; Sunfish Divers (www.sunfishdivers.com) in the Agia Napa and Protaras area; or the Pafos-based Cydive (www.cydive.com). Courses for both beginners and more experienced divers can be worked into your holiday, after which you'll be qualified to explore the rich underwater world of sea caves, shipwrecks and marine life.

The most famous Cypriot dive site is the **Zenobia wreck** off the coast of Larnaka, which is considered the finest dive site in the Med. The sunken Swedish ferry has remained remarkably intact since it sank with a cargo of over 100 articulated lorries in 1980. Divers can snoop around the ship in the company of creatures such as conger eels, barracudas and groupers which have made the wreck their home. Nearby is a British Army Air Corps **helicopter wreck** and a sunken boulder-carrying barge, which has created an artificial reef known as **Fraggle Rock**.

Between Agia Napa and Protaras, **Konnos Point** and the sea caves offer plentiful opportunities for wanders through tunnels, canyons and interesting rock formations. The waters are rich in marine life, including octupus, starfish and a variety of hunting fish, which provide quite a spectacle if you're lucky enough to catch them in action.

At the **Akrotiti Fish Reserve** in Lemesos, you can attempt to hand-feed species ranging from bream to bass. Pafos dive sites worth checking out include the **Amphorae Reef** and the **100-Foot Reef**, known for its exceptionally clear waters. These suggestions are the tip of the iceberg: the good tidings for scuba fans are that scores more intriguing sites are ripe for exploration.

Thalassa Municipal Museum of the Sea p53

Protaras is chic and simple, kitted out in white with just a splash of colour. An open kitchen lets you spy on the whereabouts of your cheap and tasty Italian meal, while the glass wall offers a view on to the street. Very European in style, Molti is a favourite with families as well as groups of friends.

Spartiatis

Konnou 79B, next to Grecian Park Hotel, Cape Greco (23 831 386). **Open** noon-4pm, 6-10.30pm daily. **€€. Fish.**
Renowned for its fish meze and for using sparklingly fresh ingredients, the restaurant also commands stunning views over Cape Greco.

Umi

Grecian Park Hotel, Konnou 81, Cape Greco (23 844 000). **Open** 7-11pm daily. **€€€. Japanese.**
The menu at this inviting fusion restaurant includes sushi and sashimi; in good weather, you can dine al fresco. Housed in a five-star hotel, this place oozes laid-back luxury – and has fantastic views to boot.

Shopping

Holi Hire

Cape Greco 501 (99 076 507/www.holihire.com). **Open** *Apr-Oct* 10am-12.45pm Mon-Sat (all other months by appointment).
This English-run company hires out various essentials, from baby cots, buggies and sterilisers to mobile phones, wheelchairs and digital cameras. Prices are low, though a refundable deposit may be required. Delivery and collection are available on request.

Arts & leisure

Agia Trias Boat Trips

Golden Coast Hotel Fishing Harbour (99 627 048). No credit cards.
Departing at 10.15am each day, this is a pleasant excursion that won't break the bank. The boat is equipped with a bar, snorkelling sets and a sun deck. Snacks are available at an extra cost.

Fantastico Mini Golf & Luna Park

Cape Greco 449 (23 833 193).
Open 10am-10pm daily.
As far as mini-golf courses go, this one is reasonably imaginative. Bumper cars, a miniature train, water rides and a snack bar make it a worthwhile stop for families.

InterYachting Catamaran Cruise

De Costa Bay Jetty (80 000 900/www.interyachting.com.cy).
Quiet and swift, these purpose-built catamarans smoothly glide you out into the open waters of the Med. Trips include food and transfers to and from your hotel, with prices starting at €46 for a half day (€23 reductions). Swimming and snorkelling are optional. There's a fully stocked bar on board; if you opt for an all-inclusive package, drinks are included. Tours depart at 9.45am or 5pm for the sunset tour.

Moonshine Ranch

NEW *Cape Greco* (99 605 042).
Open 8am-7pm daily.
Launched in summer 2008, Moonshine Ranch offers royalty-style rides in a horse-drawn carriage (great for weddings) or horse-riding treks along a local trail. Rides cost from €34 an hour.

Raptor Fast Boat Safari

Paralimni Fishing Shelter (96 596 938/www.manic-ribs.com). No credit cards.
An enjoyable three-hour trip on a high-powered boat that doesn't actually travel that fast. The price (€39 for adults) includes transfers to and from your hotel (the departure point is just outside Protaras, and the trip leaves at 10am and 2pm daily). For private parties, a high-speed boat trip (100mph), including wave-jumping and 360-degree spins, can be booked separately (€18 for 20 mins).

Undersea Walkers

De Costa Bay (99 563 506/www.underseawalkers.com). **Open** *May-Oct* 10am, 1.30pm. Closed Nov-Apr.
See box p74.

Around Agia Napa

Venture outside the boundaries of Agia Napa and Protaras and you'll hit the **Kokkinohoria**, or Red Villages. It is the fertile soil, a deep rust-red colour from the earth's high mineral content, that gives Avgorou, Dherynia, Frenaros, Vrysoulles, Liopetri, Sotira, Xylotymbou and Achna their collective name. This bountiful area is renowned for its potatoes (devotees claim that Cypriot potatoes are the most delicious in the world), strawberries and watermelons, each honoured with their own festival on different dates during the year.

On a sightseeing level, the otherwise quiet Kokkinohoria are best known for a few choice folk history museums and churches, like that of **St Peter and St Paul** in Avgorou, which houses two unusual, double-sided 17th-century icons. Natural beauty spots include the **Achna Dam**, where the rare glossy ibis stops for a well-earned rest on its migratory path every April and October. Dying traditions such as basket-weaving (Liopetri) and folk poetry (Avgorou) are also kept alive in this area.

Sights & museums

Ethnographic Museum/Pierides Foundation

Karvon 52, Avgorou (23 923 340). **Open** 8.30am-1.30pm, 4-6pm Mon, Thur; 8.30am-1.30pm Tue, Wed, Fri; 9am-1pm Sat. **Admission** €1.70; €0.85 reductions.

Take the time to hunt out this quaint little museum, housed in a beautiful example of traditional architecture. Items are in pristine condition and embrace all aspects of Cypriot life, ranging from embroidery, lace and jewellery to ceramics, metalware and more.

CYPRUS BY AREA

Detailed descriptions in English can be found at the entrance to each room.

Folk Art Museum

Demetri Liperti 2, Dherynia (23 824 526). **Open** 9.30am-7pm Mon-Sat. **Admission** €1.70; free reductions.
Frequently used as a location for civil weddings in the Famagusta region, this museum occupies a charming old house. Exhibits include a traditional Cypriot bedroom and an old-fashioned oven – once an essential feature of any self-respecting Cypriot household – in the yard. The collection includes delicate lacework, primitive farming tools and household items. The curator will happily answer questions.

Eating & drinking

Vasiliskos

NEW *Dimokratias 12, Sotira (99 176 739).* **Open** 6.30-11pm daily. **€€. International.**
Situated right in the centre of the village, Vasiliskos serves great food with an unmistakable Mediterranean focus. The service is also outstanding, making it easily the best restaurant in the area. Unsurprisingly it's often booked solid, so if you don't want to miss out, make sure you get your reservation in early.

Xylino

Trikomou 179, Agios Georgios, Vrysoulles (23 962 403). **Open** 4-11pm Mon-Sat. **€€. Taverna.**
Xylino is easily spotted (near the school, just opposite the church), as this is the only building in the village constructed from logs. In-the-know locals flock to this little gem for great food, service with a smile and low prices. The fantastic meze consists of an impressive 28 plates, many of which are made with seasonal ingredients, such as wild greens and game. Regional dishes on offer sometimes include own-made village macaroni and new potatoes sautéed in wine and coriander seeds.

Konnos Bay p55

Shopping

Ascott Pottery

Protara 210, Paralimni (23 822 428/23 822 573). **Open** 8am-sunset Mon-Sat.

A spectacular collection of Cypriot ceramics, including intricate hand-painted figurines in traditional dress. Visitors are often invited to try the potter's wheel, which is good fun for kids.

Melekkis Jewellery

Eleftherias 4, Dherynia (23 821 791/ www.melekkis.net). **Open** 8.30am-1pm, 4-8pm Mon, Tue, Thur, Fri; 8.30am-1pm Wed, Sat.

This well-known, family-run jewellery shop specialises in commissioned designs. It's especially popular with those in search of wedding rings.

Arts & leisure

EMW Go-Karts

Agias Theklas 18 (23 723 111). **Open** 10am-9pm daily. No credit cards.

Go-karting at this centre next to the Waterworld Waterpark (see above) costs from €12 for six minutes on the track. Discounts are available for tickets purchased from Waterworld.

Napa Bungee

Neophytou Poullou (99 404 208). **Open** *May-Oct* 10am-6pm daily (weather permitting). Closed Nov-Apr.

The island's only bungee jump was established a decade ago. The 200ft fall is also available to do as a tandem leap. Prices start at €70.

Waterworld Waterpark

Agia Theklas 18 (23 724 444/www. waterworldwaterpark.com). **Open** *May-Nov* 10am-6pm daily. Closed Dec-Apr.

Visible from the highway as you enter Agia Napa, Waterworld was the island's first waterpark. It has won 22 international awards as Europe's largest themed waterpark, and has a design based on Greek mythology. Restaurants and fast-food outlets are scattered around the park, and lockers can be rented for a moderate fee.

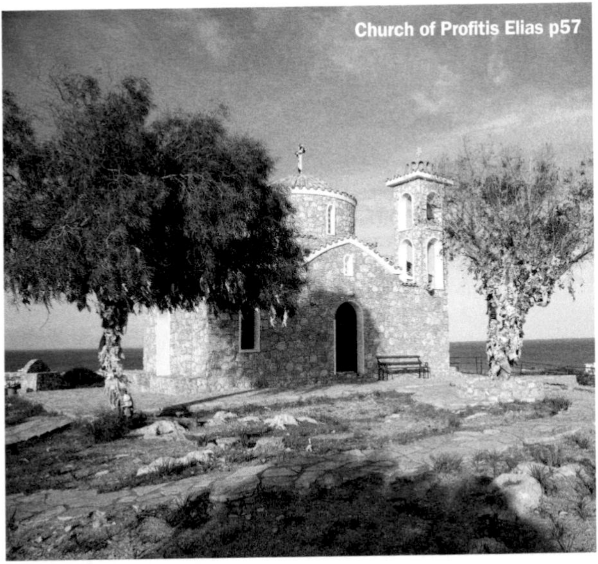

Church of Profitis Elias p57

CYPRUS BY AREA

Ammos p76

Larnaka

Larnaka ticks at a slower, less cosmopolitan pace than other Cypriot urban centres. The island's third largest town is associated with leisurely strolls along its palm-lined promenade and lazy lounging on café terraces, watching the Mediterranean lilting by.

Larnaka was founded as a city kingdom known as **Kition**, the scant ruins of which can be visited in the Chrysopolitissa area. Zenon of Kition was born here in 334BC and founded the Stoic school of philosophy in Athens. **Agios Lazaros Church**, a superb early tenth-century stone building, is the resting place of Larnaka's patron saint Lazarus. Also on site is a **Byzantine Museum** with a small but fascinating collection of religious items.

If you fly into Larnaka Airport by day you may catch a glimpse of the picturesque **Salt Lake** and its lush oasis just beyond the runway. Nestling deep in the greenery is **Hala Sultan Tekke** where Umm Haram, the Prophet Mohammed's aunt, is buried. The mosque remains one of the most important shrines in the Muslim world.
In winter, flamingos and other migratory birds line the water, but by the end of summer the salt lake is virtually dry.

If you are looking for a spot in the sun, the dark sand here is less attractive than the blond numbers further up the eastern coast, but beaches are generally very clean, many to international Blue Flag standards. Sunbeds and umbrellas are quite cheap to rent, especially along the **Phinikoudes promenade** and **Mackenzie Beach**, south of the town.

The main seaside stretch in Larnaka itself is the Phinikoudes promenade (officially named Athinon). The palm trees which give the promenade its name were first planted in 1922, and today it is surrounded by shops, bars and restaurants. At opposite ends of the promenade are Larnaka **Fort** and the **Marina**, both peaceful places to visit.

For more secluded beaches head towards **Mazotos**, a village between Larnaka and Pyla. The **Cyprus Tourism Organisation (CTO) beach** along the Dhekelia Road, between Larnaka and the British Sovereign Base of Dhekelia, hosts beach volley and handball tournaments and its facilities include a small children's playground and water sports.

Sights & museums

Agios Lazaros Byzantine Museum

Plateia Agiou Lazarou (24 652 498). **Open** 8.30am-12.30pm, 3-5.30pm Mon, Tue, Thur, Fri; 8.30am-12.30pm Wed, Sat. **Admission** €0.85; free reductions. **Map** p67 B4 ❶

The museum, located on the same site as Agios Lazaros Church (see below), is housed in a number of the cells of the old monastery that once stood here. It exhibits religious icons, artefacts and relics from the Byzantine period.

Agios Lazaros Church

Plateia Agiou Lazarou (24 652 498). **Open** 8.30am-1pm, 4-6.30pm daily. **Admission** free. **Map** p67 B4 ❷

One of the finest examples of Byzantine architecture in Cyprus, this three-aisled basilica was built in the 10th century over the tomb of Saint Lazarus, who made Larnaka his second home after his resurrection, and later became its first bishop. The gilded icon screen is considered one of the finest on the island.

Larnaka District Archaeological Museum

Plateia Kalograion (24 304 169). **Open** 8am-3pm Tue, Wed, Fri; 8am-5pm Thur; 9am-3pm Sat. **Admission** €1.70. **Map** p67 B2 ❸

Exhibits include findings from the Larnaka area's main Neolithic settlements of Choirokitia and Tenta. The pottery, ivory and alabaster exhibits provide evidence of the island's wide-ranging trade links through the years.

Larnaka District Medieval Museum

Larnaka Fort, Athinon (24 304 576). **Open** *June-Aug* 9am-7.30pm Mon-Fri. *Nov-May, Sept, Oct* 9am-5pm Mon-Fri. **Admission** €1.30; free reductions. **Map** p67 C4 ❹

Inside the fort at the southern end of the Phinikoudes, this small museum contains displays from the early Christian, Byzantine, Lusignan and Ottoman periods, as well as 12th- to 18th-century pottery, photos of historical sites and a collection of firearms, helmets and swords dating from the 15th to the 19th century. Swashbuckling stuff.

Larnaka Municipal Museum of Natural History

Grigori Afxentiou, within Larnaka Municipal Gardens (24 652 569). **Open** 9am-1pm Mon-Fri. **Admission** €0.35. **Map** p67 A3 ❺

A large collection of local reptiles, insects, birds, animals, fossils and rock formations, as well as marine life and plants from Cyprus and the surrounding countries. The museum is located in the Municipal Gardens, the greenery and playgrounds of which make for a pleasant visit, especially for children.

The Old Turkish Quarter

Around Larnaka Fort. **Map** p67 C4 ❻

In the areas south and southwest of the Fort, a maze of small, narrow streets still hums with the activity of traditional craftsmen and tiny businesses plying their trade. Most of these streets are one-way, but beware as local driving habits mean vehicles can appear from any direction. The 16th-century Grand

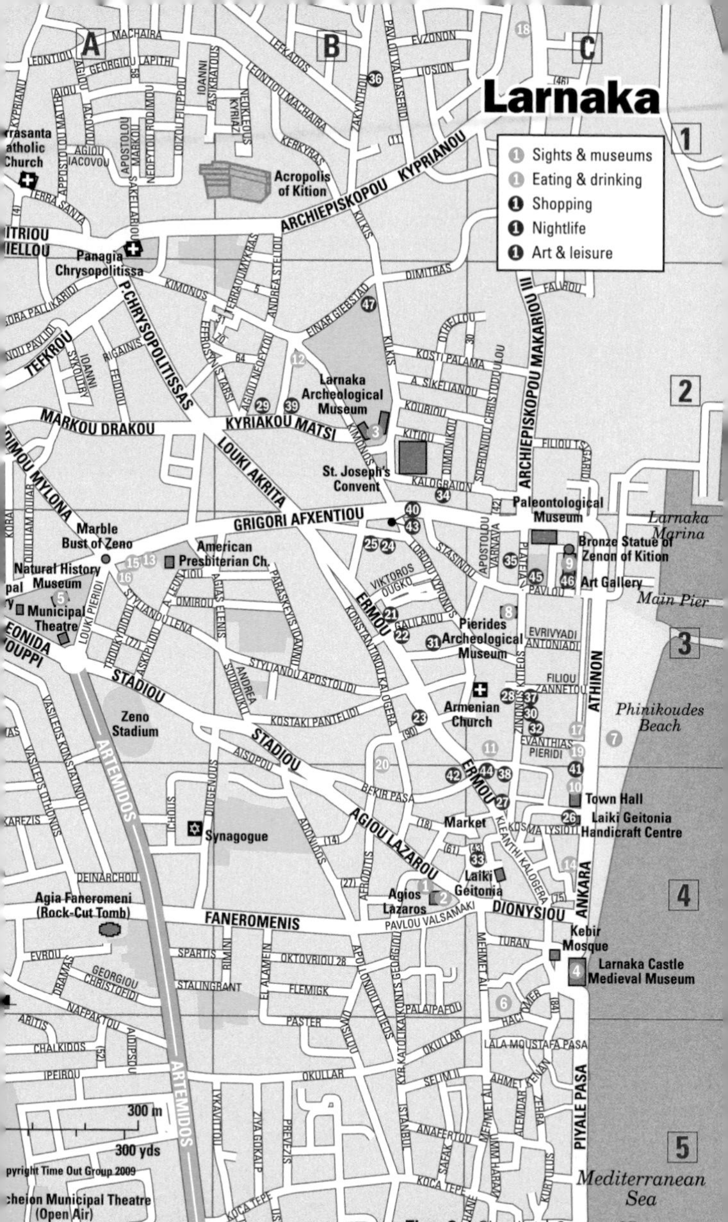
Larnaka
Sights & museums
Eating & drinking
Shopping
Nightlife
Art & leisure
A
B
C
1
2
3
4
5
Acropolis of Kitiion
Panagia Chrysopolitissa
Larnaka Archeological Museum
St. Joseph's Convent
Paleontological Museum
Bronze Statue of Zenon of Kitiion
Art Gallery
Larnaka Marina
Main Pier
Marble Bust of Zeno
American Presbiterian Ch.
Natural History Museum
Municipal Theatre
Pierides Archeological Museum
Armenian Church
Phinikoudes Beach
Zeno Stadium
Town Hall
Laiki Geitonia Handicraft Centre
Synagogue
Market
Laiki Geitonia
Agios Lazaros
Agia Faneromeni (Rock-Cut Tomb)
Kebir Mosque
Larnaka Castle Medieval Museum
Mediterranean Sea
cheion Municipal Theatre (Open Air)
rrasanta atholic Church
ARCHIEPISKOPOU KYPRIANOU
ARCHIEPISKOPOU MAKARIOU III
GRIGORI AFXENTIOU
MARKOU DRAKOU
KYRIAKOU MATSI
LOUKI AKRITA
P.CHRYSOPOLITISSAS
DIMOU MYLONA
TEFKROU
STADIOU
ERMOU
AGIOU LAZAROU
FANEROMENIS
DIONYSIOU
ATHINON
ANKARA
PIYALE PASA
ARTEMIDOS
EONIDA OUPPI
300 m
300 yds
pyright Time Out Group 2009

Nippon

Mosque (Cami Kebir) fell into a state of neglect after the 1974 invasion, but since the Green Line crossings began in 2003 has been showing greater signs of life.

Phinikoudes Promenade

The eastern edge of town. **Map** p67 C3 ❼
Rather unusually for Cyprus, this is a beach in an urban environment, with sunbeds and umbrellas on one side and cafés, restaurants and bars on the other. The middle stretch of the promenade is always busy. At the northern end is Larnaka Marina, with space for 450 yachts. Only the owners and crew are allowed inside, but you can walk freely along the pier. At the southern end, Larnaka Fort, built in the 1600s, divides the main seafront from the old Turkish quarter. The building was used as a prison during the early years of British rule. Today, it is open to the public with the Medieval Museum (see above) and often hosts events.

Pierides Foundation Museum

Laiki Group Cultural Centre, Zenonos Kitieou 4 (24 814 555). **Open** 9am-4pm Mon-Thur; 9am-1pm Fri, Sat. **Admission** €1.70; free reductions. **Map** p67 C3 ❽
The archaeological collection of the Pierides Foundation Museum was started by Demetrios Pierides in 1839 when he began purchasing ancient Cypriot artefacts to preserve them from pillaging. The collection, which now numbers over 2,500 objects, has been maintained and enriched by generations of the same family. Medieval, Byzantine, Frankish and Roman exhibits include costumes, weaponry, ceramics and needlework, alongside objects from neighbouring countries.

Tornaritis-Pierides Municipal Museum of Palaeontology

Municipal Cultural Centre, Old Customs House, Plateia Europis (24 628 587). **Open** *Sept-Apr* 9am-2pm Mon-Fri; 9am-noon Sat, Sun. *May-Aug* 9am-2pm Mon-Fri; 9am-noon Sat. **Admission** free. **Map** p67 C3 ❾
An impressive collection of shells and fossils from the Palaeozoic, Mesozoic and Caenozoic periods, housed in the warehouses of the old Customs House of 1881 that has since won a Europa Nostra restoration award. There is a guided tour once a day – call for details.

Eating & drinking

Brewery

Athinon 77 (77 772 444). **Open** 9am-2am daily. **Pub**. **Map** p67 C4 ❿

Styled as a traditional brewery, this popular pub brings beer pumps to your table, serves specialist lagers and features a menu offering international cuisine. If you like a pint it doesn't get much better than this.

Dimmers

Plateia Demetriou 16 (99 639 892). **Open** 10.30pm-3am Fri, Sat. **Bar**. **Map** p67 C3 11

DJs Harry Borg and Barry play mainstream hits in this uber-hip bar catering to a crowd of over-20s. It's popular, so if you want a table to perch at it's best to book one in advance.

Krateon

Kimonos 21 (24 622 062/99 625 117). **Open** 7.30pm-midnight Tue-Sun. **€€€**. **French**. **Map** p67 B2 12

Head here for stylish dining in a beautifully renovated house and garden. It's slightly on the expensive side by Larnaka standards but the quality never disappoints.

Momo Fusion

Gregori Afxentiou 35 (70 004 464). **Open** noon-midnight daily. **€€**. **International**. **Map** p67 A3 13

This joint occupies ultra-modern surroundings with an outdoor deck that's ideal for warm summer nights. Choose from traditional Cypriot, Oriental and Mediterranean food, plus a health corner complete with nutritional info on each dish.

Moti Mahal

Athinon 52 (70 004 484). **Open** 9am-2am daily. **€€**. **Indian**. **Map** p67 C4 14

Comfortable sofas and tasteful decoration meet great food, though it's not all Indian. Try the sushi, for example, which is unexpectedly good. Drop in on Fridays for some lively belly dancing.

Nippon

Gregori Afxentiou 57, Academia Centre (24 657 555). **Open** noon-3pm, 7pm-midnight Mon-Sat; 12.30-4pm, 7pm-midnight Sun. **€€€**. **Japanese**. **Map** p67 A3 15

This restaurant has a tremendous reputation, and lives up to expectations. The decor follows a stylishly minimalist aesthetic, with separate areas for teppanyaki and sushi/sashimi.

Spaghetteria Italia

Stylianou 1 (24 629 450). **Open** noon-3pm, 6-11pm Mon-Sat; 6-11pm Sun. **€€€**. **Italian**. **Map** p67 A3 16

This charming Italian restaurant comes highly recommended. The chef is the real deal and prepares mouth-wateringly authentic dishes from his home country. There's a selection of cheeses and a decent Italian wine list.

Spy

NEW *Athinon (24 626 627).* **Open** 9am-late daily. **€**. **Café/bar**. **Map** p67 C3 17

A new addition to the Phinikoudes promenade is this trendy place, which attracts Larnaka's twentysomethings. The menu provides a range of coffees and alcoholic beverages, and the music is mostly funky house – all in all a great place to chill out.

Taipei Town

Archiepiskopou Makariou III 63 (24 621 399/24 621 397). **Open** 1pm-3pm, 7pm-midnight daily. **€€**. **Chinese**. **Map** p67 C1 18

A great value Chinese with friendly, efficient service and good food. Reservations are strongly recommended at weekends when it gets very busy. Take-away is available.

Times Music Bar

Athinon 73 (24 625 966). **Open** 10pm-2am daily. **Bar**. **Map** p67 C3 19

One of the most popular – and loud – music bars in town, with live funky jazz on Fridays and Saturdays, and house on Sundays. Choose between the cocktail bar and chill-out lounge.

To Plakiotiko

Nikiforou Foka 5A (77 777 020). **Open** 5-11.30pm Mon-Sat. **€€**. **Taverna**. **Map** p67 B3/4 20

For an imaginative take on the taverna visit this restaurant, which impresses with postmodern Greek cuisine and an interesting wine list in a renovated traditional house. Book ahead.

At last, great protection and a stunning tan is no longer a daydream
PIZ BUIN
PIZ BUIN Tan Intensifier UVA
New PIZ BUIN Tan Intensifier combines Melitan, to naturally enhance the production of your skin's tanning pigments with the exclusive helioplex™ UVA/UVB photostable sun filter technology. The result? The tan of your dreams without compromising on protection.
Available in Spray and Lotion SPF 6, 15 and in Dry Oil SPF 6 and 10.
BUIN, Life is better in the sun.
WWW.PIZBUIN.COM ©CILAG GMBH INTERNATIONAL- DIVISION GREITER. CAREFULLY FOLLOW
PIZ BUIN
TAN INTENSIFIER
UVA-UVB
In Sun Lotion
15 MEDIUM

Shopping

Adidas Concept Store

Ermou 31 (24 628 856/www.adidas.com). **Open** 9.30am-7pm Mon-Fri; 9.30am-3pm Wed; 9.30am-5pm Sat. **Map** p67 B3 ㉑

If you're a fan of the sports brand then this is your mecca. It's all here, at the largest Adidas store on the island, including the Performance (for hard-core sports enthusiasts) and Originals lines. Also stocked are Adidas by Stella McCartney, Adidas Respect Me by Missy Elliot and Adidas Porsche Design.

Beauty Line

Ermou 51 (24 650 181). **Open** *Nov-Mar* 9am-6pm Mon, Tue, Thur; 9am-2pm Wed; 9am-3pm Sat. *Apr-Oct* 9am-7pm Mon, Tue, Thur; 9am-2pm Wed; 9am-3pm Sat. **Map** p67 B3 ㉒

Leading brands of perfume, make-up and skin care products, including Clinique, Estée Lauder and Helena Rubinstein are available at this island-wide chain. Beauty advice and makeovers are also available here on request.

Calzedonia

Ermou 101-102 (24 663 396/www.calzedonia.com). **Open** *Nov-Mar* 9am-6pm Mon, Tue, Thur; 9am-2pm Wed; 9am-3pm Sat. *Apr-Oct* 9am-7pm Mon, Tue, Thur; 9am-2pm Wed; 9am-3pm Sat. **Map** p67 B3 ㉓

A great variety of affordable and fashionable women's underwear, socks, tights and swimwear, including brightly coloured, trend-led lines. Go for everyday basics and also if you're in search of something a little more special.

Casa Del Tobacco

Gladstonos 9 (24 664 617). **Open** *Nov-Mar* 9am-6pm Mon, Tue, Thur; 9am-2pm Wed; 9am-3pm Sat. *Apr-Oct* 9am-7pm Mon, Tue, Thur; 9am-2pm Wed; 9am-3pm Sat. **Map** p67 B3 ㉔

Cigarettes, cigars, lighters, nargilehs, humidors, ashtrays and all manner of puffing paraphernalia can be procured at this specialist smoking emporium for those among you who remain dedicated smokers.

Coin Shop

Gladstonos 9 (24 817 597). **Open** *Nov-Mar* 9am-6pm Mon, Tue, Thur; 9am-2pm Wed; 9am-3pm Sat. *Apr-Oct* 9am-7pm Mon, Tue, Thur; 9am-2pm Wed; 9am-3pm Sat. **Map** p67 B3 ㉕

A collector's dream, this antiques shops sells coins, banknotes, medals, stamps, books, albums and other items. Valuations and coin cleaning are available. The dealer specialises in British and Cypriot coins and World Crowns.

Cyprus Handicraft Centre

Cosma Lysioti 6 (24 304 327). **Open** *Nov-Mar* 9am-6pm Mon, Tue, Thur; 9am-2pm Wed; 9am-3pm Sat. *Apr-Oct* 9am-7pm Mon, Tue, Thur; 9am-2pm Wed; 9am-3pm Sat. **Map** p67 C4 ㉖

The local branch of a national chain sponsored by the Ministry of Commerce, Industry and Tourism, whose mission is to preserve traditional Cypriot crafts. The shop sells a wide selection of locally produced gifts, from pottery and dolls to furniture and baskets.

Dodici

Ermou 173 (24 823 950). **Open** *Nov-Mar* 9am-6pm Mon, Tue, Thur; 9am-2pm Wed; 9am-3pm Sat. *Apr-Oct* 9am-7pm Mon, Tue, Thur; 9am-2pm Wed; 9am-3pm Sat. **Map** p67 C4 ㉗

This shoe shop has quickly gained a reputation for its classy stock and stylish retro displays. Despite the Italian-sounding name, the shoes are from Greece and they're top quality.

Kalopedis Jewellery

Zenonos Kitieos 38 (24 655 501/www.kalopedis.com). **Open** 9am-7pm Mon-Fri; 9am-2pm Sat. **Map** p67 C3 ㉘

A striking collection of jewellery honed from a 120-year-old family tradition. Everything is designed on the premises, from traditional Greek gold crosses to worry beads. You'll find the wares are extremely tempting if you like your adornments well-made and discreet.

L'Yello

Kyriakou Matsi 12 (24 621 997). **Open** *Nov-Mar* 9am-6pm Mon, Tue, Thur; 9am-2pm Wed; 9am-3pm Sat. *Apr-Oct* 9am-7pm Mon, Tue, Thur; 9am-2pm Wed; 9am-3pm Sat. **Map** p67 B2 29

This brightly decorated boutique offers beautiful handcrafted jewellery made with Swarovski crystals. Also available are nail crystals and bridal accessories. Basic jewellery begins at €8, with necklaces from €30.

Marks & Spencer

Zenonos Kitieos 57 (24 654 795). **Open** 8am-8pm Mon, Tue, Thur; 8am-2pm Wed; 8am-7.30pm Fri; 8am-6pm Sat. **Map** p67 C3 30

British favourite M&S seems to travel well, as there are branches all over Cyprus and they're hugely popular. The Larnaka one stocks the expected range of quality goods.

Monoena Exclusive Designs

Vasileos Evagora 2, Shop 1 (24 817 976). **Open** 9am-1pm, 3-7pm Mon-Fri; 9am-2pm Wed, Sat. **Map** p67 B3 31

A great place to look for that special outfit among the clothes, handbags, bijoux accessories and shoes from Italy, Denmark and Greece. Uniquely, there is also a section where clothing is made to order.

Next/Zako

Evanthias Pieridou 26-28 (Next 24626 205/Zako 24 652 900). **Open** 9am-7.30pm Mon, Tue, Thur, Fri; 9am-3pm Wed; 9am-7pm Sat. **Map** p67 C3 32

Local branch of UK clothes shop Next, which includes, on the second floor, an outpost of Cyprus-wide chain Zako – a favourite for adult and children's swimwear, underwear (including a good range of Fila, Wonderbra and Sloggi products), nightwear, towels and haberdashery items.

Oak Tree Wine Cellar

Drousioti 99G (24 815 044). **Open** 9am-6.30pm Mon,Tue, Thur, Fri; 9am-1.30pm Wed; 9am-2.30pm Sat. **Map** p67 C4 33

One of the best wine collections in town, with imports from France, Italy, Greece, America and South Africa, as well as a good selection of local bottles. Ask the enthusiastic owner about wine tastings, gastronomic events and seminars, or peruse the gadgets and accessories for both serious and amateur oenophiles.

Powder Room

Kalograion 8, Skourou Block B, Shop 4 (24 665 330). **Open** 9am-5.30pm Mon-Fri; 9am-2pm Sat. **Map** p67 B2 34

A boudoir of make-up for all occasions, from nights out to weddings. Owner Maria Thompson is highly trained, has worked with Westlife and Atomic Kitten and offers expert advice. The Powder Room also stocks handbags, as well as an excellent range of make-up, most of which you won't find anywhere else on the island.

Scan-Seller

Plateia Vasileos Pavlou 33 (24 655 748). **Open** *Nov-Mar* 9am-6pm Mon, Tue, Thur; 9am-2pm Wed; 9am-3pm Sat. *Apr-Oct* 9am-7pm Mon, Tue, Thur; 9am-2pm Wed; 9am-3pm Sat. **Map** p67 C3 35

This shop offers an upmarket selection of home accessories and collector's items, including Swarovski crystal, Lladró ornaments, Kosta Boda items, Lilliput Lane and the like.

ShoeBOX

Zakinthou 24 (24 620 784/24 627 093). **Open** *Nov-Mar* 9am-7pm Mon, Tue, Thur; 9am-2pm Wed; 9am-3pm Sat. *Apr-Oct* 9am-8.30pm Mon, Tue, Thur; 9am-2pm Wed. 9am-3pm Sat. **Map** p67 B1 36

Recently changed names from CB Emporio Festival, this is the best place to go for quality men's and women's shoes. Most are locally made, with a few international brands.

Tofarides

Zenonos Kitieou 45-47 (24 654 912). **Open** *Nov-Mar* 9am-6pm Mon, Tue, Thur; 9am-2pm Wed; 9am-3pm Sat. *Apr-Oct* 9am-7pm Mon, Tue, Thur; 9am-2pm Wed; 9am-3pm Sat. **Map** p67 C1 37

Oak Tree Wine Cellar

A general stationer and bookshop carrying a wide range of both English and Greek titles.

Zara

Zenonos Kitieou (24 828 282/www.zara.com). **Open** *Nov-Mar* 9am-6pm Mon, Tue, Thur; 9am-2pm Wed; 9am-3pm Sat. *Apr-Oct* 9am-7pm Mon, Tue, Thur; 9am-2pm Wed; 9am-3pm Sat. **Map** p67 C4 38

Zara has carved out a niche providing the latest men's, women's and children's formal and casual fashion at reasonable prices and with a turnover faster than you can say 'try this on'. If you see something you fancy, grab it or it's gone.

Nightlife

Caramel Club

NEW *Agiou Spyridonos (99 209 444).* **Open** 11pm-late Fri, Sat. **Map** p67 B2 39

A small, funky club opposite the old Attikon cinema. It has a disco feel with mirror balls and lighting effects, and plays commercial British and Greek music.

Circus

Gregori Afxentiou 17 (24 664 909). **Open** midnight-4.30am Fri, Sat. **Map** p67 B3 40

A club with the feel of an aquarium: large panes of glass allow passers-by a glimpse of the crowds swaying whenever the strobe lights send out a flash. It frequently hosts R&B nights and popular radio DJs from Cyprus and Greece. The roof bar is open during the summer months.

Encounters

Athinon 73 (24 625 966). **Open** midnight-4am Fri, Sat. **Map** p67 C4 41

Two clubs in one: Club Deep and Topaz. Deep does old-skool R&B and house. For a more mainstream chill-out evening opt to lounge about in Topaz. Fridays are specifically R&B nights with DJ Raffie; Saturdays are mainstream.

Geometry

NEW *Karaoli 8 & Plateia Demetriou (99 220 516).* **Open** midnight-4am Fri, Sat & public hols. **Map** p67 B4 42

Geometry (formerly Corridor) has undergone a major refurbishment to become one of Larnaka's hottest clubs. DJ Konstantino from Mix FM is at the decks spinning contemporary dance tracks.

Sky

Lordou Byronos & Gregori Afxentiou 15-17 (99 440 029/99 895 310). **Open** 10pm-2am daily. **Bar**. **Map** p67 B3 43

Latin, Brazilian and Cuban beats are the frisky order of the day on

Kidding around

Family fun on the east of the island.

Waterworld Waterpark

Grown-ups may be content to lie back and soak up the sun for two weeks, but lounging on a sunbed isn't going to cut it for children. Luckily, Larnaka and Agia Napa – a short drive away – have plenty of adventurous activities to occupy kids with energy to burn.

Unsurprisingly, many of the options involve water. Kids love the award-winning **Waterworld Waterpark** (p64) just outside Agia Napa. They can zip down and around Greek mythology-themed slides, or just chill in a rubber ring floating on the River Odyssey.

By the beach, water sports from banana rides to pedaloes can be found all along the coast. But for something different, head to De Costa Bay in Protaras, the home of **Undersea Walkers** (p61). Donning a wetsuit and a helmet, youngsters (aged eight and over, and at least 1.2m tall) can walk along the seabed with trained guides Rob and Christine. Newly-acquired BOBs (Breathing Observation Bubbles) use the same principle plus, there's the added excitement of an underwater scooter for older kids (aged 13 and over, and at least 1.4m tall).

Back on dry land, and high on adrenaline, enter the **Karting Center** (p78) near Larnaka Airport. There are a series of tracks including a mini go-kart track for children aged two to eight that meets European safety standards. Double-seated go-karts are available for parents who don't quite trust their offspring's driving skills. Plus, all go-karts have automatic controls and adjustable speeds based on the child's age.

For something calmer, head to **Mazotos Camel Park** (p78), 15 minutes from Larnaka, where families can make some unusual animal friends. In addition to camel rides, children can feed a Noah's Ark of creatures including donkeys, goats and ostriches with bags of carob pods, take a dip in a small swimming pool or leap around on a bouncy castle. That should tire them out.

Thursdays. Friday and Saturday nights are for letting loose to British and Greek mainstream hits, and on the seventh day you get to rest with some funky lounge tunes.

Vogue Exclusive

Plateia Demetriou 19, 4th Floor (99 654 266). **Open** midnight-late Fri, Sat. **Map** p67 C3 ㊹

With a studied grown-up feel, Vogue Exclusive attracts a well-dressed crowd which comes for the spacious dance floor, commercial hits from Greece and beyond, and sofas to receive those sore muscles afterwards. Various special events and guest DJs fill the schedule.

Arts & leisure

Guided Tours

Cyprus Tourism Organisation, Plateia Vasileos Pavlou (24 654 322). **Map** p67 C3 ㊺

These free guided tours are organised by the Cyprus Tourism Organisation (CTO) and the local municipality. 'Larnaka: Past and Present' leaves the CTO information office on Wednesday mornings for an informative walk along the seafront promenade and into the town itself. 'Skala: its Craftsmen' includes visits to local handicraft workshops around the Fort. Call for times.

Larnaka Municipal Gallery

Municipal Cultural Centre, Old Customs House, Athinon (24 658 848). **Open** *Oct-Apr* 9am-2pm Tue-Fri; 9am-noon Sat, Sun. *May-Sept* 9am-2pm Tue-Fri; 9am-noon Sat. **Map** p67 C3 ㊻

The gallery hosts regular exhibitions of works by local and international artists through an exchange programme with galleries in Athens and Dublin.

Larnaka Tennis Club

Kilkis 10 (24 656 999). **Map** p67 B2 ㊼

Non-members are welcome to play individually or in groups. The club is located behind the Archaeological Museum and you'll need to call first to make a booking. Many local hotels and gyms also have tennis courts that can be booked by the general public.

Around Larnaka

Immediately outside Larnaka is the cluster of hotels, bars and restaurants in the tourist area on the **Larnaka-Dhekelia Road**. Many Cypriots have holiday homes in **Zygi**, around which a small clutch of fish tavernas has developed. Far more intriguing, however, are the sleepy and picturesque villages in the surrounding area, which are becoming increasingly popular as agrotourism destinations.

In the village of Kiti, **Angeloktisti Church** is a lofty 12th-century building with a lantern dome said to have been built by angels. In the apse there is a rare sixth-century mosaic of the Virgin and Christ with a background of gilded glass tesserae. The villages of **Lefkara** and **Vavla** are famous for their lace and filigree silverware, which you can buy in numerous shops along the quaint cobbled streets. Watch out for the tourist traps, though, and haggle for the best prices.

The archaeological site of **Kalavasos Tenta** (under a teepee on the Limassol-Nicosia highway) is one of the island's most important Neolithic settlements, dating back to 7,000BC. Drive up to Kalavasos Dam for stunning views of the local countryside. Near the village, look out for the old abandoned railway and train that used to serve the local copper mine.

Probably the most important archaeological site in the area is **Choirokitia**. Also of interest is the **Kamares aqueduct**, a beautiful 18th-century structure that remained in use as late as 1930.

Stavrovouni Monastery (the Mountain of the Holy Cross) is one of the oldest monasteries in Cyprus, perched on a steep hill with breathtaking views. Women are not allowed within the main monastery walls, but can still light a candle in the chapel at the entrance.

Sights & museums

Choirokitia

Limassol-Nicosia Highway. **Open** *June-Aug* 9am-7.30pm daily. *Apr, May, Sept Oct* 8am-6pm daily. *Nov-Mar* 8am-5pm daily. **Admission** €1.70.

This fascinating and remarkably well-preserved Unesco World Heritage site dates from around 6,800BC and is thought to be one of the earliest permanent human settlements in Cyprus. The characteristic round houses were built on a site 2m higher than the surrounding area and could be reached by a stairway that wound for 180m around the compound. Five model dwellings reconstructed with copies of objects found on the site give an idea of everyday life in this civilisation, which disappeared suddenly in the fourth millennium BC.

Fatsa Wax Museum

Georgou Papandreou, Pano Lefkara (24 621 048). **Open** *May-Oct* 9am-7pm daily. *Nov-Apr* 9am-5pm daily. **Admission** €11; reductions free-€4.50.

Boasting more than 150 sculpted models, the Fatsa Museum waxes lyrical on eras and episodes of Cypriot life and history, from the Neolithic period to the present day.

Hala Sultan Tekke

Dromolaxia. **Open** *June-Aug* 8am-7.30pm daily. *Apr, May, Sept, Oct* 8am-6pm daily. *Nov-Mar* 8am-5pm daily. **Admission** free.

The mosque of Hala Sultan Tekke was built on the shores of this tranquil salt lake around 1760 in honour of the Prophet Mohammed's aunt, who was buried here after being thrown from her mule during the first Arab raid on Cyprus. It is now an important shrine for Muslim pilgrimage. The best times to go are in spring and autumn, when migratory flamingos stop en route to and from Africa – the pink flocks are a wonderful sight. The mosque itself is surrounded by a copse of tall palm and cypress trees. During the summer months the salt lake is dry – but the ground is not as solid as it looks, so watch your step.

Eating & drinking

Ammos

Mackenzie Beach (24 828 844). **Open** 11am-2am daily. **Bar**.

True to its name, which means sand, this restaurant and lounge bar is right on the beach. The sand here is white, just like everything else in the decor. Kick back on one of the bean bags, so comfy they might be better described as beds. There's a great selection of food – salads, platters, sushi – and funky tunes on warm summer nights.

Koutsonikolias

Kalo Chorio (24 361 690). **Open** 7.30-11.30pm Mon-Sat. **€€**. **Taverna**.

A short trek out of town, Koutsonikolias makes every kilometre worthwhile. It's housed in a traditional coffee shop and serves exceptional meze including highly unusual dishes, such as wild goose stifado (stew). And you won't have tasted anything like their grilled bread, dressed with olive oil and bitter orange juice.

Voreas

Agiou Demetriou 3, Oroklini (24 647 177). **Open** 6pm-midnight Mon-Sat; noon-midnight Sun. **€€**. **Taverna**.

One of the best tavernas in Cyprus, Voreas oozes traditional Cypriot charm. The extensive and memorable menu includes creamy tzatziki; bacon-wrapped chicken; hot village bread with olive oil; artichokes cooked to a traditional Karpas recipe; and peppers in olive oil and oregano. The meat meze is not to be missed.

Hala Sultan Tekke

Voreas p76

Nightlife

Iguana

Ithakis, Dhekelia Road (99 617 779). **Open** *Summer* 11pm-4am Fri, Sat. Closed winter.

Summer-only venue Iguana features a massive outdoor pool bar. The spacious ground level attracts younger partygoers with mainstream beats, while the older crowd tends to go to the smaller upper level with its commercial Greek music.

Secrets Freedom Club

Artemidos 67, Larnaka Airport Road (99 557 433/www.secretsfreedomclub.com). **Open** 11pm-late Tue-Sun.

The Cyprus gay scene is fairly limited, with only a few dedicated clubs and pubs scattered around the island. Secrets Freedom Club is the biggest and by far the best of them. The club welcomes both a straight and gay clientele and the atmosphere is relaxed and lively. It features a chill-out lounge, internet access, regular live performances and social events. The entry fee includes one drink.

Arts & leisure

ATV Leisure

Old Nicosia-Limassol Road, near Kofinou (99 328 821).

The island's only quad biking centre offers a race track and mountain safaris. Everyone is welcome, from beginners to experts.

Cyprus Villages

Tochni (24 332 998/ www.cyprusvillages.com.cy).

This company, in the village of Tochni, offers bike tours with good equipment and to a host of destinations. If you not a big fan of travelling on two wheels, walking and jogging activities are also organised, and nearby Drapia Farm offers horse rides and hacks through the hills, fields and woods. The company also offers treatments at their day spa and rents out agrotourism accommodation.

K-Cineplex & K-Max Bowling

Peloponissou 89 (77 778 383/ www.kcineplex.com).

The area's main cinema is a six-screen affair. Also part of the complex is a 20-lane bowling alley and eating and drinking facilities.

Karting Center

Dromolaxia (24 991 499/www.kartingcenter.com.cy).

See box p74.

KWEST Paintball Park

Old Nicosia-Limassol Road, near Kofinou (99 570 588).

From the rough-and-ready briefing shack to the strategically placed Land Rovers, this is a blast for shoot-em-up fans of all ages. It's professionally operated with a keen eye on safety at all times and features four fields, a hillside battleground and night-time floodlights.

Mazotos Camel Park

Larnaka-Mazotos Road (24 991 243/ www.camel-park.com). **Open** *Summer* 9am-7pm daily. *Winter* 9am-5pm daily.

See box p74.

View from Shacolas Tower p85

Lefkosia (Nicosia)

Set in the centre of the country, the Cypriot capital has traditionally been off most visitors' itineraries; travellers, particularly the package holiday contingent, made straight for the coast. However, the town has hit the headlines since the opening of the Green Line crossings to the Turkish occupied areas – and the landmark opening of the central Ledra Street checkpoint in April 2008.

Still commonly known as Nicosia (though road signs refer to it by its official transliteration, Lefkosia), the town's intriguing mix of old and new makes for a memorable visit. Steel and glass rub shoulders with sandstone and mudbrick in this city: in the commercial centre around Archiepiskopou Makariou III (Makarios Avenue, known simply as **Makariou**) and the posher **Stasinou**, designer shops line the streets. In the narrow streets of the old town, men gather in smoky coffee shops to exchange the day's news.

The star-shaped defence walls that encircle old Nicosia were erected by the Venetian rulers of the island between 1567 and 1570, in the hope of keeping the Ottoman army out. In the event they proved wanting but, where they still stand, are an impressive relic of the ancient fortified city. They are surpassed only by the walls in Palmanova, Italy – designed by the same engineer, Giulio Savorgnano.

The best way to discover Nicosia's charms is to adopt the laid-back pace of the locals and wander through the beguiling streets within its **Venetian walls**; this jasmine-scented town is one of the most enchanting and unique places in the eastern Mediterranean.

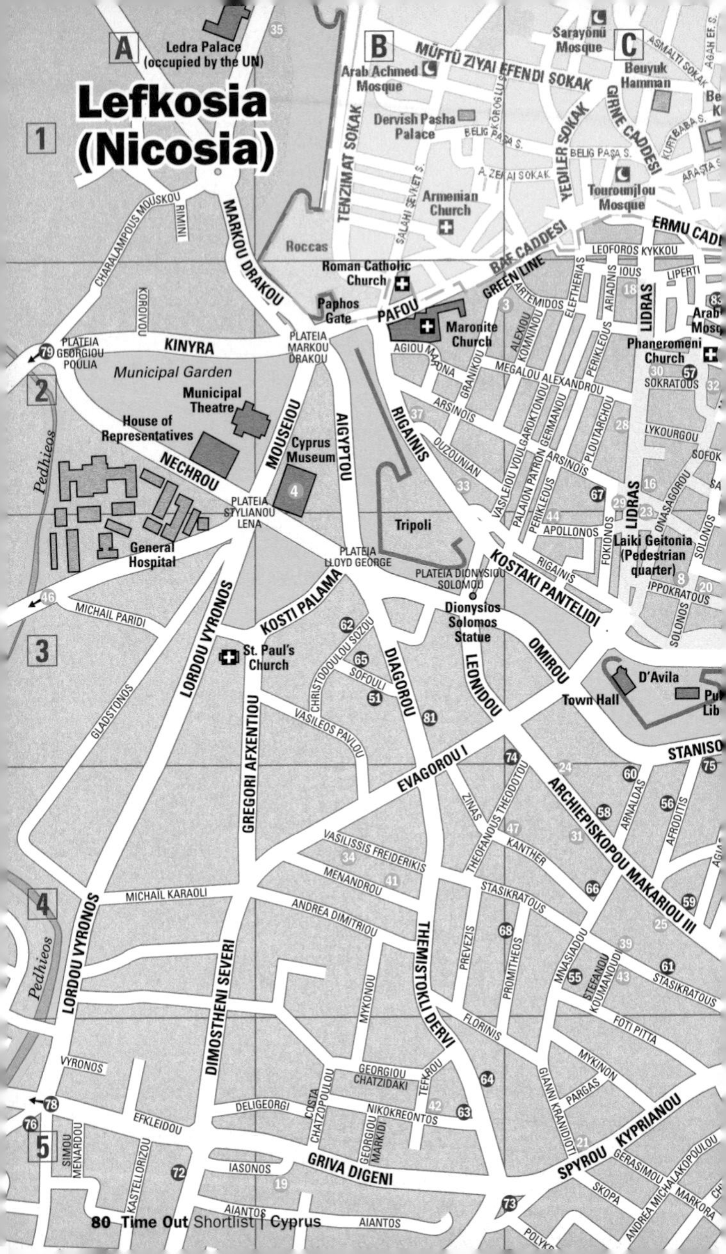
Lefkosia (Nicosia)
A
B
C
1
2
3
4
5
Ledra Palace (occupied by the UN)
Arab Achmed Mosque
Sarayönü Mosque
Beuyuk Hamman
Dervish Pasha Palace
Armenian Church
Tourounjlou Mosque
Roccas
Roman Catholic Church
Paphos Gate
Maronite Church
Municipal Garden
Municipal Theatre
House of Representatives
Cyprus Museum
General Hospital
Tripoli
Plateia Markou Drakou
Plateia Georgiou Poulia
Plateia Stylianou Lena
Plateia Lloyd George
Plateia Dionysiou Solomou
Dionysios Solomos Statue
St. Paul's Church
Phaneromeni Church
Laiki Geitonia (Pedestrian quarter)
D'Avila
Town Hall
Green Line
Müftü Ziyai Efendi Sokak
Girne Caddesi
Yediler Sokak
Tenzimat Sokak
Baf Caddesi
Ermu Cad
Leoforos Kykkou
Markou Drakou
Kinyra
Nechrou
Mouseiou
Aigyptou
Rigainis
Pafou
Kostaki Pantelidi
Omirou
Leonidou
Diagorou
Kosti Palama
Lordou Vyronos
Gregori Afxentiou
Evagorou I
Archiepiskopou Makariou III
Themistokli Dervi
Dimostheni Severi
Griva Digeni
Spyrou Kyprianou
Stasikratous
Lidras
Charalampous Mouskou
Pedhieos
Michail Karaoli
Michail Paridi
Gladstonos
Vasilissis Freiderikis
Menandrou
Andrea Dimitriou
Vasileos Pavlou
Sofouli
Christodoulou Sozou
Zinas
Theofanous Theodotou
Kanther
Prevezis
Promitheos
Mykonou
Florinis
Foti Pitta
Mykinon
Pargas
Gianni Kranidioti
Georgiou Chatzidaki
Nikokreontos
Deligeorgi
Efkleidou
Vyronos
Iasonos
Aiantos
Skopa
Gerasimou
Andrea Michalakopoulou
Markora
Arnaldas
Afroditis
Solonos
Ippokratous
Apollonos
Fokionos
Onasagorou
Lykourgou
Sokratous
Perikleous
Ploutarchou
Arsinoïs
Ouzounian
Megalou Alexandrou
Agiou Maronа
Granikou
Artemidos
Eleftherias
Ariadnis
Liperti
Koroivou
Rimini
Kastellorizou
Simou Menardou

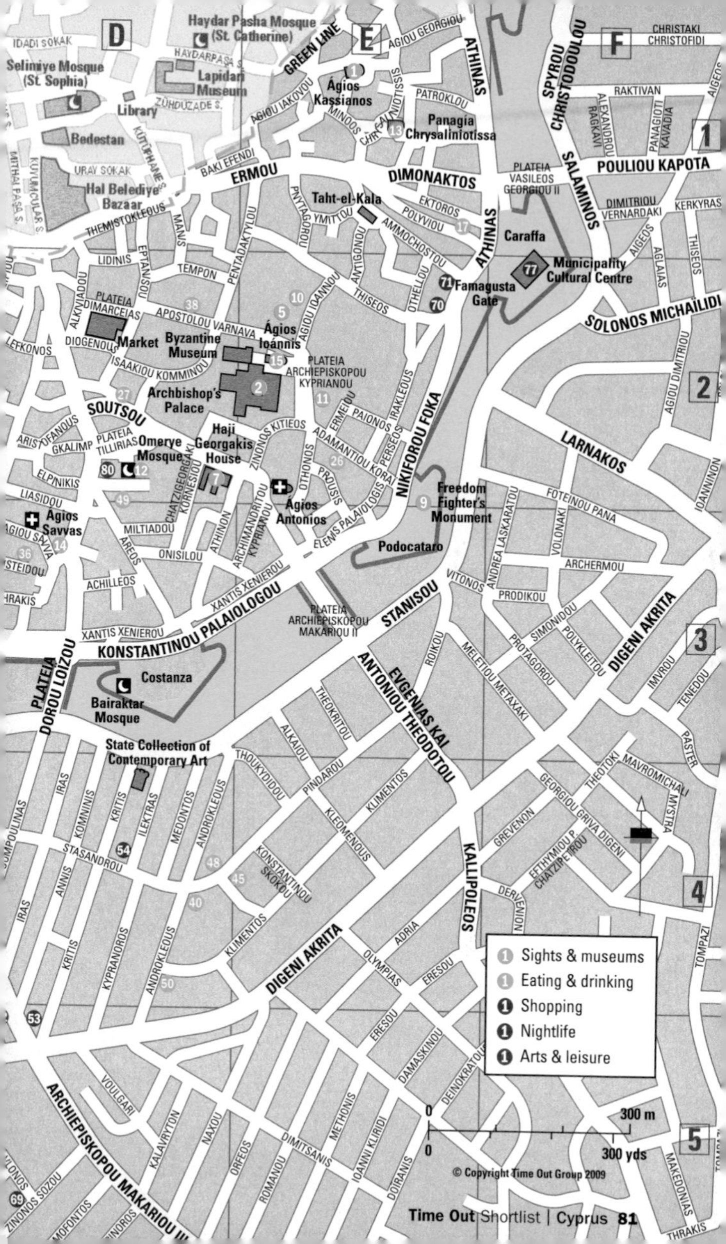
D
E
F
1
2
3
4
5
Haydar Pasha Mosque (St. Catherine)
Selimiye Mosque (St. Sophia)
Lapidari Museum
Library
Bedestan
Hal Belediye Bazaar
Ágios Kassianos
Panagia Chrysaliniotissa
Taht-el-Kala
Caraffa
Municipality Cultural Centre
Famagusta Gate
Byzantine Museum
Ágios Ioánnis
Archbishop's Palace
Market
Omerye Mosque
Haji Georgakis House
Ágios Antonios
Ágios Savvas
Freedom Fighter's Monument
Podocataro
Costanza
Bairaktar Mosque
State Collection of Contemporary Art
PLATEIA VASILEOS GEORGIOU II
PLATEIA DIMARCEIAS
PLATEIA ARCHIEPISKOPOU KYPRIANOU
PLATEIA TILLIRIAS
PLATEIA ARCHIEPISKOPOU MAKARIOU II
PLATEIA DOROU LOIZOU
GREEN LINE
IDADI SOKAK
HAYDARPASA S.
ZÜHDUZADE S.
KUTÜPHANE S.
URAY SOKAK
KUYUMCULAR S.
MITHAT PASA S.
BAKI EFENDI
THEMISTOKLEOUS
ERMOU
AGIOU IAKOVOU
MINOOS
CHRYSALINIOTISSIS
AGIOU GEORGIOU
PATROKLOU
ATHINAS
DIMONAKTOS
SPYROU CHRISTODOULOU
SALAMINOS
CHRISTAKI CHRISTOFIDI
RAKTIVAN
ALEXANDROU RAGKAVI
PANAGIOTI KAVADIA
AIGEOS
POULIOU KAPOTA
DIMITRIOU VERNARDAKI
KERKYRAS
THISEOS
AGLAIAS
PYTHAGOROU
YMITTOU
ANTIGONOU
EKTOROS
POLYVIOU
AMMOCHOSTOU
OTHELLOU
SOLONOS MICHAÏLIDI
LIDINIS
EPTANISOU
MANIS
PENTADAKTYLOU
TEMPON
APOSTOLOU VARNAVA
AGIOU IOANNOU
ALKIVIADOU
DIOGENOUS
LEFKONOS
ISAAKIOU KOMMINOU
SOUTSOU
ARISTOFANOUS
GKALIMP
ELPINIKIS
LIASIDOU
AGIOU SAVVA
STEIDOU
ERMEIOU
PAIONOS
IRAKLEOUS
KITIEOS
ADAMANTIOU KORAI
PERSEOS
NIKIFOROU FOKA
OTHONOS
PROUSIS
ZINONOS KITIEOS
CHATZIGEORGAKI KORNESIOU
ELENIS PALAIOLOGIS
MILTIADOU
ONISILOU
AREOS
ATHINON
ARCHIMANDRITOU KYPRIANOU
ACHILLEOS
XANTIS XENIEROU
KONSTANTINOU PALAIOLOGOU
AGIOU DIMITRIOU
LARNAKOS
IOANNINON
FOTEINOU PANA
VOLONAKI
ANDREA LASKARATOU
ARCHERMOU
PRODIKOU
VITONOS
SIMONIDOU
PROTAGOROU
POLYKLEITOU
DIGENI AKRITA
STANISOU
ROIKOU
MELETIOU METAXAKI
EVGENIAS KAI ANTONIOU THEODOTOU
THEOKRITOU
ALKAIOU
PINDAROU
THOUKYDIDOU
KLIMENTOS
KLEOMENOUS
IMVROU
TENEDOU
PASTER
THEOTOKI
MAVROMICHALI
MYSTRA
GEORGIOU GRIVA DIGENI
EFTHYMIOU P. CHATZIPETROU
GREVENON
DERVENION
KALLIPOLEOS
TOMPAZI
IRAS
KOMNINIS
KRITIS
ILEKTRAS
MEDONTOS
ANDROKLEOUS
STASANDROU
ANNIS
KONSTANTINOU SKOKOU
KYPRANOROS
ADRIA
OLYMPIAS
ERESOU
DAMASKINOU
DEINOKRATOUS
VOULGARI
ARCHIEPISKOPOU MAKARIOU III
KALAVRYTON
NAXOU
ORFEOS
METHONIS
DIMITSANIS
ROMANOU
IOANNI KLIRIDI
DOIRANIS
ZINONOS SOZOU
MOFONTOS
MAKEDONIAS
THRAKIS
0
300 m
300 yds
Sights & museums
Eating & drinking
Shopping
Nightlife
Arts & leisure
© Copyright Time Out Group 2009

Sights & museums

Agios Kassianos Church

Agiou Kassianou. **Admission** free. **Map** p81 E1 ❶

The original church, probably Latin, was built in the 15th century and burned down in 1570. Rebuilt in 1854, the present building is home to an exquisite panel painting of the Panagia (Virgin), dated 1400, as well as the helmet in which Kassianos, the saint whose name the church bears, is said to have been martyred. It is believed to have miraculous qualities and is donned by people suffering from severe headaches. The keyholder's name is Gia and she lives in the house to the right of the church.

Archbishop's Palace & Makarios III Cultural Foundation

Plateia Archiepiskopou Kyprianou (22 430 008). **Open** 9am-4.30pm Mon-Fri; 9am-1pm Sat. **Admission** €1.70. **Map** p81 E2 ❷

The Archbishop's Palace, which is only open to the public on special occasions, was completed just after Cyprus' independence in 1960. A 10m-high bronze statue of Archbishop Makarios III, the island's first president, was replaced in November 2008 with a more modest version. The cultural complex consists of three exhibition areas; by far the most interesting is the Byzantine Art Museum, which houses the largest collection of icons on the island. The European Art Gallery displays 17th-century European paintings (mostly religious) of the Spanish, Dutch and Flemish schools. The Greek Independence Gallery features maps, copper engravings and paintings of personalities and events from the 1821 Greek War of Independence.

Classic Motorcycle Museum

Granikou 44 (22 680 222). **Open** 9.30am-1pm, 3.30-6pm Mon-Fri; 9.30am-1pm Sat. **Admission** €5. **Map** p80 C 2 ❸

Archbishop's Palace

CYPRUS BY AREA

Born of one man's love affair with classic motorbikes, the museum has over 80 gleaming exhibits, including such gems as a 1947 Triumph Speed Twin, a 1947 Indian Chief and a 1939 Ariel Red Hunter. Also of interest are the BSAs used by the British police and military during colonial times.

Cyprus Archaeological Museum

Mouseiou 1 (22 865 854). **Open** 8am-4pm Tue, Wed, Fri; 8am-5pm Thur; 9am-4pm Sat; 10am-1pm Sun. **Admission** €3.40. **Map** p80 B2 ④

Founded in 1888, this venerable museum houses the best collection of archaeological finds in Cyprus, covering the Neolithic to the Byzantine periods. Highlights include an exemplary collection of terracotta figures excavated in 1929 at Agia Irini in Morfou, and limestone lions and sphinxes from the Tamassos necropolis. The famous Aphrodite of Soli, which has become a symbol of Cyprus, also resides here. The small but pretty Municipal Gardens are located across from the museum, behind the Municipal Theatre.

Ethnographic Museum

Plateia Archiepiskopou Kyprianou, the Old Archbishop's Palace (22 432 578). **Open** 9.30am-4pm Tue-Fri; 9am-1pm Sat. **Admission** €2. **Map** p81 E2 ⑤

The Ethnographic Museum is a showcase for local folk arts: embroidery, lace, costumes, pottery, metalwork, basketry, folk painting, leatherwork and woodcarving. The building itself was originally a Benedictine monastery, and retains a number of original 15th-century architectural features of the Frankish period.

Faneromeni Church

Onasagora. **Open** 6am-noon, 3-5.30pm daily, and for services (times vary). **Admission** free. **Map** p80 C2 ⑥

Faneromeni (or Phaneromeni), the largest church within the city walls, was built in 1871 on the site of a ruined Byzantine nunnery of the same name. It incorporates stones brought over from the remains of La Cava, the Lusignan castle at Athalassa, and has a fine 17th-century iconostasis. In the courtyard is a mausoleum containing the remains of the Orthodox clergy executed by the Turkish governor in 1821. The building attached to the church contains the Faneromeni Library, which is home to the oldest icons in Cyprus.

House of Hadjigeorgakis Kornesios

Patriarchou Grigoriou 20 (22 305 316). **Open** 8.30am-3.30pm Tue, Wed; 8.30am-4.30pm Thur; 8.30am-2.30pm Fri, Sat. **Admission** €1.70. **Map** p81 D2 ⑦

This fine example of an 18th-century mansion, or *konak*, was the official residence of Hadjigeorgakis Kornesios, the Grand Dragoman of Cyprus (Interpreter of the Sultan's Council). The impressive complex consists of Hadjigeorgakis's living quarters and offices, and includes a splendid reception room with an ornately carved and gilded ceiling; it was here that the archbishop and prelates of the Orthodox Church and foreign consuls would meet the dragoman.

Leventis Municipal Museum

Ippokratous 17 (22 661 475/22 671 997). **Open** 10am-4.30pm Tue-Sun. **Admission** free. **Map** p80 C3 ⑧

The first historical museum of Cyprus documents Nicosia's 6,000-year history through a series of permanent exhibitions. Its collection of archaeological artefacts, costumes, photographs, medieval pottery, maps, engravings, jewels and furniture tells a story of multiple occupations and hard-won independence, as well as revealing layers of social, cultural and political histories.

Liberty Monument

Nikiforou Foka. **Map** p81 E2 ⑨

Located on the Podokataro Bastion of the city walls, the imposing Liberty Monument (variously translated as the Freedom Fighters' Monument), was erected in 1970 to commemorate the island's liberation from British rule. An anthropomorphised Liberty looks

Mastic fantastic

Resin wars.

Two shops on the same street selling products incorporating the same obscure ingredient? There must be something magic about mastic.

Aromatic mastic or masticha resin is produced on the Greek island of Chios. The properties of the gum have long been known – the Romans used it to whiten teeth, and Christopher Columbus declared it should be valued by its weight in gold rather than silver.

The milky sap of the mastic tree forms translucent crystals when dried in the sun which soften when chewed, making it the original chewing gum. Apart from its refreshing and interesting flavour (an acquired but addictive taste), the gum is heralded for its medicinal and anti-bacterial properties.

You can buy toothpaste and face cream from the official shop of the growers' association at **Mastiha Shop** (p95). The association has also teamed up with Korres skincare to develop a series of luxe lotions. Across the street **Mastic Spa** (p95) specialises in delicious-smelling hair, skin and body care ranges.

Mastiha Shop also stocks traditional edible products, like sweets, biscuits and the original Elma brand chewing gum. If the unique scent of mastic wins you over, try some of their stranger products like the mastic-infused pasta or the intensely flavoured liqueur – perfect served with fresh cream over ice.

down on two life-like bronze soldiers opening the doors of a prison and releasing 14 figures, representing the various strata of Cypriot society. The area behind the statue is a firm favourite with courting couples on warm summer nights, so be warned.

Museum of the National Struggle

Plateia Archiepiskopou Kyprianou (22 305 878). **Open** 8am-2pm Mon-Fri; 3-5pm Thu. **Admission** free. **Map** p81 E2 ⑩

Located next to the Ethnographic Museum, in the side wing of the old Archbishop's Palace, the museum documents the island's liberation struggle against British rule between 1955 and 1959.

Museums of the Pancyprian Gymnasium

Plateia Archiepiskopou Kyprianou (pgmuseum@cytanet.com.cy). **Open** 9am-3.30pm Mon, Tue, Thur, Fri; 9am-5pm Wed; 9am-1pm Sat. **Admission** free. **Map** p81 E2 ⑪

The gymnasium, located opposite the Archbishop's Palace, was founded in 1812 by Archbishop Kyprianos, at a time when Cyprus was still under Ottoman occupation. It is the oldest high school still in operation on the island. Find out about famous alumni such as the late Archbishop Makarios in the museum devoted to the school's history, or browse the collections of weaponry, maps, natural history exhibits and examples of gothic architecture in the other museums here.

Omeriye Mosque

Plateia Tyllirias. **Open** daily outside prayer times. **Admission** free (donations welcome). **Map** p81 D2 ⑫

Now run by the local Muslim community, this is the only functioning mosque in south Nicosia. It was built on the ruins of the 14th-century Church of St Mary of the Augustinians, once attached to one of three important monasteries in Lusignan Nicosia and destroyed during the siege of 1570. See p97 for the Omeriye Hamam.

Panagia Chrysaliniotissa Church
Corner of Odysseos and Archiepiskopou Filotheou. **Admission** free. **Map** p81 E1 ⑬

The oldest Byzantine church in Nicosia, Panagia Chrysaliniotissa (Our Lady of the Golden Flax) was built in 1450 by Helena Palaeologou, wife of the Lusignan King John II. It owes its name to an 11th-century icon painted on linen, which depicts the Mother of God with a golden hand and golden crown which, according to tradition, was found in a field planted with flax. The icon is still in the church, the key to which can be obtained from the keyholder in the house to the right of the church.

Postal Museum
Agiou Savva 3B (22 304 711). **Open** 9am-3pm Mon-Fri; 9am-1pm Sat. **Admission** free. **Map** p81 D3 ⑭

This small museum houses a collection of Cypriot stamps from 1880, along with items relating to the history of the Cyprus Postal Services, such as scales, seals and letterboxes.

St John's Cathedral
Plateia Archiepiskopou Kyprianou, Archbishop's Palace. **Open** 9am-noon, 2-4pm Mon-Fri; 9am-noon Sat. **Admission** free. **Map** p81 E2 ⑮

The church of Agios Ioannis (St John) was erected in 1662 on the site of a Benedictine abbey's 14th-century chapel. A modest exterior (it could not be otherwise under Ottoman rule) does nothing to prepare visitors for the intricate, gilded 18th-century woodwork, crystal chandeliers and vivid frescoes inside. All Cypriot archbishops since the end of the 18th century have been consecrated here.

Shacolas Tower Museum & Observatory
Shacolas Tower, corner of Ledras & Arsinoes (22 679 369). **Open** 10am-6.30pm daily. **Admission** €0.85; free reductions. **Map** p80 C2 ⑯

Classic Motorcycle Museum p82

On the 11th floor of the Debenhams building on Ledra Street, this observatory offers unique views across the city: north and south, traditional and modern, and across to the Pentadaktylos mountain range and beyond. There are telescopes, binoculars and a recorded feature on the history of the capital.

Eating & drinking

Aigaio

Ektoros 40 (22 433 297). **Open** 7pm-midnight Mon-Sat. **€€**. **Taverna**. **Map** p81 E1 ⑰

Aigaio has been holding the fort in the old town since the 1980s, before anyone else dared venture into what was then a dark, dead-end part of town. It has also steadfastly held its number one position in locals' hearts (and stomachs) with its truly exceptional food. It is probably the best restaurant of its kind in Nicosia, if not the entire island, offering unusual meze from the Greek mainland alongside classic dishes. A bookshop is attached, while the owner's strongly felt politics are displayed all over the walls. Booking is essential.

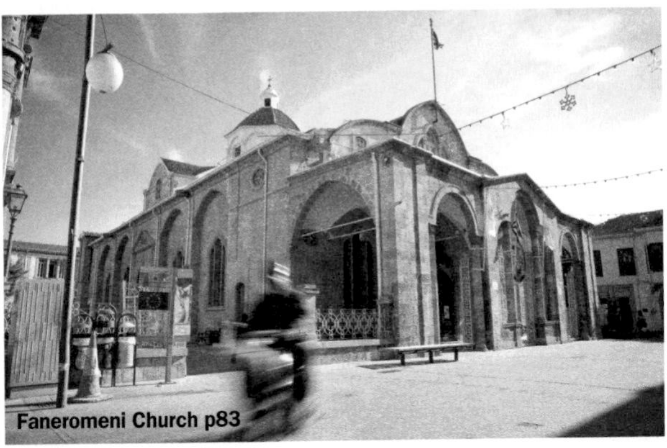

Faneromeni Church p83

Aztecas

NEW *Ledras 51, in Faneromeni parking area (22 680 610).* **Open** 11am-midnight daily. **€€. Mexican. Map** p80 C2 18

Tucked away just off the northern end of Ledra Street, this Mexican eaterie offers good food and great cocktails. Save room for the fried vanilla ice-cream dessert.

Babylon

Iasonos 6 (22 665 757). **Open** 8pm-2am daily. **Pub. Map** p80 B5 19

Babylon is one of the oldest pubs in the city, and its patio is the perfect place to spend a summer's night; in the winter, punters huddle under old Rolling Stones posters or gather round the pool table. Offering a vast selection of cool beers and tasty meals, it's easy to see why it's so popular. There is usually a busy beer festival in the first week of September, with drinks promotions and gifts aplenty.

Brewery

NEW *Corner Spyrou Kyprianou & Yianni Kranidioti (70 004 424).* **Open** 9am-2am daily. **€€. Café/bar. Map** p80 C5 21

Juicy burgers, Caribbean chicken and other such bites are on the menu in this hip and very popular all day café-restaurant-bar, which recently opened its doors in the capital after successful launches in Larnaka and Limassol.

Brew Lounge & Tea Bar

NEW *Ippocratous 30B (22 100 133).* **Open** 11.30am-2am Tue-Thur, Sun; 11.30am-3am Fri, Sat. **€. Café/bar. Map** p80 C3 20

This new addition to the Laiki Geitonia area of the old town is turning into a hangout for British expats and repatriated UK Cypriots, which is not surprising given the 24 types of teas on offer. Both the music and atmosphere are suitably relaxed.

Casa Vieja

Archangelou Michael 3 (22 673 371/www.casavieja.com.cy). **Open** 7.30-11.30pm Mon-Sat; 12.30-3.30pm, 7.30-11.30pm Sun. **€€. Spanish. Map** p80 C2/3 22

Casa Vieja is the only Spanish restaurant in town, but puts on an authentic show: there's decent tapas, strong sangria and a quaint little back garden for al fresco dining in the warmer months.

Chop't

Ledras 207 (22 818 781). **Open** 11am-11pm Mon-Sat; 11am-5pm Sun. **€. Salad bar. Map** p80 C2/3 23

You can style your own salad at this trendy salad bar, set in an old arcade in Ledra Street, choosing from a list of fresh ingredients and dressings. Still hungry? Try the dips or order a slice of quiche.

Cos'altro

Archiepiskopou Makariou III 9 (77 778 055). **Open** 7.30-11.30pm daily. **€€€. Italian. Map** p80 C3/4 24

This trendy, busy eaterie is located at the top end of Makariou, one of the capital's main shopping streets. Modern decor is paired with a wide-ranging, upmarket Italian menu.

Da Capo

Archiepiskopou Makariou III 30B (22 757 427). **Open** 8.30am-2.30am daily. **€€. Café. Map** p80 C4 25

The fashionable place to be seen taking a break from Saturday shopping sprees. Da Capo's food is reliably good and comes in generous portions, served either in the sleek dining area or under a parasol on the outdoor deck. There's also free Wi-Fi. See box p91.

Domus Lounge Bar

Korae 5 (22 433 722). **Open** 8.30pm-2am Mon-Sat. **€€. Bar/restaurant. Map** p81 E2 26

This minimalist designer haven, decked out in black and shimmering shades of gold and silver with a splash of red, comprises a stylish, upscale restaurant and bar with innovative international cuisine and a laid-back atmosphere.

Hamam Pre-Club

Soutsou 9 (22 766 202). **Open** 9am-2am Tue-Sun. **Bar. Map** p81 D2 27

A strong contender for the title of the capital's best bar. Expect a great vibe, cool, sociable crowds and (on Wednesdays, Fridays and Saturdays) an eclectic blend of jazz, funk and freestyle electronica. On summer evenings, the front courtyard is one of the most atmospheric places in town.

Heraklis Garden Café

Ledras 110 (22 664 198). **Open** 8.30am-midnight daily. **€. Café. Map** p80 C2 28

The most famous place in Nicosia for ice-cream, Heraklis is located at just the right spot to be the highlight of many a Sunday family walk. The large garden at the back is child-friendly, with a free playground. The café also serves snacks such as burgers and pasta.

Il Forno

Ledras 216-218 (22 456 454). **Open** 11am-11.30pm daily. **€. Italian. Map** p80 C2 29

An excellent Italian pasta and pizza restaurant, Il Forno is small and always busy. Make sure you try its special version of garlic bread with cheese and olives.

Kala Kathoumena

Stoa Papadopolou, at the north end of Ledras (22 664 654). **Open** 11am-10pm Sun-Thur; 11am-midnight Fri, Sat. **€. Café. Map** p80 C2 30

A welcome change from the franchise café scene, and a favourite with the arty brigade. There are a few tables inside, but most customers prefer to sit outside in the narrow arcade and watch the world go by. See box p91.

Le Café

Archiepiskopou Makariou III 16C (22 466 566). **Open** 9.30am-2am daily. **€€. Café. Map** p80 C4 31

Possibly the most popular café in town, and the capital's prime people-watching vantage point. The atmosphere is chic and the food gives many pricier restaurants a run for their money. See box p91.

Loxandras

Faneromenis 67-69 (22 675 757). **Open** 6pm-midnight Mon-Sat. **€€. Taverna. Map** p80 C2 32

Invariably packed with locals, Loxandras is always lively, with tables lining the pedestrian street leading to Faneromeni church in summer. The food is good and the surroundings picturesque. It's ideal if you enjoy a walk after dinner, as you can wander the narrow streets of the old town.

Marco Polo

Holiday Inn, Rigainis 70 (22 712 712). **Open** 7pm-2am daily, weather permitting. **€€€. Bar/restaurant. Map** p80 B2 33

An excellent rooftop restaurant overlooking Nicosia, with a good seafood menu and a well-stocked bar. There's live music in the evenings with in-house Colombian band Majagua.

New Division

Vasilissis Frederikis 2 (22 679 957). **Open** 5pm-2am Mon-Sat; 9.30pm-2am Sun. **Bar. Map** p80 B4 34

Pretty much the best rock bar in Nicosia, New Division is friendly, unpretentious and a firm favourite with those in the know. Here your three-day stubble is welcome, your black clothing approved of and your social sciences degree feels right at home.

Oinohoos

NEW *Markou Drakou 12 (77 771 167).* **Open** noon-2am daily. **€€€. International. Map** p80 B1 35

Set in the new and fashionable Chateau Status complex near the Ledra Palace check point (which also houses the Harley Davidson Café and the Arabian Lounge Bar), this great restaurant offers grills and fusion cuisine from around the globe. The decor is a glammed-up take on a rustic Greek taverna.

Oktana/Uqbar

Aristidou 6 (22 760 099). **Open** *Oktana* noon-2am Mon-Fri; 10am-2am Sat, Sun. *Uqbar* 5pm-2am daily. **Café/bar. Map** p81 D3 36

One of the most popular hangouts in the old city, Oktana gets crowded, especially in the evenings. People come here not only to chill out and sip on excellent hot chocolate, but also to thrash out a game of backgammon and tuck into some masterful crêpes. There's a beautiful courtyard at the back, and the basement is

given over to the relaxed and cosy Uqbar, where you can smoke nargiles (hookahs). See box p91.

Pago Pago

Castelli Hotel, Ouzounian 38 (22 712 812). **Open** 3.30-11.30pm daily. **€€€. Polynesian.** **Map** p80 B2 ㊲

Perfect for a cosy dinner for two, this establishment has a tropical feel and serves a unique Polynesian menu. In the evenings the in-house band conjures up the beats of the South Pacific.

Palia Electriki

Powerhouse, Apostolou Varnava 19 (22 432 559). **Open** 11am-2.30pm, 7pm-midnight Tue-Sat; 11am-2.30pm Sun. **€€. Mediterranean.** **Map** p81 D2 ㊳

This sophisticated restaurant sits side by side with the Municipal Arts Centre, so you can combine lunch with a cultural experience. Located in an old electricity powerhouse, it's discreet, stylish and quiet, serving creative Mediterranean cuisine. In summer, dine outdoors in the beautiful garden.

Pralina

Stasikratous 31 (22 660 491). **Open** 9am-midnight Mon-Sat; 10pm-midnight Sun. **€€. Café.** **Map** p80 C4 ㊴

In a prime spot on one of Nicosia's most fashionable shopping streets and frequented by a well-dressed clientele, Pralina's decor is suitably trendy and minimalist. Stop by for a coffee, or Italian-influenced mains.

Puzzle Coffeeplays

Pindarou 29D (22 441 111). **Open** 9am-2am daily. **Café/bar.** **Map** p81 D4 ㊵

This cheerful café-bar was the first in town to kick off the trend for playing board games while you sip and munch. There's a large selection of games to choose from, and staff are happy to explain the rules. Snacks, waffles, hot apple pie, fresh juices and good coffee sustain players throughout the day.

Pyxida

Meneandrou 5 (22 445 636). **Open** 12.30-4pm, 9pm-midnight daily. **€€. Fish.** **Map** p80 B4 ㊶

One of the best recent openings in the fish taverna sector, Pyxida ('compass') offers 24 different meze dishes as well as seafood pasta dishes. The setting is stylish and the service professional.

Scarabeo

Nikokreontos 4 (99 935 777). **Open** 6pm-2.30am daily. **Bar.** **Map** p80 B5 ㊷

An interesting spot for coffee, food or drinks. The decor is effortlessly cool, and a roster of rotating DJs spins eclectic tunes: depending on the prevailing mood of the day you could hear anything from reggae or rock to electronica. Various events, including art exhibitions, take place here.

Seiko

Stasikratous 26-28 (77 777 375). **Open** noon-3pm, 7pm-midnight Mon-Sat; 7pm-midnight Sun. **€€. Japanese.** **Map** p80 C4 43

Sleek and ultra-modern, Seiko spoils diners for choice with a menu of more than 100 Japanese dishes. Prices are reasonable, even though it's perched on trendy Stasikratous.

Shiantris

Pericleous 38 (22 671 549). **Open** noon-4pm Mon; noon-10.30pm Tue-Sat. €. No credit cards. **Taverna.** **Map** p80 C3 44

Having recently moved to new premises just down the road, this small eaterie has always drawn a dedicated clientele from tourists and Cypriots alike. It serves home-cooked dishes such as pea and artichoke casserole; only fresh, seasonal ingredients are used, so the menu is generally quite concise. Shiantris serves the best traditionally prepared pulses around, as well as great stuffed vegetables, roast pork and scrambled eggs with courgettes. Prices are a bargain and the quality is excellent.

Leventis Municipal Museum p83

Sushi La

NEW *Pindarou 27, Agios Antonios (22 375 036).* **Open** noon-midnight daily. **€€. Japanese.** **Map** p81 E4 45

A fun, cosmopolitan venue with strikingly futuristic decor, sexy Sushi La is the place to be. Bright white, geometric fittings and low lighting create a stylish atmosphere in which to partake of light bites such as spicy salmon rolls and chicken teriyaki. Staff are attentive and offer helpful advice on what to choose.

Syrian Arab Friendship Club

Vasilissis Amalias 17 (22 776 246). **Open** 11am-midnight daily. **€. Syrian.** **Map** p80A3 46

This down-to-earth, homely restaurant serves very good Arabian meze, including paper-thin *mar'ouk* bread made on the premises. The intense Middle Eastern flavours make a welcome change if you're all Cypriot meze'd out, and there's plenty of choice for vegetarians. Generous portions make it excellent value for money. Nab a garden table in warm weather and round the evening off with an aromatic puff on a nargile.

Taj Mahal

NEW *Zenas Kanther 1B (22 672 324).* **Open** 10pm-2am daily. **Bar/club.** **Map** p80 C4 47

A popular downtown bar and club decked out in a glam oriental theme, Taj Mahal is part of a Greek chain. Well-known local and Athenian DJs spin a variety of Greek and international pop hits.

Toy

Pindarou, Alpha Business Centre (22 817 040). **Open** 8.30pm-2am Mon-Thur; 8.30pm-3am Fri, Sat. **Bar.** **Map** p81 D4 48

The red-and-white interior of this hip downtown lounge bar looks like the set for a White Stripes video. During

Coffee culture

Where to sample the legendary frappé.

Coffee culture

The British may be famed for their love of tea, but in Cyprus the most revered caffeinated beverage is definitely coffee. Trendy cafés and old-school coffee shops line the streets of every city and village on the island, and it's not just the old folk that like to sip the good stuff and watch the world go by.

Traditional Cypriot coffee is similar to its Mediterranean cousin, the espresso, in that it's taken short and strong. It is also drunk black and in some villages you may still find it cooked slowly in a tray of hot sand placed over the cooker, to give the drink a fuller aroma. Wash it down with a cool glass of water, but don't drink the unfiltered dregs at the bottom of the cup; not only can the grounds be read to tell your fortune, they are also quite gritty.

The coffee drink you will also undoubtedly encounter is the ubiquitous frappé. Served in tall glasses with lots of ice, this milkshake-like concoction is what summer on the island is really about. Both traditional coffee and its beach-friendly counterpart have three measures of sweetness: you can order it *gliko* (sweet), *metrio* (medium) or *sketto* (plain/no sugar). When ordering a frappé, you also need to specify how milky you want it: either *olo gala* (all milk), *miso-miso* (half-milk and half-water) or *mavro* (black/no milk).

Join the Cypriot posing posse at Nicosia hotspots like **Da Capo** (p87) or **Le Café** (p88), where the drink is made to last as long as possible; gossiping, people-watching (and, more crucially, being seen) are the main events. Alternatively, try **Oktana** (p88) or **Kala Kathoumena** (p88) for a more laid-back vibe, where a leisurely coffee is the perfect accompaniment to a lively game of backgammon or a fragrant shisha pipe.

Liberty Monument p83

the week there are occasional jazz performances or a sax player accompanying the jazzy house spun by the resident DJs. Finger food and an array of imaginative cocktails are on offer.

Zanettos

Trikoupi 65 (22 765 501). **Open** 7pm-midnight daily. **€€. Taverna. Map** p81 D2/3 (49)

Hidden away in the narrow streets of the old city, Zanettos can be difficult to locate. Ask any taxi driver, however, and they'll speed you straight to this local landmark. Going strong since 1938, the taverna serves old-school Greek Cypriot meze in a lively atmosphere.

Zebras Steakhouse

Klimentos Towers, Klimentos 43 (22 458 600/www.zebras.com.cy). **Open** 11am-midnight daily. **€€. African. Map** p81 D4 (50)

Run by chef Andros Vassiliades (who owned restaurants in South Africa for more than 20 years), stylishly quirky Zebras provides an unusual dining experience. Recipes come from different parts of Africa, with specialities such as ostrich and biltong; overall, though, the cuisine is best described as international, as familar dishes like steak and seafood platters also feature.

Shopping

All Records

Sofouli 32-34 (22 669 040). **Open** 9.30am-1pm, 3.30-6.30pm Mon, Tue, Thur, Fri; 9.30am-1.30pm Wed; 9.30am-2pm Sat. **Map** p80 B3 (51)

This is the place to go if you're looking for British, European or American CDs. There's also plenty of Greek music, as well as DVDs and videos.

Bershka

Archiepiskopou Makariou III 48B (22 763 434). **Open** 9am-8pm Mon, Tue, Thur, Fri; 9am-2.30pm Wed; 9.30am-7.30pm Sat. **Map** p81 D5 (52)

Bershka targets teens and twenty-somethings, offering budget, trendy clothing. A little Spanish high-street enclave is in place at this end of Makariou, with Pull and Bear and Stradivarius, owned by the same company, nearby.

Other location Ledras 161 (22 873 940).

Debenhams

Corner of Archiepiskopou Makariou III & Kritis (22 758 801). **Open** 9am-8pm Mon, Tue, Thur, Fri; 9am-3pm Wed; 9am-7.30pm Sat. **Map** p81 D5 (53)

The British department store has three branches in the centre of Nicosia.

Other locations Archiepiskopu Makariou III 22 (22 849 000); Ledras 171-179 (22 679 369).

Dora Schabel

Elektras 14B (22 757 740). **Open** 9am-6pm Mon-Fri; 10am-2pm Sat. **Map** p81 D4 54

Head here for unconventional, ultra modern bags and accessories. They're made from a wide variety of leathers, including stingray, ostrich and snake skin, in a colourful array of shades.

Fetish

NEW *Mnasiadou 8 (22 662 015).* **Open** 9.30am-1.30pm, 3-7pm Mon, Tue, Thur, Fri; 9.30am-2.30pm Wed, Sat. **Map** p80 C4 55

The name says it all: if you get palpitations every time you're near a shoe shop, then this new boutique just off stylish Stasikratous will send your pulse racing. Accessorise with shoes and bags by the likes of Alessandro Dell' Acqua, Prada, Louboutin and Jimmy Choo.

Flexi

Aphrodites 23 (22 767 003). **Open** 10am-7pm Mon, Tue, Thur, Fri; 10am-1.30pm Wed; 10am-2.30pm Sat. **Map** p80 C4 56

The best place to catch up with Cypriot designers who've made it big in the fashion centres of London, Paris, Athens and New York, this boutique stocks pieces by hot names such as Joanna Louca, Elena Pavlou, Dora Schabel, Ioanna Kourbela and Sia Dimitriadi.

Gatapou

Stoa Papadopoulou (22 667 741). **Open** 11am-2pm, 4-7.30pm Mon, Tue, Thur, Fri; 4am-7.30pm Wed; 11am-4pm Sat. **Map** p80 C2 57

This colourful Aladdin's cave features decorative items large and small, along with pleasingly original gifts from nine different artists: tobacco cases, hats, bags, candles, paintings and handmade dolls are among the offerings.

G Stephanides Son & Co

Archiepiskopou Makariou III 23 (22 754 419/www.stephanides.com.cy). **Open** 9am-1pm, 3-7pm Mon, Tue, Thur, Fri; 9am-1pm Wed, Sat. **Map** p80 C4 58

Panagia Chrysaliniotissa Church p85

This long-established shop, founded in 1906, sells silverware and a range of watches from luxury brands such as Tag Heuer. Its main strength, though, is its lines of beautiful jewellery designs, including contemporary pieces and a Cypriot heritage range inspired by local museum artefacts. **Other location** Griva Digheni 75G (22 661 776).

Korres

NEW *Galaxias Centre, Archiepiskopou Makariou III 33 & 38 (22 375 730/www.korres.com).* **Open** 9am-7pm Mon, Tue, Thur, Fri; 9am-3pm Wed, Sat. **Map** p80 C4 59

New to the Galaxias shopping centre is this stand-alone store for the Korres bodycare ranges. Fans of the skincare line, based on all-natural ingredients and sold abroad in high-end shops such as Liberty and Sephora, can take the opportunity to stock up on the full range of wonderfully fragrant products.

Krama

Arnaldas 3E (22 761 655). **Open** *June-Aug* 9.30am-1pm, 5-8pm Mon, Tue, Thur, Fri; 9.30am-1.30pm Wed; 10am-1.30pm Sat. *Feb-May* 9.30am-1pm, 3-6pm Mon, Tue, Thur, Fri; 10am-1pm Wed, Sat. **Map** p80 C4 60

This jewellery gallery showcases highly original necklaces, rings, bracelets and earrings in silver and gold, by Cypriot designer Skevi Afantiti. Her sought-after work is also on sale at the Benaki Museum in Athens and gallery shops in Greece, Ireland and the UK.

La Perla

Stasikratous 37B (22 374 774). **Open** 9.30am-1pm, 3.30-7pm Mon, Tue, Thur, Fri; 9.30am-1pm Wed; 10am-2pm Sat. **Map** p80 C4 61

If you need some deliciously extravagent undergarments to go with your purchases from the neighbouring designer boutiques, La Perla comes to the rescue with its provocatively designed but blissfully comfortable lingerie. Bra fittings are available, and there's a small swimwear range.

Levinia K

Christodoulou Sozou 23-25 (22 662 488). **Open** 9.30am-1.30pm, 3-7pm Mon, Tue, Thur, Fri; 9.30am-1.30pm Wed; 10am-2pm Sat. **Map** p80 B3 62

Local fashion designer Levinia Konyalian, who has styled and designed for some of the biggest names in the Greek music world, has returned home with her own collections. She also offers image consulting services.

Kala Kathoumena p88

Mastic Spa

Themistocle Dervi 42A (22 667 771). **Open** 9.30am-7pm Mon, Tue, Thur, Fri; 9.30am-2pm Wed, Sat. **Map** p80 B5 63

This shop specialises in beauty products made from natural ingredients, including mastic – the resin of a shrub cultivated on the Greek island of Chios. See box p84.

Mastiha Shop

Themistocle Dervi 9D (22 445 690). **Open** 9.30am-1pm, 2.30-6pm Mon, Tue, Thur, Fri; 9.30am-2pm Wed, Sat. **Map** p80 B5 64

Over the road from Mastic Spa (see above), this tiny shop has a different range of mastic products. Its scent is unmistakable and harnessed here in everything from chewing gum to a beautifully aromatic liqueur. It's a wonderful place for a unique gift. See box p84.

Moufflon Bookshop

Sofouli 3 (22 665 155). **Open** 9.30am-7pm Mon, Tue, Thur, Fri; 9.30am-2pm Wed; 9.30am-3pm Sat. **Map** p80 B3 65

Established in 1967 by Kevork Keshishian, Moufflon Bookshop is currently run by his daughter, Ruth. The shop has an impressively comprehensive selection of books on Cyprus, among many other categories.

Odd Fish

NEW *Mnasiadou 11 K (22 660 181).* **Open** 9.30am-1.30pm, 3-6.30pm Mon, Tue, Thu, Fri; 9.30am-1.30pm Wed; 9.30am-2.30pm Sat. **Map** p80 C4 66

This new arrival caused a stir in Nicosia. Its minimal space crams in one-of-a-kind clothes from Italy, Spain and Brazil, as well as shoes, bags and accessories by well-known brands such as the Spanish Desigual, and popular Greek designer George Eleftheriades.

Psema

Fokionos 16 (99 578 949/99 664 554). **Open** 10am-1pm & 5pm-8pm Tue-Fri; 10am-1pm Sat. **Map** p80 C2 67

Each room in this renovated 1950s house features one-of-a-kind artworks plus bags, jewellery, T-shirts, books and CDs. Most of the stock is imported from the US, UK, Germany and Greece.

Room

Promitheos 14A (22 104 602). **Open** 10am-8pm Mon, Tue, Thur, Fri; 10am-3pm Wed; 9am-3pm Sat. **Map** p80 C4 68

The owners of this little designer haven wanted to create a space with a relaxed, intimate feel, dotted with gorgeous pieces. As well as evening dresses, dreamy blouses and trendy

Sushi La p90

men's shirts from their own Chi line, you'll find a treasure trove of vintage items by D&G, Gucci, Moschino, Oscar de la Renta, Versace and more.

Vitrine Designer Boutique

Zenonos Sozou 5A (22 760 860). **Open** 10am-1pm, 3-7pm Mon, Tue, Thur, Fri; 10am-3pm Wed, Sat. **Map** p81 D5 ⑥⑨

After 14 years in New York, designer Maria Zachariou has opened up her own little boutique in the heart of Nicosia. The shop stocks her jewellery, clothing and bag designs, as well as brands such as Stella McCartney and Marc Jacobs. Don't forget to ask if you can visit the secret pink room.

Nightlife

Enallax

Athinas 16-17 (22 430 121). **Open** 11pm-3am Thur-Sat. **Map** p81 E2 ⑦⓪

Open three nights a week, Enallax is an interesting place to go if you fancy sampling live Greek music with a local crowd on Thursdays and Saturdays, or rock on Fridays. There are several little bars on the same street, so you can wander from one to another.

Klubd

NEW *Ammohostou 36, opposite Famagusta Gate (22 104 841).* **Open** 11pm-3.45am Fri, Sat. **Admission** €20 incl two drinks (until 12.30am) or one drink (until 2.30am). **Map** p81 E2 ⑦①

After a three-year absence, this club reopened in late 2009 – much to the delight of the island's techno, minimal and house music fans. Complete with its own digital sky (made of LED lights) and thumping sound system, the club fosters local talents such as Alex Tomb and Gomez, alongside regular appearances from international DJs.

Loop

NEW *Demostheni Severi 6 (22 680 800).* **Open** 11pm-late Fri, Sat. **Map** p80 A5 ⑦②

This new arrival in the capital caters to a well turned out crowd of twenty- and thirty-somethings, with a backdrop of mainstream '80s and '90s hits.

Sfinakia

Corner of Spyrou Kyprianou & Themistocle Dervi (22 766 661). **Open** 10pm-late Wed-Sun. **Map** p80 C5 ⑦③

You'll need to make a reservation if you want a table or couch, as Sfinakia is one of the most popular and overcrowded (some might say overrated) clubs in town.

Versus

Archiepiskopou Makariou III 2, Capital Centre, 3rd floor (99 393 009). **Open** 11.30pm-late Wed-Sat. **Map** p80 C3 ⑦④

Versus is the destination of the moment for progressive dance sounds, mainly spun by resident DJ Manic Mike. The crowd is hip, the interior design is smart and the sound and light systems are state-of-the-art.

Zoo

Stasinou 15 (22 458 811). **Open** *Lounge bar* 9am-2am Wed, Thur; 9am-3am Fri, Sat. *Club* 11pm-3am Fri, Sat. **Map** p80 C3/4 ⑦⑤

Domus Lounge Bar p87

CYPRUS BY AREA

Arguably the most popular club in town, Zoo is a lively, stylish spot with a breathtaking view of the walled city and a music list that spans international hits to Greek pop. Food (salads, tandoori chicken) is served in the lounge bar, but might be hard to stomach after midnight once the music is turned up.

Arts & leisure

Artos Foundation

Agion Omologiton 64 (22 445 455/www.artosfoundation.org). **Map** p80 A5 76

Once the premises of the parish bakery, this atmospheric space is a powerhouse of cultural and educational activity, organising exhibitions, art talks, film screenings and conferences. Check the website for details.

Famagusta Gate Cultural Centre

Athinon (22 430 877). **Map** p81 F2 77

Once a main point of entry to the walled city, the beautifully restored Famagusta Gate now functions as an arts hub, hosting exhibitions, talks and concerts.

Micromania

Stasinou 15C (22 661 517). **Open** 9am-1pm, 4-7pm Mon-Fri; 9am-2pm Sat. **Map** p80 A5 78

Cycling is an ideal way to explore Nicosia's old town, providing the weather isn't too hot. The guys who run Micromania sell and rent excellent bikes (rental €6 per day), and also organise weekend excursions to scenic spots such as Akamas in Pafos, the Karpas peninsula in the north or Cape Greco near Agia Napa.

Municipality Swimming Pool

Louki Akrita 8 (22 781 155). **Open** 10am-6pm daily. **Map** p80 A2 79

To avoid the crowds at this popular swimming pool, go for a dip first thing in the morning. Alternatively, the Hilton hotel at the southern end of Makariou offers a more refined spot to lounge pool-side.

Omeriye Hamam

Plateia Tyllirias (22 460 570/22 750 550). **Open** 11am-7pm Mon; 9am-9pm Tue-Sun (men Tue, Thur, Sat; women Wed, Fri, Sun; couples Mon). **Map** p81 D2 80

The Omeriye Hamam was built in the 16th century opposite the Omeriye Mosque, and used as a community baths until 2002. Extensive renovations have transformed it into the most luxurious hamam in Cyprus. It's a great place to relax and rejuvenate the way Cypriots did 100 years ago (for €18, nowadays). Around the hot slab – the hottest spot in the hamam – there are seven rooms, each at a different temperature. Massages, body wraps, spa treatments and mud therapy are also available. Once steamed and scrubbed, you can unwind on plush divans in an atmosphere of complete calm.

Pantheon Art Cinema

Diagorou 29 (22 675 787). **Map** p80 B3 81

One of the oldest cinemas in town, the Pantheon is carving out a niche for itself as the only art house cinema on the island.

Walking Tours of Nicosia

Cyprus Tourism Organisation (CTO), Aristokyprou 11 (22 674 264/www.visitcyprus.com). **Tickets** free. **Map** p80 C3 82

A series of free walks start at 10am at the tourist information office in the old town. Monday is 'Chrysaliniotissa and Kaimakli: The Past Restored', Thursday is the 'Tour of Old Nicosia' – visiting workshops and shops where craftsmen still work in the traditional way, and Friday is 'Nicosia Outside the Walls.'

Weaving Mill

Lefkonos 67-71 (22 762 275/www.ifantourgio.org.cy). **Map** p80 C2 83

Head to this converted factory to sip wine while watching alternative movies, listening to live jazz or enjoying a poetry reading. It has the largest public library of cinema books on the island, plus a film archive of more than 600 titles.

Lemesos beachfront.

Lemesos (Limassol)

Located less than an hour's drive from Nicosia, Larnaka, Pafos and the Troodos mountains, the island's second largest town and main port is an ideal base for exploring the whole country. On either side of the outskirts of town lie the archaeological sites of **Ancient Amathus** in the east and **Kourion (Curium) Amphitheatre** in the west; the latter is one of the island's greatest treasures.

Split into two areas linked by a long seafront promenade, Lemesos consists of the **Germasogeia Tourist Area**, which leads to the more interesting **Old Town** further west. On the seafront road is the rather unusual **Sculpture Park**. Entrance is free to view the 16 metal, stone, concrete and marble sculptures by local artists, which are atmospherically illuminated at night. Every Sunday a busy market, catering mostly to the local Asian population, takes place here.

Across the road from the park, next to the **Cyprus Tourism Organisation** (CTO) office, is a narrow road leading north to Anexartisias Street, one of the main shopping areas. Behind this is the central bus station, which is traversed by Agiou Andrea, a cobbled pedestrian thoroughfare lined with small trinket and leather shops. It's overlooked by a roundabout, upon which is the surprisingly interesting **Sea Sponge Exhibition Centre**.

The old port alongside it looks rather neglected and run down, but plans have been announced for its renovation (see box p110). Less than 50 metres from the old port roundabout is the **Medieval Castle and Museum**. If you're also planning to visit the out-of-town historic sites (and you should), buses bound for **Kourion Amphitheatre** and its magnificent mosaics, as well as for the 12th-century **Kolossi Castle**, stop in front of the castle.

Old Town

Sights & museums

Archaeological Museum

Corner Kanningos & Vyronos (25 305 157). **Open** 9am-5pm Mon-Fri; 10am-1pm Sat. **Admission** €1.70. **Map** p101 E2 ❶

Spanning 10,000 years of history, the displays in this museum offer a cross-section of discoveries from multiple archaeological sites in and around Lemesos. Pottery, jewellery, tools and statuary relating to the goddess Aphrodite feature prominently.

Folk Art Museum

Agiou Andreou 253 (25 362 303). **Open** *June-Sept* 8.30am-1.30pm, 4-6.30pm Mon, Tue, Wed, Fri. *Oct-May* 8.30am-1.30pm, 3-5.30pm Mon, Tue, Wed, Fri. **Admission** €0.85. **Map** p101 D3 ❷

Kept in a faithfully preserved traditional house, this quaint collection of more than 500 original artefacts from the last 200 years includes examples of Cypriot dress, crafts, household items and furnishings.

Medieval Castle & Museum

Near the Old Port (25 305 419). **Open** 9am-5pm Mon-Sat; 10am-1pm Sun. **Admission** €3.40. **Map** p100 C4 ❸

This atmospheric little museum is housed inside a 13th-century castle whose main claim to fame is that it stands on the site of the castle where, in 1191, Richard the Lionheart married Berengaria of Navarre and crowned her Queen of England. Cells in the basement were used as a prison until 1950. Items displayed in the museum date as far back as 620AD, and include a collection of Lusignan armour as well as treasures from Kyrenia.

Natural Sea Sponge Exhibition Centre

Old Port Roundabout (25 871 656). **Open** 9am-7pm Mon-Fri; 9am-3pm Sat. **Admission** free. **Map** p100 C4 ❹

An unusual little place offering an intriguing insight into the harvesting and production of sea sponges.

Eating & drinking

127

Elenis Paleologinas 5 (25 343 990). **Open** 10am-1am Mon-Thur; noon-1am Sat, Sun. €. **Café/bar**. **Map** p101 D3 ❺

Hidden in a side street in the heart of the Old Town, this recently renovated café and lounge bar offers gourmet salads and sandwiches. Chillout music and bohemian decor make for a relaxed atmosphere, and the large garden area is perfect for balmy evenings.

7 Seas Music Bar

NEW *Columbia Plaza, Agiou Andreou 223 (25 278 000).* **Open** 8pm-2am daily. **Bar**. **Map** p101 D3 ❻

This twinkling new lounge bar on the second floor of the Columbia Plaza cultivates a groovy mood with live R&B from house band Soft Touch. International guest acts also drop in, playing anything from salsa to acoustic singer-songwriter musings.

Aliada

Irinis 117 (25 340 758). **Open** 8pm-11pm Mon-Sat. €€. **International**. **Map** p100 C3 ❼

This appealing restaurant, occupying a grand old house with high ceilings and a pretty garden, has been around for years. It offers an extravagant four-course set menu, attractively presented and at a price so low (€23) you'll think they made a mistake.

Anotera

Gladstonos 5 (25 354 033). **Open** noon-3.30pm, 7.30-11pm Tue-Fri, Sun; 7.30-11pm Sat. €€. **Taverna**. **Map** p100 C3 ❽

Deceptively large thanks to the charming garden area at the rear, this taverna has the enviable reputation of

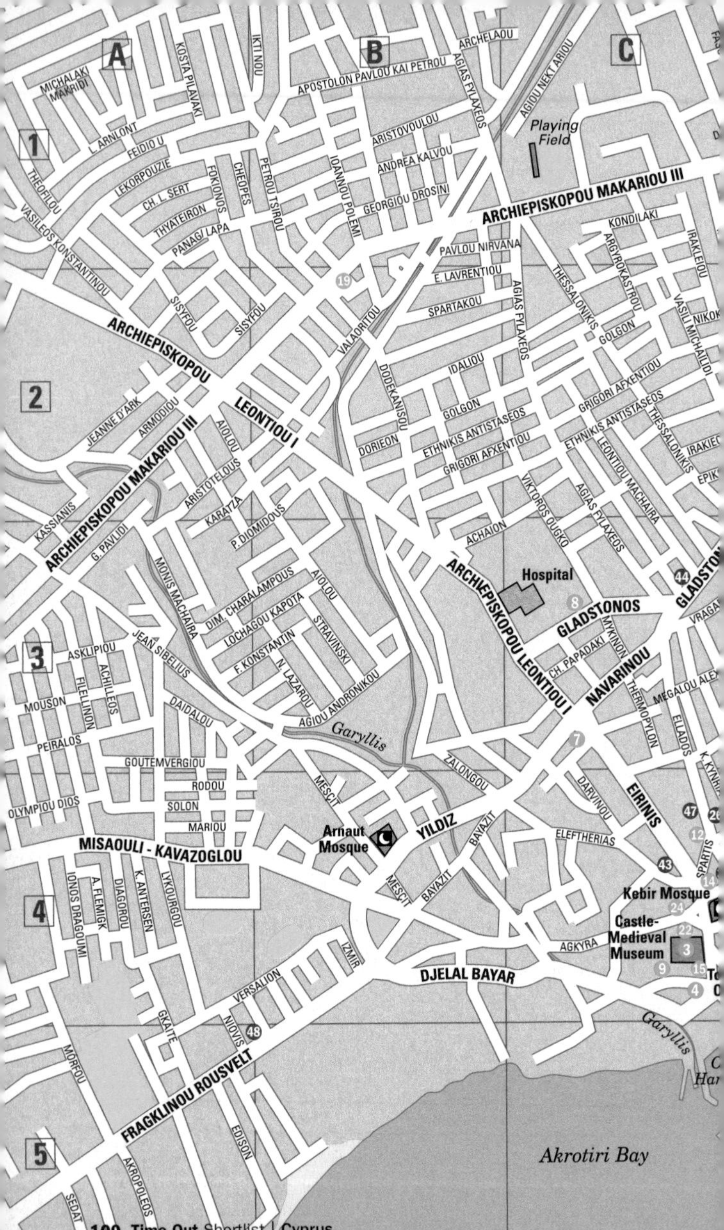
A
B
C
1
2
3
4
5
MICHALAKI MAKRIDI
KOSTA PILAVAKI
IKTI NOU
APOSTOLON PAVLOU KAI PETROU
ARCHELAOU
AGIAS FYLAXEOS
AGIOU NEKT ARIOU
Playing Field
L. ARNLONT
FEIDIO U
LEKORPOUZIE
CH. L. SERT
THYATEIRON
PANAGI LAPA
FOKIONOS
CHEOPES
PETROU TSIROU
IOANNOU POLEMI
ARISTOVOULOU
ANDREA KALVOU
GEORGIOU DROSINI
ARCHIEPISKOPOU MAKARIOU III
KONDILAKI
THEOFILOU
VASILEOS KONSTANTINOU
PAVLOU NIRVANA
E. LAVRENTIOU
SPARTAKOU
THESSALONIKIS
ARGYROKASTROU
IRAKLEIOU
VASILI MICHAILIDI
NIKOK
19
SISYFOU
VALAORITOU
GOLGON
ARCHIEPISKOPOU
LEONTIOU I
DODEKANISOU
IDALIOU
GRIGORI AFXENTIOU
ETHNIKIS ANTISTASEOS
JEANNE D'ARK
ARMODIOU
AIOLOU
DORIEON
IRAKIEC
EPIK
ARCHIEPISKOPOU MAKARIOU III
ARISTOTELOUS
KARATZA
P. DIOMIDOUS
VIKTOROS OUGKO
LEONTIOU MACHAIRA
KASSIANIS
G. PAVLIDI
ACHAION
Hospital
8
44
GLADSTONOS
GLADSTON
MONIS MACHAIRA
DIM. CHARALAMPOUS
LOCHAGOU KAPOTA
STRAVINSKI
ARCHIEPISKOPOU LEONTIOU I
MYKINON
CH. PAPADAKI
VRAGA
NAVARINOU
ASKLIPIOU
JEAN SIBELIUS
F. KONSTANTIN
N. LAZAROU
THERMOPYLON
MEGALOU ALEX
ACHILLEOS
FILELLINON
MOUSON
DAIDALOU
AGIOU ANDRONIKOU
ELLADOS
PEIRALOS
Garyllis
7
K. KYNIKI
GOUTEMVERGIOU
ZALONGOU
DARVINOU
EIRINIS
RODOU
MESCIT
SOLON
OLYMPIOU DIOS
47
26
MARIOU
Arnaut Mosque
YILDIZ
BAYAZIT
ELEFTHERIAS
12
SPARTIS
MISAOULI - KAVAZOGLOU
43
14
IONOS DRAGOUMI
A. FLEMIGK
DIAGOROU
K. ANTERSEN
LYKOURGOU
Kebir Mosque
24
Castle-Medieval Museum
22
3
AGKYRA
IZMIR
DJELAL BAYAR
9
15
4
VERSALION
GKAITE
NIOVIS
48
MORFOU
Garyllis
FRAGKLINOU ROUSVELT
EDISON
Akrotiri Bay
AKROPOLEOS
SEDAT

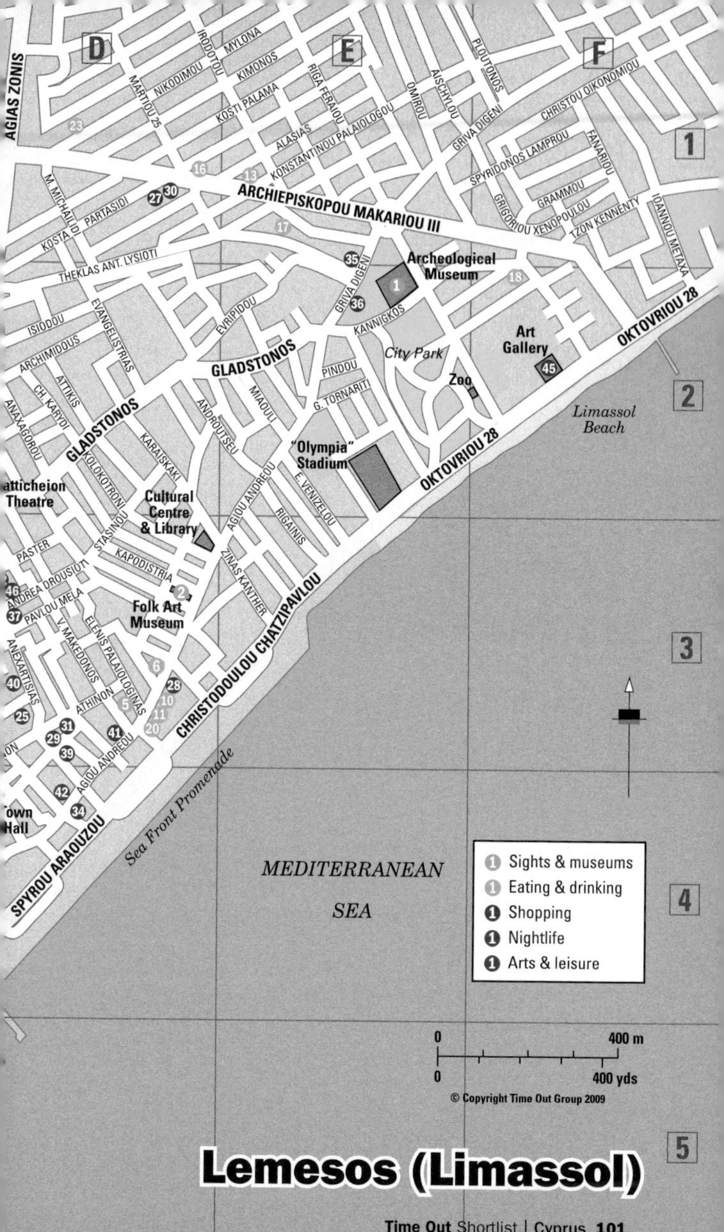

Lemesos (Limassol)

being the best in town. Unusually, an à la carte menu is offered in addition to the traditional meze.

Artima

Lanitis Carob Mill Complex, Vasilissis (25 820 466). **Open** 1-3pm, 7.30-11pm daily. **€€€. Italian. Map** p100 C4 9
Set just off the old port roundabout, this Italian lends itself to business lunches. Nonetheless, its imaginative menu and slick service can also tempt weary, shopped-out sightseers.

Barolo

Agiou Andreou 248 (25 760 767). **Open** 7-11pm Mon-Sat. **€€€. International. Map** p101 D3 10
There is no substitute for quality, and no restaurant knows it better than this ultra-stylish establishment. Barolo boasts a subtly lit and decorated interior, a gorgeous outdoor deck, creative and flavoursome dishes (duck and deer are on the menu), sumptuous desserts and an award-winning wine list.

Beige

Agiou Andreou 238 (25 818 860). **Open** 6pm-midnight daily. **€€€. International. Map** p101 D3 11
One of the few true fusion restaurants on the island, Beige offers chichi sushi alongside a global array of dishes; the regularly changing menu could include the likes of Angus steak, lobster spaghetti or black cod fillet in miso sauce. Decor is understated, with stone walls and natural-toned furnishings.

Central Surf and Turf

NEW *Ellados 28 (25 373 760).* **Open** 7.30-11pm daily. **€€€. International. Map** p100 C4 12
This place serves a bit of everything, from steaks to seafood, and has a comprehensive wine list. The setting, in a renovated old house, is warm and comfortable, and service is unwaveringly efficient.

Chocolate Soup

Archiepiskopou Makariou III 197 (25 344 141/www.chocolatesoup.com.cy). **Open** 9am-1am daily. **€. Café. Map** p101 E1 13
Choose from a decadent array of chocolate treats, including chocolate platters, hot and cold chocolatey drinks and the 'Suckao' – a shot of melted chocolate served in an espresso cup. A handful of savoury choices combat sugar overload.

Dino Art Café

Irinis 62-66 (25 762 030). **Open** 10.30am-midnight Mon-Sat; 4pm-midnight Sun. **€. Café. Map** p100 C4 14
A stellar array of homemade dishes ensures repeat business to this buzzy café. The sociable owner and chef Dino oversees the preparation of every dish, and is known for his divine desserts. The art exhibited on the walls is all for sale, if you're looking to pick up a holiday souvenir with a difference.

Draught Microbrewery

Lanitis Carob Mill Complex, Vasilissis (25 820 470). **Open** 11am-2am daily. **Pub. Map** p100 C4 15
Drop in to sample the golden nectar from Cyprus's first ever microbrewery. Tex-mex dips keep hunger at bay as the DJ mixes 1970s and '80s tunes. It's jumping at weekends.

Gioia

Archiepiskopou Makariou III 193 (25 761 761). **Open** 10.30pm-2am Wed, Fri, Sat. **Bar. Map** p101 D1 16
If you're looking to try out a local place that plays exclusively Greek music, Gioia is a good bet.

Ibsen Tea & Coffee House

Chrysanthou Mylona 16 (25 340 714). **Open** 8am-6pm Mon-Fri; 9am-3pm Sat. **No credit cards. €. Café. Map** p101 E1 17
A variety of international and unusual teas are on offer at this intimate little tea and coffee house, while chunky sandwiches, homemade quiches and carrot cake can be enjoyed from the comfort of plush chairs and sofas.

Itilo

Amathountos 12 (25 590 970). **Open** noon-3pm, 7.30-11pm Mon-Sat. **€€. Mediterranean. Map** p101 F2 18
Accented with touches of blue, this centrally located Mediterranean

CYPRUS BY AREA

restaurant is stylish yet welcoming. Divine salads, meat and seafood dishes arrive beautifully presented and taste just as good as they look.

Kyprion Gevsis

Archiepiskopou Makariou III 126B (77 778 877). **Open** 6pm-late daily. **€€.** **Taverna**. **Map** p100 B2 ⓳

This typical Cypriot kitchen offers a rich meze of 30 plates, including meat and fish dishes. To listen to live traditional music as you dine, come on Friday or Saturday. This is also one of the few establishments to provide disabled access.

Peaches 'n' Cream by Graffiti

Agiou Andreou 236 (25 747 552). **Open** 9pm-2am daily. **Bar**. **Map** p101 D3 ⓴

Adding a new name to the recently renovated, minimalist space, Graffiti has retained its original charm. The music has evolved into an eclectic mix of house, tribal, ethnic and oriental sounds, interspersed with European chart hits. The back yard opens up during the summer months.

Pi

Kitiou Kyprianou 27 (25 341 944). **Open** 10am-1am Mon-Sat; 4pm-1am Sun. **€**. **Café/bar**. **Map** p100 C4 ㉑

Buried in the back streets, this diminutive café and bar occupies a gorgeous stone building. Customers delve into posh salads, cheese and meat platters, while jazz and chill-out tunes tinkle in the background.

Stretto

Lanitis Carob Mill Complex, Vasilissis (25 820 465). **Open** 9am-1am daily. **€€**. **Café**. **Map** p100 C4 ㉒

Chic red seats and inviting sofas warm the mood in this super-trendy café, which serves light Mediterranean dishes.

Ta Piatakia

Nicodemou Mylona 7 (25 745 017). **Open** 7-11.30pm Mon-Sat. **€**. **International**. **Map** p101 D1 ㉓

This gem of a restaurant (the name translates as 'Little Plates') is nothing short of a culinary revelation. Owner/chef Roddy happily reels off the specials, which are prepared using only fresh, local produce. Fried celery leaves are an unexpectedly delicious start to the meal, the duck is to die for, and you can't leave the premises without trying the pavlova. Smokers are banished to outside tables or sent upstairs.

Ta Psarakia tou Nikou

Angyras 14 (25 376 082). **Open** 5pm-midnight Mon-Sat. **€€**. **Fish**. **Map** p100 C4 ㉔

Conveniently close to the castle, this simple, authentic fish taverna (also known as the Old Neighbourhood) is the ideal place to recover after a hard day's shopping in town. Impeccably fresh food and speedy service make it a winner.

Shopping

34 the Shop

Andrea Themistokleous 20 (25 878 555/www.34theshop.com). **Open** 9am-7pm Mon, Tue, Thur; 9am-2pm Wed; 9am-7.30pm Fri; 9am-2.30pm Sat. **Map** p101 D3 ㉕

Just off Anexartisias street, this hip boutique is filled with upbeat and casual clothes by European brands like Paul Smith, Paul Frank and Pepe.

Other location Anexartisias 120 (25 310 808).

Bags of Fun

Ellados 44 (25 762 575). **Open** *May-Sept* 9am-1pm, 2.30-6.30pm Mon, Tue, Thur, Fri; 9am-1pm Wed, Sat. *Oct-Apr* 9am-1pm, 2.30-6pm Mon, Tue, Thur, Fri; 10am-1.30pm Wed, Sat. **Map** p100 C4 ㉖

There are bargains to discover here amid a treasure trove of antique costume jewellery. A good selection of handbags, gloves and other vintage fripperies completes the stock.

Bear Factory

Costa Partassidi 34, off Archiepiskopou Makariou III (25 341 040). **Open** 9am-7pm Mon, Tue, Thur; 9am-8pm Fri; 9am-3pm Wed, Sat. **Map** p101 D1 ㉗

Children can design their own soft toy, choosing an animal and giving it a heart and a name, then watching as it's fluffed into life before their eyes. The whole affair is quite magical.

Boukla Boukla

Agiou Andreou 252 (25 363 737). **Open** 10am-1pm, 4-7pm Mon, Tue, Thur, Fri; 10am-2pm Wed, Sat. **Map** p101 D3 ㉘

Fans of cutting-edge fashion will adore this boutique, with womenswear and accessories by three Greek designers.

Brent Cross

Anexartisias 32 (25 378 344). **Open** *May-Sept* 8.30am-1pm, 4-7pm Mon, Tue, Thur, Fri; 8.30am-2pm Wed, Sat. *Oct-Apr* 8.30am-5.30pm Mon, Tue, Thur, Fri; 8.30am-2pm Wed, Sat. **Map** p101 D3 ㉙

A well-established chain, stocking an enormous variety of music and DVDs. **Other location** Archiepiskopou Makariou III 175 (25 747 814).

Calvin Klein Jeans

Archiepiskopou Makariou III 216B (25 342 810). **Open** 9am-1pm, 3.30-7.30pm Mon-Fri; 9am-2pm Wed; 9.30am-2.30pm Sat. **Map** p101 D1 ㉚

Only a couple of years old, this specialist shop stocks the entire range of Calvin Klein jeans, as well as T-shirts and casualwear for men and women.

Cyprus Handicraft Centre

Themidos 25 (25 305 118). **Open** *May-Sept* 8am-1pm, 4-7pm Mon, Tue, Thur, Fri; 8am-1pm Wed, Sat. *Oct-Apr* 8am-1pm, 2.30-5.30pm Mon, Tue, Thur, Fri; 8am-1pm Wed, Sat. **Map** p101 D3 ㉛

This is a great place to buy souvenirs, as all the products are handmade locally: painted and woven objects, pottery, silver jewellery and decorative handicrafts with traditional patterns.

Damart

Anexartisias (25 358 333/www.damart.com.cy). **Open** 9.30am-7.30pm Mon, Tue, Thur, Fri; 9.30am-2pm Wed, Sat. **Map** p101 D3 ㉜

Head here for an expert bra-fitting service and a full range of sizes. The top-of-the-range brands stocked include Fantasie and Rigby & Peller.

Design Plus

Ellados 7 (25 109 000). **Open** 9am-1pm, 3-7pm Mon-Fri; 9am-2pm Wed, Sat. **Map** p100 C4 ㉝

A feast of Italian design, with outfits from Kartell, Moooi, Lapalma and more.

Ecco Shoes

Agiou Andreou 123 (25 343 867). **Open** 8am-7pm Mon, Tue, Thur, Fri; 8am-2pm Wed; 8.30am-2pm Sat. **Map** p101 D4 ㉞

Danish brand Ecco costs considerably less in Cyprus, as the shoes are locally produced under licence.

Kyriakou Bookshop

Griva Digheni 3 (25 747 555). **Open** *Mar-June* 8am-1pm, 3-7pm Mon, Tue, Thur, Fri; 8am-1.30pm Wed, Sat. *July-Aug* 8am-1pm, 4-7.30pm Mon, Tue, Thur, Fri; 8am-1.30pm Wed, Sat. *Sept-Feb* 8am-1pm, 3.30-6.30pm Mon, Tue, Thur, Fri; 8am-1.30pm Wed, Sat. **Map** p101 E1 ㉟

The shelves here are lined with an impressive range of local and international books; you can also buy magazines, cards and stationery.

M&M Kovis Jewellery

Griva Digeni 2, Shop 8 (25 343 771). **Open** *Summer* 9.30am-1pm, 4-7pm Mon-Sat. *Winter* 9.30am-1pm, 3-6.30pm Mon-Sat. **Map** p101 E2 ㊱

Handmade and Italian-imported gold and silver jewellery are on display in this highly regarded shop. Commissions are also welcomed.

MAC

Anexartisias 100 (25 871 387). **Open** 9am-7pm Mon, Tue, Thur, Fri; 9am-3pm Wed; 9am-5pm Sat. **Map** p101 D3 ㊲

Professional make-up with a flawless finish and long durability is this global beauty brand's forte. Stock is updated on a regular basis.

Made to Measure Shoes

Tzami Tzetik 14 (25 372 898). **Open** 8am-6pm Mon-Fri. **Map** p100 C4 ㊳

This shop near the castle offers custom-made footwear, including orthopaedic shoes, riding boots and golf shoes. Orders for tourists are finished in two to three days.

Precious Metal Gallery

Agora Anexartisias, Anexartisias, Shop 17 (25 353 639). **Open** *May-Oct* 10am-1.30pm, 4.30-8pm Mon, Tue, Thur, Fri; 10am-2pm Wed, Sat. *Nov-Apr* 10am-1pm, 3-6pm Mon, Tue, Thu, Fri; 10am-2pm Wed, Sat. **Map** p101 D3 ❸❾

The handmade gold and silver jewellery in this little shop, sometimes incorporating precious stones, is influenced by geometric shapes. Commissions welcome.

Stradivarius

Anexartisias 107 (25 350 469). **Open** Mon, Tue, Thur, Fri 9.30am-8pm; 9.30am-3pm Wed; 9.30am-7.30pm Sat. **Map** p101 D3 ❹⓿

This trend-led clothes shop oozes appeal for the younger generation, who flock here after school and at weekends.

Thesis

Agiou Andreou 201 (25 369 479/www.thesis.com.cy). **Open** 9am-1pm, 3.30pm-7pm Mon, Tue, Thur, Fri; 9am-1pm Wed; 9am-2pm Sat. **Map** p101 D3 ❹❶

A beautiful, well-established shop, selling decorative and practical items for the home; lines are modern and simple, with an ethnic accent. Natural materials (wood, bamboo, cotton) and muted, restful colours dominate. There's also an on-site café and petite bookshop, well-stocked with art and design titles.

Nightlife

Metropole Retro Music Club

Metropole Hotel, Ifigeneias 6 (25 357 676). **Open** 11pm-late Fri-Sat. **Map** p101 D4 ❹❷

Reopened after a considerable hiatus, this 500-capacity venue plays, as its name suggests, 1970s and '80s music.

Sesto Senso

Promachon Eleftherias 45 (25 879 080). **Open** 11pm-4am. **Map** p100 C4 ❹❸

Playing all the latest international and Greek hits, this stylish and expensive club (drinks cost €10-€15) administers 'face control' at the door to ensure that only the beautiful people get in.

Arts & leisure

Century House of Billiards

Gladstonos 29 (25 745 547). **Open** 10am-1am daily. **Map** p100 C3 ❹❹

The only establishment of its kind in Lemesos, Century houses a dozen fine snooker and American pool tables and holds snooker, eight-ball and nine-ball tournaments on a weekly and monthly basis. An ideal place for amateurs and professionals alike.

Municipal Art Gallery

Ocktovriou 28 103 (25 586 212). **Open** 8.30am-1.30pm, 3-5.30pm Mon, Tue, Wed, Fri; 8.30am-1.30pm Thur. **Map** p101 F2 ❹❺

There are some remarkable works on display in this striking building, located on the seafront road. The main displays showcase oil, watercolour and acrylic paintings by local artists, while the basement focuses on the EOKA Struggle of 1955-59 for independence from the British.

Rialto Theatre

Andrea Drousioti 19, Plateia Iroon (25 343 900/www.rialto.com.cy). **Map** p101 D3 ❹❻

This lovely, restored old theatre offers an exceptional variety of events, spanning all the performing arts. Shows are often free, although it's a goor idea to book in advance.

Rio

Ellados 125 (25 871 410). **Map** p100 C4 ❹❼

This unique complex boasts an ex-Gold Class cinema (with a small room and large seats), as well as two traditional screens. It even has an outdoor cinema which operates during the summer months.

Tehnohoros Ethal

NEW *Franklin Roosevelt 76 (25 877 827).* **Map** p100 B5 ❹❽

On occasion, English theatre companies perform their productions at this new arts space. Call ahead to find out what's on.

Beach bars

The new trend upping the nightlife style stakes.

Guaba Beach Bar

With Agia Napa's heyday as the clubbing destination of choice a more distant memory every year, a new breed of fairweather going-out options is vying for the crown. Lemesos is making a name for itself with its sophisticated beach bars, most of which have replaced run-down, soulless pubs along the main drag of Germasogeia.

Brand new **Cote D'Azur** (p108) combines floaty white sails and comfy couches for an impressive alfresco clubbing experience on a wooden deck. Another popular nightspot on the stretch is **Breeze** (p108), where the locals are dressed to the nines; it's made for posing and preening, as its street level café/restaurant provides a bird's eye view of the dancefloor. Be prepared to queue for this one.

For daytime scenesters, Greek coffee chain **Flo Café** (p108) combines seaside views, a wide selection of caffeine-rich drinks and tasty food. Further down the coast, the beach at Agios Tychonas hosts **Drops** (p108), a laid-back option serving cocktails and iced coffees with a smile.

The hottest seaside spot du jour, however, is **Guaba** (p108), where a hip crowd dance on the beach to tunes spun by international DJs. At the time of going to press, Guaba's licence had not been renewed for its location at Agios Tychonas beach, but the organisers were confident a new venue would be found; go to www.guababeachbar.com for info.

Beach-starved capital-dwellers now make the trip from Lefkosia especially for the lively nightlife in Lemesos, with its combination of chic bars and seaside surroundings. Just make sure you dress the part if you don't want to stick out like a tourist thumb – Cypriots love to glam it up.

Germasogeia Tourist Area

Stretching east along the coast from the centre of Lemesos, the overdeveloped concrete jungle of the tourist strip at least has convenience on its side – most venues are located on the long beachfront road. One thing this area does well is nightlife, with several stylish bars to be found among the endless line of hotels.

Eating & drinking

Akakiko

Louis Apollonia Beach Hotel, Georgiou I (25 323 351). **Open** 7.30-11pm daily. **€. Japanese.**

This budget-priced Japanese restaurant turns out a high standard of food: sushi, sashimi, salads, tempura, teppanyaki and combination platters.

Breeze

Georgiou I 90 (25 321 294). **Open** *Summer* 10am-3am daily. **Bar.**

See box p107.

Caprice at Londa

Londa Hotel, Georgiou I 72 (25 865 555). **Open** 12.30-3pm, 7.30-11pm daily. **€€€. Italian.**

Located in a tasteful boutique hotel, the sister restaurant of Mykonos's Caprice luxuriates in spectacular sea views and subtle decor. In summer, barbecue platters are served by the pool.

Cote D'Azur

NEW *Georgiou I 89 (70 00 5008).* **Open** *May-Oct* 11am-3am daily. Closed Nov-Apr. **Bar.**

See box p107.

Drops

Amathountos 17, Agios Tychonas (25 310 310). **Open** 10am-2am daily. **Bar.**

See box p107.

Flo Café

Georgiou I 106 (25 879 610). **Open** 10am-12.30am Mon-Thur; 10am-1am Fri, Sat. **€. Café/bar.**

See box p107.

Guaba Beach Bar

(99 520 129/www.guababeachbar.com). **Open** *May-Oct* Closed Nov-Apr. **Bar/club.**

See box p107.

Mandaloun

Yiannou Kranidioti, near Le Meridien Hotel (25 636 845). **Open** 6-11pm Tue-Sun. **€€. Lebanese.**

Wonderful, authentic Lebanese food in upmarket bohemian surroundings extending outdoors to a large marquee-covered terrace. The meze is brilliant value and nargilehs (shishas) are available for a post-prandial puff.

Mavromatis

Four Seasons Hotel, Amathountos (25 858 000). **Open** 7.30-11pm Tue-Sat. **€€€. International.**

A superb dining experience, courtesy of an acclaimed Paris-based chef who has raised Greek and Cypriot dishes to new heights. No fewer than seven cooks toil away to conjure up this gourmet magic, which is accompanied by an equally impressive wine list.

Pebbles

Amathountos (25 322 277). **Open** 9am-late daily. **Bar.**

You pay that little bit extra for the view at this multi-level bar, which is open all year round and has hammocks by the sea. The music policy covers all the latest hits, interspersed with Latin parties and salsa dancing on the odd Sunday afternoon in summer.

Plaz

Georgiou I (25 812 291). **Open** 5pm-2am daily. **Bar.**

Previously known as Pralina by the Sea, this newly redecorated beach bar pumps out Greek and global hits to accompany its café menu.

Surfers

Georgiou I, Galaxy House (99 662 741). **Open** 10am-2am daily. **Pub.**

A complete overhaul has transformed this dowdy pub into a trendy, ultra-modern venue with oversized bamboo sofas in lime green and orange and

Oleastro Olive Park p111

multi-coloured neon lights. It features international music (sometimes with a live DJ), an interesting cocktail selection and four sports screens.

Zen Room

Amathountos 194, Pareklissia (25 812 659). **Open** noon-2am daily. **€€.**
Japanese.
A trendy, New York-style restaurant serving Japanese specialities with some Thai influences. Service is good and the chefs work in an open kitchen, so you have a lively view while you wait.

Nightlife

Basement

Georgiou I 91 (25 325 752). **Open** 11pm-4am daily.
Attracting a particularly young crowd, this freshly renovated and very popular club is one of the oldest on the strip. It churns out the latest hits, R&B and old skool tunes, and hosts regular progressive house and trance nights.

Arts & leisure

Onisilos Seaside Theatre

Amathountos, Agios Tychonas (info 25 323 567).
This charming open-air theatre plays host to Musical Sundays, organised by the CTO in conjunction with the local municipality. An extensive programme of short music and dance events are held free of charge at 11am (Nov-May), 8pm (May), and 9pm (June-July) to disappointingly small audiences.

Around Lemesos

There are exactly 100 villages within the Lemesos district, as well as the spectacular Troodos mountain range. Fresh mountain air, a leisurely pace of life, quaint cobbled streets, stone houses and fresh produce entice both locals and tourists all year round.

One of the most popular – and interesting – rural communities to visit is **Lania**, whose exquisite views have attracted numerous foreign artists over the years (two remain, and open their studios to the public). **Lofou** was virtually abandoned for many years, but is now in the midst of an extensive restoration project. It boasts striking stonework and unparalleled eating options; the tourism board has commended all three of its tavernas. Tucked away in the folds of the hills, **Vouni** keeps visitors busy with the Friends of the Cyprus Donkey Sanctuary (25 945 488) and the Vouni Art Gallery.

Sights & museums

Ancient Amathus

11km east of Lemesos centre. **Open** *Nov-Mar* 8am-5pm daily. *Apr-May, Sept-Oct* 8am-6pm daily. *June-Aug* 8am-7.30pm daily. **Admission** €1.70.
Dating back to 1100 BC, Amathus came to be one of the most significant city-kingdoms of Cyprus in antiquity. Myth has it that Theseus left the pregnant Ariadne here to be cared for after his battle with the minotaur. Today, you can peruse the ruins of Hellenistic and Roman baths, walk across the stones of the agora between tall carved pillars or peer down at the ancient sunken harbour.

Cruise control

Lemesos marina smartens up its image.

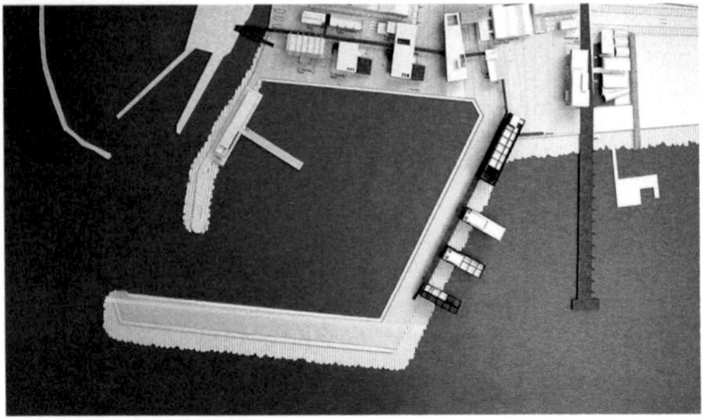

After long years of neglect and lingering roadworks, Lemesos, blighted for years by its image of a concrete jungle by the sea, is finally getting a makeover.

Several factors have come into play – not least the renovation of the Lanitis Carob Mill complex (near the castle), with its exhibition spaces and eating venues. A spate of new, good-quality restaurants, museums and stylish bars have opened up in the area, and there have been some key improvements to the city's infrastructure: the newly cobbled stretches along the seafront road, designated cycling routes and the extraordinary seafront promenade. Slowly but surely, the city is regaining some of its lost charm.

At long last, the old port area of Lemesos is also to be given a facelift. However, with plans to increase the berthing capacity of the marina from 70 to 120 vessels, to resurrect the original stone buildings and to open new fish restaurants both on land and 'at sea', it's hard to see how the project will be finished within the one-year time limit in early 2010.

Designed as a fishermen's port accepting only professional vessels, it will undoubtedly improve tourism in the city. The old incarnation wasn't the most welcoming to holidaymakers arriving by ship; a dilapidated old shed acted as a makeshift terminal for the past 30 years, and an upgrade was urgently needed.

The unusual design of the new terminal – a series of simple elliptical shells – will cut a strong, singular image. The interior will be reminiscent of seashells and bubbles, portholes and binoculars; the wood-lined, zinc-clad shells are intended to create an acoustic space familiar to that found onboard early sailing ships.

The Lemesos Port Authority, which is financing the entire €7 million project, is nevertheless optimistic that the awaited planning permission will soon be granted, so that work on the port can begin immediately.

Ancient Kourion

19km west of Lemesos on Lemesos-Pafos Road (25 934 250). **Open** *June-Aug* 8am-7.30pm daily. *Sept-Mar* 8am-5pm daily. *Apr-May* 8am-6pm daily. **Admission** €1.70.

This is one of the island's most important archaeological sites, and it's hard to decide which is more impressive: the Greco-Roman amphitheatre perched on the clifftop, or the view it provides. Constructed in the second century BC, the theatre has undergone extensive renovation in recent years – mostly to protect the spectacular floor mosaics that were previously exposed to the elements. During the summer, Kourion (or Curium) is used for its original purpose of staging arts performances. Any production, be it music, theatre, dance or ancient drama, takes on a new dimension at this stunning venue. Bring a cushion to alleviate the effects of the stone seating – though minor discomfort is a small price to pay for such a tremendous experience.

Kolossi Castle

Kolossi, 11km west of Lemesos (25 934 907). **Open** *June-Aug* 9am-7.30pm daily. *Sept-May* 9am-6pm daily. **Admission** €1.70.

Kolossi is the perfect example of a 13th-century medieval castle, originally built by the Knights of St John and rebuilt in the 15th century after a Genoese attack. The crenellated rooftop offers wonderful views of the surrounding vineyards, which produce Commandaria (Cyprus's sweet dessert wine, commonly used for communion and the world's oldest named wine still in production). The remains of a 14th-century sugar factory are also nearby. The castle is around 20 minutes' drive from Lemesos.

Sanctuary of Apollo

2.5km west of Kourion on Lemesos-Episkopi Road (25 991 049). **Open** *June-Aug* 9am-7.30pm daily. *Sept-May* 9am-5pm daily. **Admission** €1.70.

Discoveries on this archaeological site include the ruins of a bath house, the main gates of the sanctuary, and the walls and floors of the house of Apollo Hylates (god of the woodlands), who was worshipped here from the eighth to the fourth century BC and was protector of the nearby kingdom of Kourion.

Arts & leisure

Amathus Park Riding Club

Parekklissia, take the motorway exit opposite Hawaii Beach Hotel (99 604 109).

Provides guided treks for competent riders around the quaint, picturesque villages in the area.

Fasouri Watermania Waterpark

Lanitis Orange Groves, Fasouri (25 714 235/www.fasouri-watermania.com).

What's a holiday in the sun without a waterpark? This one is a scream, with black holes and kamikaze slides for adrenaline junkies and paddling pools for younger visitors. Shuttle buses to the waterpark stop at larger hotels along the seafront road between Le Meridien and Holiday Inn.

Oleastro Olive Park

Anogyra (99 525 093/www.oleastro.com.cy).

This themed attraction is based around the organic olive oil produced on the premises. From the short but fascinating guided tours around the mill to the organic food at the restaurant, everything here is in line with traditional Cypriot life. Attractions include a small museum tracing the use and production of olive oil through the centuries, as well as pony rides for children and a great olive-themed gift shop.

Vikla Golf & Country Club

Vikla-Kellaki, 18km from Lemesos (25 622 894/www.vikla-golf.com). **Open** 9am-sunset daily.

A wonderfully laid-back amateur golf course. A free introductory lesson is offered to newcomers, and there's a swimming pool that opens in summer.

Pafos castle

Pafos

Pafos seems to be in a constant state of frenetic commercial and tourist development. At the same time, the town has managed to retain a very human face, with pockets of deep tranquility, luxuriant gardens and clean, enchanting beaches. The city is composed of two distinct districts: Kato Pafos (Lower Pafos), and the older, more characterful Ktima (Upper Pafos). Visitors to this region, rich in archaeological sites, are never more than ten minutes' walk from an ancient monument: it was this remarkable historical legacy that compelled UNESCO to add the entire town to its World Cultural Heritage list.

As with all towns on the island, Pafos is within easy reach of rural Cyprus. Equipped with a set of wheels, you can embark on a memorable day trip or a longer stay, letting your curiosity draw you around blind corners, over pine-clad hills, and through astoundingly beautiful and varied land and seascapes.

The jewel in the region's crown is the **Akamas Peninsula**, an area of unspoilt, often breathtaking wilderness, which is locked in an ongoing bureaucratic battle to achieve national park status and ensure its continued protection.

Pafos is not a 'tourist behaving badly' place, nor the ultimate hangout for hip young urbanites. Neither is it awash with twin-sets and safari suits, though: the area draws a healthy cross-section of visitors, especially those looking for a more action-packed holiday. Walking, mountain biking, golf, scuba diving and sailing are among the outdoor activities on offer.

Then there is omnipresent Aphrodite, goddess of love, whose myth originated just on the outskirts of Pafos, at a place called Kouklia. She is said to have risen from the sea foam beneath the monolithic **Petra tou Romiou**. It's appropriate then, that 5,000 years later, Pafos has become a prime destination for weddings and honeymoons, with over 5,000 soon-to-be brides arriving annually to take their vows from the UK alone.

Sights & museums

Agia Kyriaki (Chrysopolitissa) Church

Stilis Apostolou Pavlou, Kato Pafos (26 931 308). **Admission** free. **Map** p115 C5 ❶

One of the most impressive structures of the early Christian period was the Chrysopolitissa basilica, which survived to the middle of the seventh century, when it was ransacked during an Arab invasion. The small church of Agia Kyriaki was later built on the same spot, and today is a regular place of worship for Anglicans and Roman Catholics with services held every Sunday. It is also the church of choice for non-Orthodox wedding services. Take a walk around the site and enjoy the peace and quiet; this is a place mainly populated by stray cats, wildflowers and sightseers looking for St Paul's Pillar – the spot where the saint is said to have been tied and lashed 40 times on orders given by the then Roman governor. The pillar is one of a number of similar column remains on the site, in addition to mosaics from the Chrysopolitissa church floor.

Byzantine Museum

Pafos Bishopric, Andrea Ioannou 5, Ktima (26 931 393). **Open** 9am-5pm Mon-Fri; 9am-1pm Sat. **Admission** €2. **Map** p114 D2 ❷

With an impressive array of gold leaf-encrusted icons, wall paintings, carvings and a stash of beautifully illuminated books and manuscripts, with some of the exhibits dating back to the seventh century, this is a brilliant Byzantine feast for the eyes. The museum is next door to the church and headquarters used by the Bishop of Pafos: walk round to the offices and you can admire a superb display of the incumbent's precious jewels in the entrance hall – Orthodox prelates take their bling very seriously.

Pafos Mosaics p117

Pafos

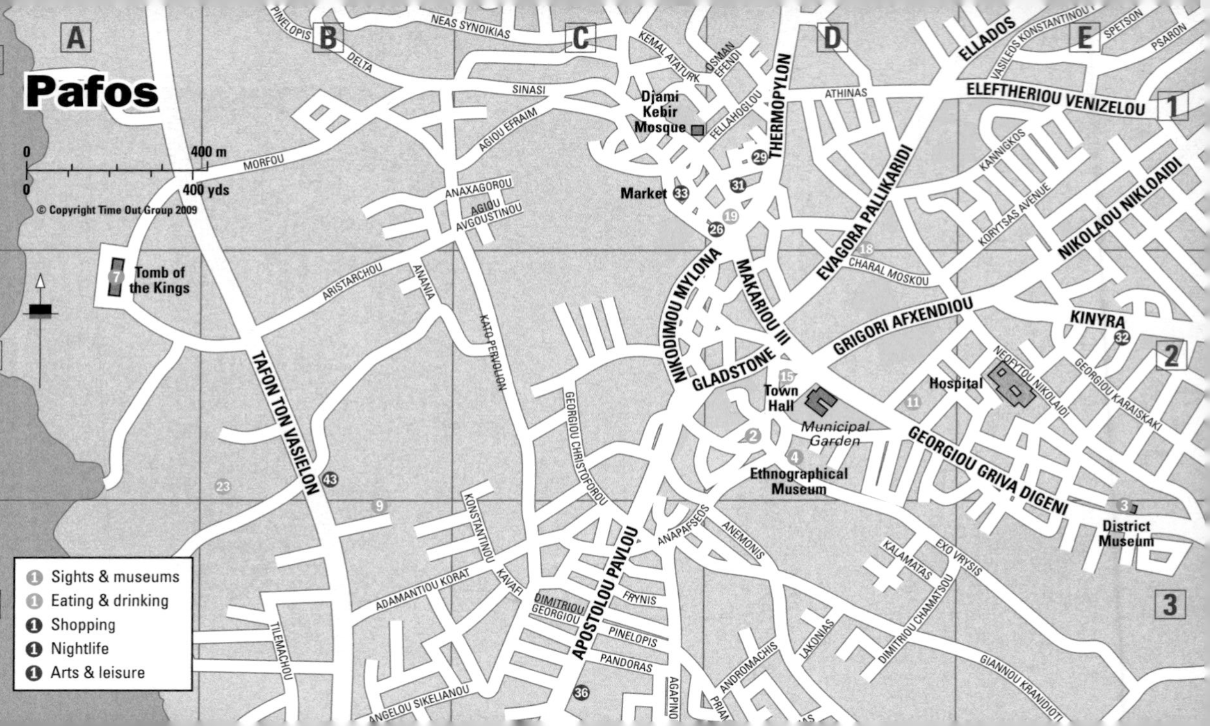
Pafos
A
B
C
D
E
1
2
3
0
400 m
0
400 yds
© Copyright Time Out Group 2009
Tomb of the Kings
7
NEAS SYNOIKIAS
PINELOPIS
DELTA
SINASI
AGIOU EFRAIM
MORFOU
ANAXAGOROU
AGIOU AVGOUSTINOU
ARISTARCHOU
ANANIA
KATO PERVOLION
TAFON TON VASIELON
KEMAL ATATURK
OSMAN EFENDI
FELLAHOGLOU
Djami Kebir Mosque
THERMOPYLON
Market
33
29
31
19
26
ATHINAS
ELLADOS
VASILEOS KONSTANTINOU I
SPETSON
PSARON
ELEFTHERIOU VENIZELOU
KANNIGKOS
KORYTSAS AVENUE
NIKOLAOU NIKLOAIDI
EVAGORA PALLIKARIDI
18
CHARAL MOSKOU
NIKODIMOU MYLONA
MAKARIOU III
GRIGORI AFXENDIOU
KINYRA
32
GLADSTONE
15
Town Hall
Hospital
NEOFYTOU NIKOLAIDI
GEORGIOU KARAISKAKI
11
Municipal Garden
2
4
Ethnographical Museum
GEORGIOU GRIVA DIGENI
3
District Museum
GEORGIOU CHRISTOFOROU
KONSTANTINOU
43
23
9
ANAPAFSEOS
ANEMONIS
KALAMATAS
EXO VRYSIS
ADAMANTIOU KORAT
KAVAFI
DIMITRIOU GEORGIOU
FRYNIS
APOSTOLOU PAVLOU
PINELOPIS
PANDORAS
AGAPINO
PRIAM
ANDROMACHIS
LAKONIAS
DIMITRIOU CHAMATSOU
GIANNOU KRANIDIOTI
TILEMACHOU
ANGELOU SIKELIANOU
36
Sights & museums
Eating & drinking
Shopping
Nightlife
Arts & leisure

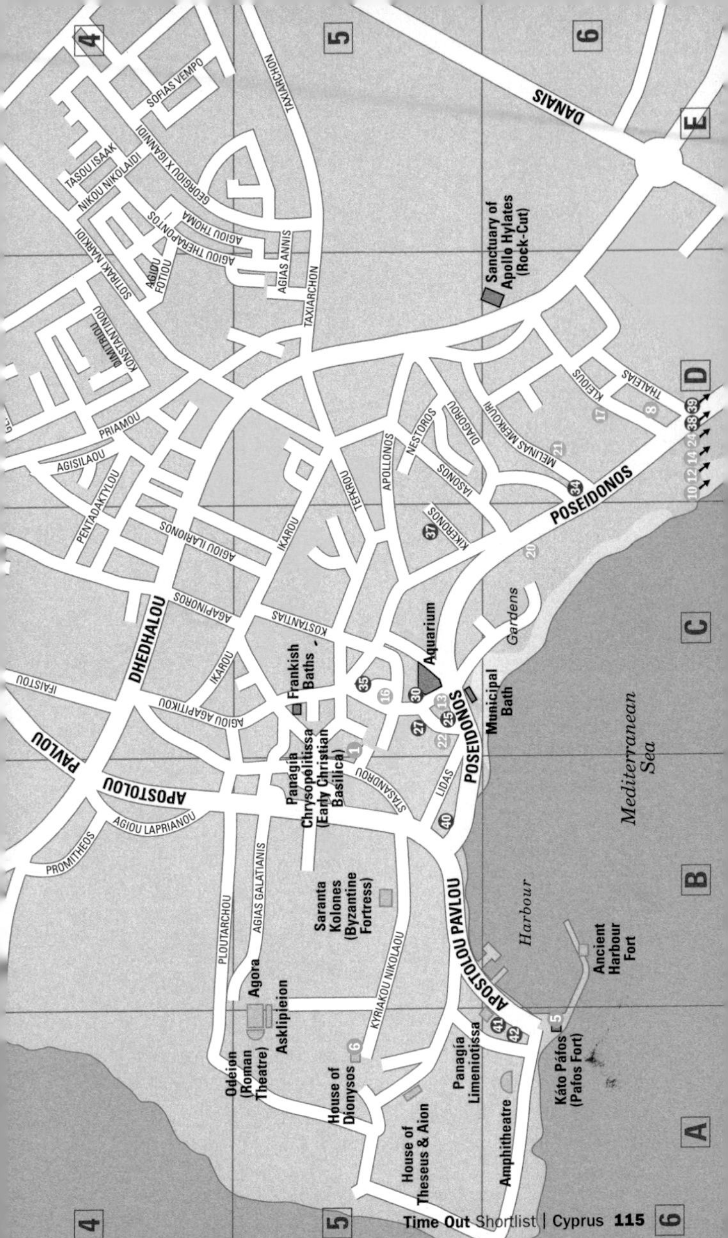

Mediterranean Sea
Harbour
Gardens
Sanctuary of Apollo Hylates (Rock-Cut)
Aquarium
Frankish Baths
Municipal Bath
Panagia Chrysopolitissa (Early Christian Basilica)
Saranta Kolones (Byzantine Fortress)
Agora
Asklipieion
Odeion (Roman Theatre)
House of Dionysos
House of Theseus & Aion
Panagía Limeniotissa
Amphitheatre
Ancient Harbour Fort
Káto Páfos (Pafos Fort)
APOSTOLOU PAVLOU
POSEIDONOS
DHEDHALOU
DANAIS
TAXIARCHON
AGIAS ANNIS
AGIOU THOMA
AGIOU THERAPONTOS
GEORGIOU X IOANNIDI
SOFIAS VEMPO
TASOU ISAAK
NIKOU NIKOLAIDI
SOTIRAKI NARKIDI
AGIOU FOTIOU
KONSTANTINOU
DIMITRIOU
PRIAMOU
AGISILAOU
PENTADAKTYLOU
AGIOU ILARIONOS
AGAPINOROS
IKAROU
TEFKROU
APOLLONOS
NESTOROS
DIAGOROU
IASONOS
KIKERONOS
MELINAS MERKOURI
KLEIOUS
THALEIAS
KOSTANTIAS
AGIOU AGAPITIKOU
IFAISTOU
AGIOU LAPRIANOU
PROMITHEOS
STASANDROU
LIDAS
PLOUTARCHOU
AGIAS GALATIANIS
KYRIAKOU NIKOLAOU
A
B
C
D
E
4
5
6

District Archeological Museum

Griva Digheni, Ktima (26 940 215). **Open** 9am-5pm Mon-Fri; 10am-1pm Sat. **Admission** €2. **Map** p114 E3 ❸

Most curators would swoon if given stewardship of this museum, which is literally overflowing with an embarrassment of riches. Many of the exhibits are now stored outside as there is little room left inside for all the statues, wall carvings, tomb artifacts, tools and decorative wares that have been – and are still being – dug up within the local area. It's a small museum but one that gives a remarkable snapshot of the history of the region and its inhabitants, from Neolithic times right through to the Byzantine and Frankish periods.

Ethnographic Museum

Exo Vrisi, Ktima (26 932 010). **Open** Mon-Fri 9am-1pm, 2-5pm; Sat 9am-1pm **Admission** €2. **Map** p114 D2 ❹

A little gem of a place, the Ethnographic Museum stands just a few metres along from the Bishopric. The house itself is over 300 years old, built by the current owner's wealthy ancestors. Visitors are warmly welcomed, and even invited to peek into the rooms still occupied by the family. In the courtyard, a series of rooms are devoted to the way Cypriots lived in the past, with a kitchen laid out as it would have been a century ago and a bedroom hung with Lefkara lace and traditional costumes worn by the family on feast days and holidays.

Medieval Fort

Pafos Harbour, Kato Pafos. **Open** *Nov-Mar* 8am-5pm daily. *Apr, May, Sept, Oct* 8am-6pm daily. *June-Aug* 8am-7.30pm daily. **Admission** €1.70. **Map** p115 A6 ❺

Originally Byzantine, the fort was rebuilt in the late 13th century by the Lusignans. It failed to protect the

Tombs of the Kings

town from the Ottoman invaders in 1570 and was subsequently abandoned. Later it was used as a prison, but under British rule it became a dry goods storage area. It's now the focal point of the picturesque harbour area and serves as a backdrop to the Pafos opera festival which takes place here under the stars every September.

Pafos Mosaics

Kyriakou Nikolaou, Kato Pafos.
Open *Nov-Mar* 8am-5pm daily. *Apr, May, Sept, Oct* 8am-6pm daily. *June-Aug* 8am-7.30pm daily. **Admission** €3.40. **Map** p115 A5 6

Discovered in 1962 by a farmer ploughing his field, these spectacular ruins have been acclaimed as some of the best examples of Roman floor mosaics discovered to date. The mosaics date from the third to the fifth centuries AD and can be seen in the archaeological park in five separate houses which would have made up a Roman noble's villa. They are named after the scenes they depict: the House of Dionysos focuses on the god of wine, while the House of Theseus shows the hero battling the Minotaur. A guide available at the ticket office has details on all five houses, the others being the Houses of Aion, Orpheus and the Four Seasons. Also nearby are the remains of the Saranta Kolones ('forty columns') castle, a modern-day lighthouse and the ancient agora (place of assembly) and odeon (theatre), the latter still used for the odd performance.

Tombs of the Kings

Tafon ton Vasileon, Kato Pafos.
Open *Nov-Mar* 8am-5pm daily. *Apr, May, Sept, Oct* 8am-6pm daily. *June-Aug* 8am-7.30pm daily. **Admission** €1.70. **Map** p114 A2 7

The name of this huge necropolis refers to the imposing character of the tombs rather than the regal nature of their inmates. Carved into the rock, these tombs for noblemen and their families were built over a period of 600 years, between the third century BC and the third century AD. About 100 tombs have been uncovered for public view. The best are situated in the majestic atrium area, with its soaring Doric columns. Intricate frescoes once decorated its walls, although scant traces remain. The site is best visited early in the morning, particularly in high summer when the sun beats down mercilessly.

Eating & drinking

Ano Kato Soures

Cleious 6, Kato Pafos (26 960 063).
Open 6-11pm daily. **Main courses** €€. **Taverna**. **Map** p115 D6 8

This rustic taverna offers meat and fish meze and an à la carte menu, featuring traditional dishes as well as more creative propositions. There is a good selection of wines from Cyprus and Greece, plus live music on Fridays and Saturdays.

Artio Brasserie

Pyramou 6, off Tafon ton Vasileon, Kato Pafos (26 942 800/www.artio brasserie.com). **Open** 6.30-11.30pm Mon-Sat. **€€€€**. **Mediterranean**. **Map** p114 B3 9

Despite the name, this is more of a full-blown formal restaurant than a casual brasserie. Rack of lamb often appears on the Mediterranean menu. The lovely garden is open in summer, making it a popular wedding venue for brides wanting to add a bit of class to their nuptials.

Asiachi

Amathus Hotel, Poseidonos, Kato Pafos (26 883 300). **Open** 7pm-midnight daily. **€€€**. **Japanese**. **Map** p115 D6 10

A vision of understated, tasteful design, Asiachi delivers accomplished pan-Asian cuisine and top-notch sushi. It's pricey, but attention to detail is immaculate.

Casa

NEW *Apriliou 1 12, Ktima (99 673 961).* **Open** 9am-11pm daily. **€€**. **Café/bar**. **Map** p114 D2 11

Set in an old house renovated along modern, minimalist lines, this new café, bar and restaurant is the place to be. Drop by for drinks or a light meal, accompanied by a soundtrack of laid-back lounge music.

Cavallini

Poseidonos 65, Kato Pafos (26 964 164). **Open** 6.30-10.30pm daily. **€€€**. **Italian**. **Map** p115 D6 12

One of the most established Italian eateries in town, Cavallini has garnered itself a loyal following. Chef Pietro Ribone is responsible for the handmade pasta, while executive chef Christos Mavrommatis takes care of the rest; the consistently high-quality dishes taste even better eaten outdoors in the garden area.

Chloe's No 1

Poseidonos 13, Kato Pafos (26 934 676). **Open** 11.30am-3pm, 6-10pm Mon-Sat; 5.30-10.30pm Sun. **€€**. **Chinese**. **Map** p115 C5 13

The seafront in this area has recently been transformed into a pedestrian-only thoroughfare, and Chloe's has been one of the lucky beneficiaries of the change. Serving competent Chinese fare, Chloe's is also famous for its vibrant – if a little OTT – Beijing-inspired decor. Locals come here to sample wines from one of the best-stocked in-house cellars in the area. The sister branch, near the Tombs of the Kings, also has an alfresco dining area.
Other location Chloe's No 2, Tafon ton Vasileon, opposite Venus Beach Hotel (77 771 737).

Dodici

Poseidonos, next to Aliathon Hotel, Kato Pafos (77 778 83). **Open** 7pm-late Fri, Sat & public hols. **Bar/club**. **Map** p115 D6 14

Minimalist decor and maximum entertainment characterise this stylish over-21s venue. In the early evening it's a friendly lounge bar, turning into party central as the night wears on. The space features two large bars, along with chill-out areas and private lounges.

Fettas Corner

Ioanni Agroti 33, Ktima (26 937 822). **Open** 6.30-11pm Mon-Sat. **€€**. **Tavernas**. **Map** p114 D2 15

The 20-dish meze (€16.20) is put together according to your tastes, from a list that includes snails, wild asparagus, spare ribs, beef liver, sausages and pork in wine. Try the wine from the family's vineyards and the sinfully delicious *lokmades* (honey doughnuts) for dessert. One of the best tavernas in the area.

Grazie

Corner of Anastasias 3-5 & Theoskepastis, Kato Pafos (26 964 164/ www.grazie-ristorante.com). **Open** 6-11pm daily. **€€€**. **Italian**. **Map** p115 C5 16

Grazie offers a classic Italian menu with authentic pastas and an emphasis on steak and seafood (the menu specifies if the catch is frozen or fresh and local). Black fetuccini with local prawns, salmon and mussels is heartily recommended.

New-wave tavernas

Giving standard grub a grilling.

Araouzos Taverna

It's hard to get excited about the so-so taverna fare rustled up in the island's tourist traps, but don't despair. There are just as many brilliant establishments where the food is guaranteed to thrill the soul of any discerning meze enthusiast. That said, you have to know where to look. Most of the respected tavernas on the island are advertised by word-of-mouth alone, and are usually found outside the main visitor hotspots, in small villages a short drive from the towns.

One exception (although still fairly hidden) is **Mageirion to Elliniko** (p120), tucked away in the alleys of Pafos old town. The menu combines Cypriot and Greek staples with some forgotten flavours such as *yaourtlu* chicken or *Pera* kebab, which bring the refined recipes of Greek Constantinople to your palate. Live strains of *rembetika* complete the Greek atmosphere.

Outside Pafos, in the village of Kathikas, **Araouzos Taverna** (p127) offers *stifado* (casserole) of wild boar and *tsikles* (wild fowl), which are neatly rounded off with little sweet carob rusks for dessert.

For an authentic and filling smörgåsborg around Larnaka, head to Kalo Chorio. Here, the tables at **Koutsonikolias** (p76) groan under the weight of delicacies such as *kerpasto* (salted lamb on charcoal), baked asparagus, deer and wild boar. If you want to sample exquisite seafood dishes involving sea urchins, crab and pandora fish, you need to call two days in advance, thus guaranteeing a fresh catch.

Koh-i-Noor

Cleious 7, Kato Pafos (26 964 083/4). **Open** 5-11pm daily. **Main courses** €€. **Indian**. **Map** p115 D6 17

This Pafos stalwart specialises in northern Indian cuisine and offers some milder dishes for those with more delicate palettes, alongside blisteringly hot curries. The extensive menu, good wine list, relaxed atmosphere and friendly service make it a local favourite.

Kourides

Charalambous Mouskou 1 & Evagora Pallikaride, Ktima (26 941 604). **Open** 6am-6pm Mon-Sat. €. No credit cards. **Taverna**. **Map** p114 D1/2 18

Authentic Cypriot cuisine is served in hearty portions at this good-value taverna. Excellent choices include kid goat baked in a clay pot, pork with *kolokasi* (an indigenous root vegetable), *afelia* (pork chunks in wine and coriander seeds) or traditional *souvla* kebabs (the big brother of *souvlaki*).

Mageirion to Elliniko

Votsi 8-10, Ktima (26 955 989). **Open** 11am-midnight Mon-Sat. **€€**. **Taverna**. **Map** p114 D1 19

A hot destination hidden away in the old town, this beautiful little taverna showcases genuine Greek flavours. The chef is well versed in Greek cuisine and serves original, little-known dishes – a refreshing change for this corner of Pafos. Live music is played on Wednesdays, Fridays and Saturdays.

Notios

Almyra Hotel, Poseidonos, Kato Pafos (26 888 700). **Open** *Apr-Oct* 12.30-3pm, 7.30-11pm daily. *Nov-Mar* weather permitting. **€€**. **Fusion**. **Map** p115 C6 20

A harmonious blend of Mediterranean and Far Eastern gastronomy, with two different menus for lunch and dinner, served outdoors in the modern, elegant surroundings of the super-stylish Almyra hotel. The wine list includes some interesting and international vintages. An *omakase* menu has recently been introduced, based on the concept that the chef is entrusted to prepare what he chooses following a discussion with the customer.

Pagoda

Poseidonos 85, Kato Pafos (26 813 232). **Open** noon-3pm, 5pm-midnight daily. **€€**. **Chinese**. **Map** p115 D6 21

The Pafos branch of this Cypriot mini-chain is popular with locals and tourists alike; families with small children are especially welcome. The standard of food is good, with lots of house specialities on the menu, and the service is friendly and reliable.

Risto la Piazza

Alkminis 11-12, Kato Pafos (26 819 921/www.ristolapiazza.com). **Open** noon-3pm, 6-11.30pm daily. **€€€**. **Italian**. **Map** p115 C5 22

With a Venetian chef in the kitchen, the food at this chic, authentic Italian restaurant is the real deal. The menu is ever-changing, but pastas are a speciality; the wine list is possibly the best on the island.

Ristorante Bacco

Elysium Hotel, Vasilissis Verenikis, Kato Pafos (26 844 444). **Open** 7.30-10-30pm Mon-Sat. **€€€. International. Map** p114 B2 ㉓

It's a little on the pricey side (€41 for two courses, €71 for four courses), but if you're after an indulgent dining experience with highly attentive staff and an extensive list of fine wines, then you can't do much better than Ristorante Bacco. Ingredients are always fresh and seasonal, with herbs and vegetables grown in a plot adjacent to the hotel.

Taste of India

Leoforos Poseidonos, Kato Pafos (26 961 700). **Open** 5pm-midnight Mon-Sat. **€. Indian. Map** p115 D6 ㉔

If you're tiring of meze and Cypriot cuisine, head to this Indian restaurant to feast on classic curries. Service is friendly and efficient and prices modest; it's a popular place, so booking is advised.

Shopping

Athos Diamond Centre

Poseidonos, Lighthouse Shop 80, Kato Pafos (26 811 630). **Open** *Summer* 9am-8-30pm Mon-Sat. *Winter* 9am-7pm Mon, Tue, Thur-Sat; 9am-3pm Wed. **Map** p115 C5 ㉕

You'll be tempted to flex the plastic in this jewellery shop, with its dazzling displays of gold and platinum pieces, diamonds the size of eggs and a kaleidoscope of precious stones.

Beauty Line

Archiepiskopou Makriou III 12, Ktima (26 933 731). **Open** *Apr-Oct* 9am-8.30pm Mon, Tue, Thur; 9am-2pm Wed; 9am-3pm Sat. *Nov-Mar* 9am-7pm Mon, Tue, Thur; 9am-2pm Wed; 9am-3pm Sat. **Map** p114 D1 ㉖

This cosmetics emporium, part of an island-wide chain, offers everything you need to look and smell gorgeous. It stocks all the big beauty brands: Clinique, Clarins, Chanel and so on. **Other location** Gladstonos 3A (26 945 765).

Centroptical

Alkiminis 5, Kato Pafos (26 933 611). **Open** *Summer* 9am-10pm daily. *Winter* 9am-7pm Mon, Tue, Thur-Sat; 9am-6pm Wed. **Map** p115 C5 ㉗

Owned by a qualified ophthalmologist and devotee of Italian-style frames, Centroptical offers speedy, professional service and some great lines of prescription sunglasses. Prices are cheaper than in the UK (although the gap is closing since the adoption of the euro) and eye tests are free.

Cyprus Handicraft Centre

Apostolou Pavlou 64, Kato Pafos (26 306 243). **Open** *Summer* 7am-2pm, 4-7pm Mon, Tue, Thur, Fri; 7.30am-2pm Wed; 8am-1pm Sat. *Winter* 7am-2pm, 2.30-5.30pm Mon, Tue, Thur, Fri; 7.30am-2pm; 8am-1pm Sat. **Map** p114 C3 ㉘

A government-backed enterprise to help keep local traditions alive, the Handicraft Centre offers beautiful lacework, pottery, carvings, baskets, jewellery and other craft items at fair prices.

Gas Point

Leontiou & Thermopylon, Ktima (26 954 700). **Open** *Apr-Oct* 9am-8.30pm Mon, Tue, Thur; 9am-2pm Wed; 9am-3pm Sat. *Nov-Mar* 9am-7pm Mon, Tue, Thur; 9am-2pm Wed; 9am-3pm Sat. **Map** p114 D1 ㉙

Cool and casual, this is *the* place to buy your jeans, combats, caps, hats and bags. Great for everyday staples.

Liza's Boutique

Dimitra Hotel Apartments, Artemidos, Kato Pafos (26 938 211). **Open** *Apr-Oct* 9am-8.30pm Mon, Tue, Thur; 9am-2pm Wed; 9am-3pm Sat. *Nov-Mar* 9am-7pm Mon, Tue, Thur; 9am-2pm Wed; 9am-3pm Sat. **Map** p115 C5 ㉚

If you're into a sophisticated look and have a few euros to splash on chic designer gear, this is the place for you.

Motivo Gallery

Kanari 30, Agas Centre, Ktima (26 935 116). **Open** *Summer* 9am-8.30pm Mon, Tue, Thur, Fri; 9am-2pm Wed; 9am-3pm Sat. *Winter* 9am-7pm Mon, Tue, Thur, Fri; 9am-2pm Wed; 9am-3pm Sat. **Map** p114 D1 ㉛

This may be one of the most exclusive shops on the island, but its prices aren't too steep considering the quality. Its focus is unique jewellery made by Greek silver- and goldsmiths, as well as eye-catching interior design pieces that include marvellous ceramics and glassware. Phoebe, who runs the shop, is utterly charming and a talented mosaic artist.

Moufflon Bookshop

Kinyras 30, Ktima (26 934 850/www.moufflonpaphos.com). **Open** *Summer* 9am-1pm, 3.30-7pm Mon, Tue, Thur, Fri; 9am-1pm Wed, Sat. *Winter* 9am-1pm, 2.30-5.30pm Mon, Tue, Thur, Fri; 9am-1pm Wed, Sat. **Map** p114 E2 32

Dealing mainly in English-language titles, the Moufflon has a good selection of books dedicated to all things Cypriot, including its birds, flowers, plants, food and culture. An out-of-print search service and interesting selection of wrapping paper and cards are also offered.

Pafos Market

Agoras, Ktima. **Open** *Summer* 9am-8pm Wed-Sun. *Winter* 9am-6pm Wed-Sun. **Map** p114 C1 33

Situated in the old town, this is a fun place to browse. As well as knock-off Gucci, Louis Vuitton and Chanel bags for around €50 and other tourist tat, there are some decent silver shops selling well-priced, quality pieces. Invest in some luggage or leather goods, select some wine or stock up on herbs, spices and bags of fruit and vegetables, freshly picked by local farmers. The Friday Food Fayre brings an abundance of local delicacies, from Cypriot olive pies to Russian salads.

Nightlife

Cartel

Poseidonos 31, Kato Pafos (77 777 793). **Open** 9.30pm-3am Fri, Sat. **Map** p115 D6 34

Older, mainly non-tourist posers come here to see and be seen, so make sure you look the part; no flip-flops or football shirts. A lovely rooftop area comes into operation in the summer.

Different

6-7 Agias Napas, Kato Pafos (26 934 668). **Open** 9pm-2am Sun-Thur; 9pm-4am Fri, Sat. **Map** p115 C5 35

One of the better venues among Pafos's less than inspired drinking options, Different so is named as it welcomes a gay as well as straight clientele. In summer it's perfect for people-watching as tables are set out on the pedestrian walkway. Great bar service and reasonably priced drinks add to the appeal.

Level

Carob Mills Complex, Apostolou Pavlou, Kato Pafos (99 673 961). **Open** 11pm-late Fri, Sat & public hols. **Map** p114 C3 36

Formerly known as Glamour but now completely redesigned, Level plays to a mainly over-25s crowd. DJ Ody spins mainstream hits on Saturdays, while Fridays bring special events with guest DJs from Greece. A private area can be booked for large groups.

Loft

Archemidous 1, Kato Pafos (77 777 742). **Open** 10pm-late Mon-Sat. **Map** p115 C5 37

This recently refurbished club has emerged with stylish decor and clever lighting. A friendly, local crowd congregates here to dance to a mix of light Greek and popular world music. In warm weather it's a great open-air venue.

Arts & leisure

Aphrodite Water Park

Poseidonos, Kato Pafos (26 913 638/www.aphroditewaterpark.com). **Open** *May-June* 10am-5.30pm daily. *July-Aug* 10am-6pm daily. *Sept-Oct* 10am-5pm daily. **Closed** Nov-Apr. **Admission** €28; free-€15 reductions. **Map** p115 D6 38

There are slippery slides and waterborne modes of transport galore here, but it's the vertigo-inducing Free Fall that elicits the loudest shrieks. Less frantic activities can be enjoyed in the lazy river and wave pool, and kids can

Coral Beach Hotel p176

clamber on to the pirate ship slide. If you want to make a day of it, the complex is dotted with restaurants and refreshment kiosks.

BikeTrek Cyprus

Aliathon Holiday Village, Poseidonos, Kato Pafos (26 913 676). **Map** p115 D6 39

This company organises mountain biking treks for adventurous types, although arrangements can also be made for those looking for a gentler ride. Tours can be taken through the rocky trails of Troodos or in the wilderness of the Akamas Peninsula. The firm also organises an annual biking and swimming competition.

Cydive

Poseidonos, Kato Pafos (26 934 271). **Open** 9am-7pm Mon-Sat. **Map** p115 B5 40

One of the oldest and most respected Scuba diving schools in Pafos, Cydive offers a wide variety of dives, lessons and packages. At the popular Bubbles Club, young diving enthusiasts can learn the basics in a safe environment. All instructors are Padi-qualified professionals.

Paphos Sea Cruises

Pafos Harbour, Kato Paphos (26 910 200/www.paphosseacruises.com). **Map** p115 A6 41

Enjoy the Mediterranean waters and explore the island's coastline in delightfully stress-free fashion by embarking on a day cruise from Pafos harbour. The boats sail around the cliffs of the Akamas Peninsula towards Polis and back, stopping halfway in a quiet cove of turquoise water for long enough to take a dip and an alfresco lunch. The company's offices are located on Apostolou Pavlou and yachts depart from the harbour.

Tiger Trips

Pafos Harbour, Kato Pafos (99 665 753/www.tiger-trips.com). **Map** p115 A6 42

Imagine the bounciest bouncy castle in the world, partnered with a level of speed that makes the fillings in your mouth quiver. Welcome to the adrenaline-soaked experience of riding a tiger boat. This British-owned company promises (and delivers) a thrilling white-knuckle ride in two fully-licensed, inflatable boats, powered by a 450 twin 6cc 225 horsepower Yamaha engine. Don't worry about feeling sick: you'll be far too preoccupied by the challenge of holding on. Under-16s need an adult signature and under-12s must be accompanied by an adult. Gentler coastal tours are also available.

Zephyros Adventure Sports

Tafon ton Vasileon, Shop 7, Royal Complex, Kato Pafos (26 930 037/ www.enjoycyprus.com). **Map** p114 B2 43

Satisfaction for thrill-seekers is guaranteed with this activities company. They help raise your adrenaline count with rock climbs, diving, kayaking, snorkelling and mountain biking, led by professionally trained guides and instructors. In winter the company also organises skiing trips to Troodos, if the weather is compliant.

Around Pafos

A remarkable, untamed wilderness can be found close by Pafos, in the protected area of the **Akamas Peninsula**. So wild, in fact, that you will need to tackle it either on foot, by mountain bike or in a 4x4 vehicle. The area is home to 530 indigenous plant species and 168 species of birds, including kestrels, falcons and vultures; some rare butterflies and rather shy snakes and reptiles also reside here.

Aleppo pines and juniper cover the rough terrain of hills that run along this spine of coastland, most of it made up of white sandy beaches such as **Coral Bay** (not too far from Pafos, and definitely worth a visit). The remote **Lara Bay** offers a more secluded bathing experience, and is the protected nesting area of the island's endangered green turtles. For information on turtle-watching and conservation volunteering opportunities, contact Episkopi Turtlewatch (25 325 292). Inland, **Avakas Gorge** offers respite from the heat, with a miniature waterfall at the end of a shaded hiking route.

The towns of **Polis** and **Latchi** provide more opportunities to get back to nature. The popular campsite is located near a marina, where you can hire out a boat for the day and go scuba diving around the Agios Georgios islet.

Sights & museums

Agios Neophytos Monastery

North of Pafos, off route B7. **Open** *Apr-Oct* 9am-1pm, 2-6pm daily. *Nov-Mar* 9am-1pm, 2-4pm daily.
Admission €0.85.
Ten kilometres from the centre of town and 410m above sea level, the monastery of Agios Neophytos offers a unique insight into the secluded and serene life of a great theologian. It was founded by a 12th-century hermit, who made his home in a small cave carved out from the rock face. The bright Byzantine frescoes on the walls retain an astonishing freshness. A short walk away stands the church, with fine examples of later Byzantine wall paintings and hand-carved woodwork. The views are spectacular, and in summer you can order a simple lunch under the cool shade of the pines at the nearby coffee shop. The souvenir shop sells everything from icons to locally made honey and sticky confections such as pistachio-nut brittle.

Kalogirou Candle Factory

Off B7, Agia Marinouda (99 539 951).
Open 8am-4.30 pm Mon-Fri; 8am-2pm Sat. **Admission** free.
On the outskirts of Yeroskipou (take the road to Agia Marinouda) is the

Artistic stimulation

Express art with your espresso.

Cafés serving up a side of cultural stimulation alongside daily doses of caffeine are on the rise, with exhibitions popping up at coffeehouses and bars as a way of keeping the feel fresh, fluid and fashionable.

In Pafos, **Casa** (p118), which opened in 2008, has put the culture into coffee drinking. Occupying a restored mansion, it adds a contemporary twist with an outdoor, granite-topped bar and transparent green seating. This restaurant/bar/café exhibits mostly photographic work by Pafos artists, spicing up the internationally-inspired dishes on the menu.

Over in Lemesos, **Dino Art Café** (p99) is another arty spot for a caffeine fix. The pieces on display are all by Lemesos-based artists, and change monthly. The stripped-down surrounds let the paintings, photographs and sculptures set the mood; plus, everything's for sale.

In Nicosia, **Oinohoos** (p88) sits right on the border of the dead zone. Fittingly, it has teamed up with various UN agencies to showcase works that highlight human rights and refugee issues. Meanwhile, **Scarabeo** (p89) sets the standard for the gallery/nightspot hybrid. Head here to hang with the cool kids amongst paintings, photos, sculptures or jewellery by local bright young things. Gallery-going has never been so hip.

Petra tou Romiou

family-run Kalogirou Candle Factory, which has been fulfilling the needs of Orthodox religious rituals for over a century. The new factory looks modern enough, but certainly traditions remain – the family's grandmother still makes her beeswax candles by hand. Visitors are welcome to watch how candles are made and hear tales of brave workers who go out searching for the best beeswax. The sweet-smelling showroom also stocks a tempting range of scented candles.

Sanctuary of Aphrodite

Road F612 off B6, Kouklia (26 432 180). **Open** 8am-4pm Mon-Wed, Fri-Sun; 8am-5pm Thur. **Admission** €3.40.

It was in the village of Kouklia that the most sensual goddess of the island was lavishly worshipped. Although the original sanctuary has been ravaged by time and earthquakes, with a little imagination you can visualise its former opulence. The palace here was renowned throughout the ancient world not only as a place of fabulous wealth – a veritable Versailles of its time – but also as one of the great religious centres of the Greek and Roman world. Today, only the sun-baked ruins of the shrine remain. Park in the shade of the trees and make your way to the museum, housed in an impressive medieval Lusignan Manor which was built on the actual site. It's home to a fascinating collection of artifacts, gleaned from the cult of Aphrodite.

Petra tou Romiou

Aphrodite's Rock. On the old Pafos-Limassol road B6, 25km from Pafos.

Along the old coastal road, about 15 minutes from the Sanctuary of Aphrodite, you will come to the Rock of Aphrodite. It's here that the irresistibly lovely goddess was born, rising from the waters. As legend dictates, those who manage to swim round the rock three times gain perpetual beauty (a promise not guaranteed by this publication).

Eating & drinking

Ais Georgis Pegeias

Off Agiou Georgiou (26 621 306). **Open** 9am-10pm daily. **€€**. **Fish**.

En route to Akamas, turn off the main road, travel down the E714 to the bay by Agios Georgios village and settle down next to the church to a sensational lunchtime vista. This simply decorated restaurant is set high on the cliff, so the stunning views keep you distracted while the rather slow service gets going. After you've selected your fish from the fridge it is weighed and cooked, and an appetising meal eventually makes its appearance. Brits come here en masse to relish a plate of fried calamari and properly cooked chips. Wash it all down with a cool KEO beer.

Anavargos Tavern

Anavargos opposite the church (26 938 214). **Open** 7-11pm Mon-Sat; noon-2pm Sun. **€**. No credit cards. **Taverna**.

The taverna is set in what was once the schoolhouse in the village of Anavargos; its owner attended school here. She cooks meze in what once formed part of the playground, offering home-cooked food and excellent value for money. This family-run business has consistently been voted as one of the best tavernas in Pafos by both visiting and resident Brits. Try the homemade chicken pie and juicy moussaka, five-star dishes both.

Araouzos Taverna

Georgiou Kleanthous 17, Kathikas (26 632 076). **Open** 12.30-11.30pm daily. **€**. **Taverna**.

This old, long-established eaterie is located in a traditional stonebuilt house, decorated with ancient tools and artifacts. It offers a 25-plate meze that includes wild mushrooms, snails, moussaka and meatballs. The quality food is well worth the 25-minute drive from Pafos.

Chillingtons

Griva Digeni 57, St George Commercial Centre, Chloraka (26 911 480/www.chillingtonsrestaurant.com.cy). **Open** 7-11pm Mon-Sat; noon-4pm Sun. **€€€**. **International**.

Set in Chloraka village, between Kato Pafos and Coral Bay, this luxury establishment is run by a British couple, Paul and Paula Chillington. It boasts a modern decor and, unusually for Cyprus, both smoking and non-smoking areas. The fish-focused menu offers a selection of international dishes – Alaska king crab, fine de Claire oysters and seafood spring rolls. Dotted with trees, the garden features sleek white couches for pre- or post-dinner drinks.

Fast Good Takeaway

Archiepiskopou Makariou III, Geroskipou, on main road close to the main square (77 777 464). **Open** 11am-11pm daily. **€**. **International**.

Great if you want to grab a quick bite instead of a sit-down meal, this is one of the best takeaways around. The chef is health-conscious, so fatty dishes are off the menu – try the grilled salmon or prawns, or delicious marinated chicken in pitta bread. You can eat in or take away.

Keralam South Indian Restaurant

Aristo Complex, Coral Bay (26 622 877). **Open** 6-11pm daily. **€€**. **Indian**.

The all-you-can-eat Sunday buffet is great value for money, though the food is equally good on other days. Its delicate, distinctive Keralan dishes include plenty of vegetarian options, as well as the fish dishes for which the region is famed. A nicely laid-back ambience and friendly service add to the whole effect.

Konia Tavern

*Konia, opposite the main village church (26 864 807).***Open** 7-11pm Mon-Sat. **€**. No credit cards. **Taverna**.

One of the best, most reliable tavernas around, Konia serves a slap-up meze as well as individual mixed grills, lamb chops and very good grilled chicken breast. The owner clearly understands the simple philosophy behind running a successful eaterie: serve the freshest seasonal food, offer good service, don't rip the customer off, and always be consistent. It's a winning formula so booking is essential, especially if you want to eat outside in summer time.

La Frescoe

Pegeia, opposite Jail Pub (26 623 123). **Open** 11am-11pm Mon-Sat. **€€**. **International**.

Located in the village of Pegeia, which is hugely popular with the expat crowd, this upmarket takeway deals in gourmet sandwiches, ideal for a day at the beach. Also on offer are chicken breast stuffed with goat's cheese in a Pernod sauce, home-made lamb burgers and peri peri chicken. Self-catering? Pre-cooked, frozen dishes using quality ingredients are available to take away and cook at your apartment.

Mylos Restaurant

Pano Gialia, 2km along the Gialia-Stavrou Road travelling from Pomos towards Polis (26 342 676). **Open** 11am-10pm Mon-Sat. **€€**. No credit cards. **Taverna**.

This converted schoolhouse is set in a shady, wonderfully peaceful forested area. It boasts a fantastic selection of stuffed vegetables, accompanied by homemade bread and excellent *sheftalia* (a Cypriot sausage-like delicacy). This is a true family-owned business, run by seven enthusiastic siblings. It's a great spot to pause for a rest if you're driving through the area.

Old Town

Gregoriade Kyproleonta 9, Polis (26 322 758). **Open** 7-11pm Mon-Sat. **€€**. **Mediterranean**.

Old Town is a romantic spot, ideal for summer dining in the secluded garden. Plus points include quality local wines, pleasant service and a bill at the end that won't trigger a panic attack. The chef's appreciation of good seasonal food makes it difficult to single out any particular dish, as everything is always first class.

Paradise Place

Charalambou Fournidi 12, Pomos (26 342 537). **Open** 10am-2am daily. **€€**. **Café/bar**.

This dreamy little place is located just outside the village of Pomos. It's a bit of a makeshift coffeeshop/ restaurant, with odd chairs and tables, but the view is amazing; the sunset is one of the most breathtaking on the island. Order ouzo and a tasty dish of the day as you chill out to the eclectic music, chosen by the owner Socrates. A one-of-a-kind experience.

Psaropoulos

Polis-Latsi Road (26 321 989). **Open** 11.30am-11pm daily. **€€**. **Fish**.
Set on the route from Polis to Latsi, this beachfront fish restaurant is the perfect place to take a break from driving. Barbecued octopus is the house special, while the grilled sea bream drizzled with olive oil is not to be missed. The owners hail from a long line of fishermen, so the freshness of the catch is guaranteed.

Seven St Georges Tavern

Geroskipou (26 963 176/www.7stgeorgestavern.com). **Open** 11am-3pm, 6-30-11.30pm Tue-Sun. **€€**. **Taverna**.
Menus are notably absent from the tables here. Instead, George, the effusive owner, will kneel down at your feet to tell you what's on offer. From this unique vantage point he'll enthusiastically seduce you into sampling his decidedly different meze. Expect lots of tiny dishes, many made with organic, hand-picked, local and seasonal ingredients (they couldn't tick more sustainability boxes if they tried) with plenty of opportunity to explore unusual flavours.

Viklari Observation Point Restaurant

Avakas Gorge (99 489 000). **Open** *Apr-Oct* 10.30am-5pm daily. **Closed** Nov-Mar. **€€**. No credit cards. **Taverna**.
Set high on a hill and commanding superb sea views, this is the place to lunch at if you're walking through the Lara Bay area, or exploring in a 4x4. You won't regret the steep climb up to the family-run taverna. The tables, chairs and weird and wonderful decor that make up this outdoor 'stone oasis' were literally hewn from the rock by the owner. Don't expect too much in the way of a menu, as it's made up entirely of chicken or meat *souvla*, kebab, salad, bread, potatoes and beer. It's good, no-nonsense fare, though – ideal if you've built up an appetite exploring the Avakas Gorge, which is just below this quirky establishment.

Shopping

Hearn's Bookshop

Coral Bay Plaza, Coral Bay (26 622 441). **Open** 9.30am-5.30pm Mon, Tue, Thur, Fri; 9.30am-2pm Wed, Sat.
Hearn's stocks a sterling array of English titles and an excellent selection of local interest books and maps. Assorted greeting cards, gifts, games and stationery complete the stock.

Nightlife

Bario Del Mar

Geroskipou Beach (99 632 229). **Open** *Summer* 11.30pm-4am daily. Closed winter. **Admission** €12.
Generally not for anyone over thirty or with auditory problems. The music can blast the sand off the beach as you boogie to Greek hits, garage, rap and anything that fits the moment, under a vast canopy of stars. Geroskipou Beach is located at the south-eastern reach of Poseidonos Avenue.

Arts & leisure

Trident Boat Hire Company

Agiou Georgiou 10, Neo Chorio (99 112 144/99 994 281). **Tickets** €60-€380.
The Trident Boat Hire Company can take you on an exploration of the hidden secrets of the Akamas Peninsula. The trip starts off at Latsi then navigates past the Baths of Aphrodite and all the way to Fontana Amoroza and the tiny Mazaki island. A lovely way to spend the day.

Archangelos Michael Church p136

The Troodos Mountains

The Troodos Mountain range sprawls across the centre of the island like a dusty green giant that's easily reached from every town. It consists of the central Troodos reaches that catch most of the snow during winter, and the surrounding valleys and ridges densely planted with vineyards and orchards that cling precariously to the steep mountainsides. The area provides a totally different experience to the typical beach holiday Cyprus is known for, with great opportunities for hiking, cycling or simply picnicking your way through sleepy villages and admimring the many Byzantine churches in the region.

For a map of the Troodos region, see the back cover flap.

Central Troodos

Home to the highest reaches and ergo the lowest temperatures on the island, the central Troodos region offers refreshing pools of shade under dark pine canopies for the sun-beaten traveller. In the late 19th century, the cooler climes lured British personnel here to establish a hill station and the first tourist hotels in the village of **Platres**, long before it became fashionable to bronze post-Victorian complexions on the white sands of Agia Napa.

Having emerged from the depths of the sea centuries ago, Cyprus's highest peak **Mount Olympus** stands at 1,951 metres. A number of CTO **nature paths**, such as the

Artemis trail, will take you on hiking and cycling routes around the peak; in the winter months, you can enjoy a run on the snowy ski slopes.

Sights & museums

Hantara Waterfalls

Follow dirt track off from F804, Phini (Foini).

A pleasant spot to rest, this small waterfall is around 1.5km from the main road, providing a good excuse to get out of the car and stretch your legs. Nearby you can find the foundations of an old watermill, thought to date from the 1900s.

Kalidonia

Caledonian Falls. Platres.

Just outside the village of Platres, this waterfall is one of the most famous attractions in the area. Though it only stands 12m high, the cool, shady cascade is worth a visit. It can be reached by car, or by following the nature trail that begins 350m off the main road from Troodos to Platres, near the presidential summer house.

Millomeris Waterfalls

Take marked exit approximately 2km before reaching Platres, on B8 Limassol-Troodos Road.

Until recently, these falls (which are higher than the Kalidonia) were little known, simply because they were so hard to reach. In the last few years the area has become more accessible, with a loose-surface (but manageable) road and then a stairway leading to the base of the falls, or via a 1km hike from Platres village church. If you get a chance to stop by in the winter the waters are much fiercer.

Pilavakion Museum

Phini (Foini) (information 25 421 508/caretaker 99 421 508). **Open** By appointment, daily. **Admission** €2.

These 16th-century stone-built rooms house humble objects that were traditionally used in village life. Relics range from milking utensils to the ancestors of the ubiquitous coffee-shop chairs that are still hand-made in the village to this day. Most impressive is an extensive collection of the ceramics Phini is famous for, ranging from small clay pot holders to oversized *pitharia*, used for storing wine.

Trooditissa Monastery

On F807 route, 5km northwest of Platres.

A monastery has stood here since the 13th century, though the current structure was built in 1731. It's still very much in use, so you'll have to admire it from the outside. Nearby, a little mountain cave is open to visitors; it's been a place of pilgrimage for centuries, ever since a glimmering icon of the Virgin Mary mysteriously appeared.

Verengaria Hotel

1km from Prodromos.

On the approach to the central Troodos region from the Marathasa Valley, you may spot a grand-looking building overlooking Prodromos village. It is the abandoned Verengaria Hotel, once a beacon of 1930s decadence. Originally decked out with heavy leather chairs and plush carpets, the interior has long since been stripped and sits in ghostly emptiness. You can walk around and explore inside if you're brave enough. Though the outdoor swimming pool only catches autumn leaves, there are rumours that the Verengaria will one day be restored to its former glory.

Eating & drinking

Psilo Dendro Restaurant

Aedonion 13, Platres (25 421 350). **Open** *Apr-Nov* 9am-5pm daily. **Closed** Dec-Mar. **€€. Taverna.**

This typical mountain eaterie is famous for its pink trout, fresh from the adjacent fish farm. The salads are also fresh, but the rest of the menu is standard tourist fare: greasy chips, kebabs and dips.

Village Tavern

Archiepiskopou Makariou III 26, Platres (25 422 777). **Open** 9am-8pm daily. **€€. Taverna.**

Drop by this pleasant taverna to feast on traditional Greek and Cypriot dishes such as meaty, no-nonsense stews and lemon-drizzled grilled mushrooms.

Trooditissa Monastery p131

Shopping

Chocolate Workshop

NEW *Archiepiskopou Makariou III 29, Platres (99 766 446/www.platres-chocolate-workshop.com).* **Open** 10am-5pm daily.

The first shop of its kind, this place serves handmade luxury chocolates with some interesting Cypriot-inspired fillings; Commandaria (dessert wine), say, or syrup-preserved cherries. The shop's loquacious founder is happy to share a few of his secrets (learnt while training in France and Holland), offering two-hour courses on how to make your own bar of delight. Classes cost €50 per person, with a minimum booking of two people.

Cleopatra's Shop

Archiepiskopou Makariou III, Platres. **Open** 9am-6pm daily.

With a wide selection of trinkets to take home, this souvenir shop opened to serve the first bus-loads of tourists that began swarming the area decades ago. Now only one of the three sisters who came here from a neighbouring village remains, but she'll gladly tell you a story or two about how things have changed on the island.

Phini Delights

Antoniou & Evgenias Theodorou 8, Phini (Foini) (25 423 060). **Open** 10am-7pm daily.

Heavy boxes of 'Cyprus Delight' make for deliciously satisfying gifts and Cypriots often go the extra mile to pick them up from this village, whose confectioners have been perfecting the recipe since 1930. Philaktis Pilavaki set up shop here after having earned his culinary stripes in Egypt, firmly establishing loukoumia as a local speciality. Even if the shop is shut, there is generally someone in the attached house to buy from.

Phini Pottery

Follow signs from Grigori Afxentiou, Phini (Foini). **Open** *Summer* daily (no set hours). **Closed** winter.

More of an open, ramshackle workshop than a shop, this is the place to find traditional pottery. The pieces are crafted by celebrated octogenarian Sophronia Theodorou, who has been working the clay for over 65 years now. She is the last of her generation in Phini keeping the art form alive, but hopes to see her daughter open her own pottery shop in the village. Her vases, decorated with flowers and birds (as featured on the now-redundant Cypriot ten cent coin), cost from €10 to €20.

Arts & leisure

Cyprus Ski Federation & Club

Ski shop located next to Sun Valley lift, Troodos (25 420 104/www.cyprusski.com). **Open** Jan-Apr, depending on snowfall.

When the powder settles in Cyprus, this area is soon packed with eager skiers, with two beginners' slopes, one intermediate and a black run for the experienced (aptly named Zeus), as well as cross country tracks. An afternoon ski lift pass costs €16 (€23 for a day), and you can rent adult or child-sized skis and boots from the shop.

Cyprus Tourism Organisation

Olympou, Platres (25 421 316/ platresinfo@cto.org.cy). **Open** *Sept-June* 9am-3.30pm Mon-Fri; 9am-2.30pm Sat. *July-Aug* 9am-3pm Mon-Fri; 9am-2pm Sat.

This local CTO office has information and maps on cycling and hiking beats in the area, from the leisurely 45-minute Persephone Trail to a 65km 'long and easy' downhill cycling itinerary from Troodos to Pafos. Whether you take a slow-paced bird-spotting detour or trek around the highest peak on the island, central Troodos is the perfect starting point for breathing in the fresh mountain air and soaking up the views.

Lambouri Winery

On E805 in Kato Platres (99 440 048/www.lambouri.com). **Open** By appointment 10am-3pm Mon-Fri; 10am-2pm Sat, Sun.

This award-winning winery has gone from strength to strength since its official founding in 1988, and now produces 75,000 bottles a year. It offers some interesting wines, blending indigenous grape varieties with famous strains such as cabernet and merlot. It ventured into organic wines with its 2006 Pure range, and also offers the 'first Kosher wine in Cyprus in over 2,000 years'. The ruby-coloured Lambouri sweet red is especially recommended for its dense-bodied, warm and spicy palate. Tours of the winery and tastings of up to three wines are free; for €2 you can sample all 18. For groups of four or more, tastings cost €3.50, and you will need to book three days in advance.

Around Central Troodos

Located just south of Platres is the charming village of **Pera Pedi**, where you can visit the old (yet still functional) water-powered mill, sample the region's

Phini Delights

famed apples and visit the workshop of Cypriot painter Kikkos Lanitis. His work features on the bottles of the local wine producer, Constantinou Winery.

Omodos is one of the most famous wine villages in the area – and for this reason receives coach-loads of tourists every year. Don't let this put you off though, as the cluster of souvenir shops can't ruin the charm of its cobbled streets, flower-decorated balconies and carefully restored old houses, open to visitors as private museums. There are also various public museums to explore, including one dedicated to the national liberation struggle. For more information on both villages, see p48.

Sights & museums

Venetian Bridges

F810 leads to Elaia (Elias) bridge, near Treis Elies village.

From 1489 to 1570 AD, Cyprus was under Venetian control; it was during this period that the famed Venetian walls of Nicosia were constructed. The Venetians also built camel-caravan routes for transporting copper mined in the Troodos mountains to trading cities such as Pafos, but today little remains of these medieval tracks. A number of eloquently executed stone bridges from the trails still stand, though, the most accessible being Elaia bridge. From here you can follow the 'Enetika Gefyria' (Venetian Bridges) CTO trail to Kelefos bridge, approximately 3.5km further west. For keen walkers, the 17km trek from Kaminaria to the abandoned village of Vretsia passes all three bridges in the area. Alternatively, it's possible to drive to Kelefos bridge from Agios Nikolaos via an unsealed dirt road. It's worth the hunt when you find the graceful arch, framed by fairytale woodland.

Marathasa Valley

The black cherries produced in this fertile valley are famous the island over, and when the trees and wildflowers blossom, the area takes on a staggering beauty. Among the heavily-laden fruit trees you'll find some of the best-known of Troodos's frescoed Byzantine churches, such as the church of **Archangelos Michael** in Pedoulas and **Agios Ioannis Lambadistis** in Kalopanagiotis.

Further afield, Marathasa provides a through-road to the **Kykkos Monastery**. It's a site of national significance, since it produced the first president of the Republic, Archbishop Makarios III. His tomb (admittedly unglamorous in itself) lies two kilometres from the monastery, while a nearby shrine presides over captivating, unobstructed views of the Troodos summit and Tillyrian hills.

Sights & museums

Agios Ioannis Lambadistis Monastery

Kalopanagiotis. **Open** 9am-1pm, 4-6pm Tue-Sun. **Admission** free (donations welcome).

One of ten designated UNESCO World Heritage Sites in the area, this is in fact an amalgamation of three churches, built at different times under one pitched roof. It is speculated that the Orthodox church was built on an earlier pagan site, due to its location overlooking the cold sulphur streams that run through Kalopanagiotis. The earliest structure dates from the 11th century (though its second nave followed 100 years later); a narthex was subsequently added before a 15th-century Latin chapel completed the picture. In the Latin portion you will find the most complete Italo-Byzantine frescoes in Cyprus, their panels illustrating an acrostic hymn which takes the first letter of its stanzas from the Greek alphabet.

Kalopanagiotis

Agios Ioannis Lambadistis Museum & Monastery

CYPRUS BY AREA

Agios Ioannis Lambadistis Museum

Kalopanagiotis. **Open** *Dec-Feb* 10am-3.30pm daily. *Mar-May* 9.30am-5pm daily. *June-Aug* 9.30am-1pm, 3-7pm Mon-Sat; 11am-1pm, 3-7pm Sun. *Sept* 9.30am-5pm daily. *Oct-Nov* 10am-3pm daily. **Admission** free (donations welcome).

Adjoining the monastery of the same name is a museum of Byzantine icons from local churches, with works dating from the 12th to the 16th centuries. Many of the items in the collection are rare, as the priest will most likely inform you. If you've been to Kykkos Monastery (see below) and have seen the icon encased in silver there, feast your eyes on an approximation of what lies beneath in the local version of the Virgin Eleousa (Merciful). Especially fascinating is a series of 13th-century icons which are all but blank, having been destroyed by damp when they were hidden in a basement by priests fleeing the invading Ottomans.

Archangelos Michael Church

Archangelou Michael, Pedoulas (22 952 704). **Admission** free (donations welcome).

Another church that features on UNESCO's list of World Heritage Sites, this little church dates from 1474. The frescoes, characteristic of the post-Byzantine revival style, are more naturalistic than others found in Cypriot churches. Note, too, the apse, which does not depict the usual Christ Pantocrator but instead shows the Ascension to heaven. The key-keeper is the friendly Stella Efthimiou, whose family preserved the church for decades with no government funds or assistance until Cypriot sovereignty was gained from the British in 1960.

Folkloric Museum

Vasou Hadjiioannou, next to Platanos Restaurant, Pedoulas (22 952 140). **Open** 10am-4pm Tue-Sun. **Admission** free (donations welcome).

Essentially consisting of two large rooms, carefully laid out with items used in Cypriot crafts such as shoe making, distilling roses and working the loom, this museum has some fine examples of 'folk' utensils. It also provides an insight into traditional village living, with examples of bedroom and kitchen furniture. Look out for the pretty silk wedding dress, dating from 1929.

Kykkos Monastery

On the E912, Tillyria Valley, west of Kalopanagiotis (22 942 736). **Open** *June-Oct* 10am-6pm daily. *Nov-May* 10am-4pm daily. **Admission** free (donations welcome).

The richest monastery in Cyprus, this place demands attention for its political and cultural relevance rather than its decorative or cosmetic merits. The origins of the monastery can be traced to the 11th century, when a monk cured the daughter of the Byzantine emperor Alexios Komnenos in exchange for an icon of Panagia Eleousa (the Merciful Virgin), ascribed to the hand of Luke the Evangelist. The icon itself was shielded in silver gilt 400 years ago; and the monastery that stands today dates from the 1830s.

What still draws the crowds in droves are the monastery's associations with the first president of Cyprus, elected after a hard-won independence. Archbishop Makarios III received his secondary education here, served as a monk in his early career and later returned to hide out while active in the guerrilla war against the British. His memory is passionately cherished by most Cypriots, who overcrowd the monastery on Sundays to baptise their babies. Make sure you bring something to cover exposed arms and knees, or you will have to rent trousers and shawls from stalls outside the church in order to enter.

Archangelos Michael Church

The holy trail

Troodos basks in an embarassment of religious riches.

Cyprus's rich religious history is as heady as the incense used for services in Greek Orthodox churches all over the island. From the early fourth century to the end of the 12th century, the Byzantine Empire ruled supreme over the island, and ecclesiastical art and architecture flourished.

One of the greatest concentrations of churches and monasteries in the former Byzantine Empire is strewn around Troodos; Unesco's shortlist of painted churches – although by no means a definitive list – comes in handy. Ten monuments in the Cyprus heartland have been granted the status of World Heritage Sites thanks to their wonderfully vivid murals, which demonstrate the style shifts in Christian art from the 11th to the 16th centuries.

The churches' exteriors are often dominated by steep-pitched tiled roofs that shroud the squat-looking masonry beneath – a beautiful and distinctively Cypriot characteristic of religious architecture. Among the finest examples of this 'vernacular architecture' trend is Agios Nikolaos tis Stegis (p141), which gets its name from the huge roof protecting the church from heavy snowfall. For protective as well as religious reasons, many churches, like Panagia tou Moutoulla in Moutoullas village, also had an external wall or narthex built around them centuries after the outer frescoes were painted.

The interiors of the painted churches usually encompass more than one artistic style, as different artists over various periods added their own influences to the mix. In the church of Timios Stavros in Pelendri, the earliest wall painting dates from 1171, while the later 14th-century frescoes betray at least two separate artist's touches. The result is a decidedly local amalgamation of crusader, Armenian, Western Roman Empire and Byzantine iconography.

Elsewhere, as in Panagia Forviotissa (p141) and Panagia tou Araka (p144), the brushwork indicates the artist probably originated in Constantinople. In most of these churches, New Testament stories are depicted in panels, like a cartoon-strip for the illiterate congregation. In many, you'll notice traces of pagan beliefs slipped in, as water sprites and sun deities take their places among the apostles and saints.

Kykkos Museum

On the E912, Tillyria Valley, west of Kalopanagiotis (22 942 736). **Open** *June-Oct* 10am-6pm daily. *Nov-May* 10am-4pm daily. **Admission** €5.

The Kykkos museum houses an extensive collection of objects, ranging from antiquities of the Copper Age through to post-Byzantine ecclesiastical silver vessels, with a whole gamut of interesting ornaments in between: precious oil lamps, seventh-century jewellery, embroidered cloths, woodcarvings and manuscripts.

Pedoulas Byzantine Museum

Archangelou Michael, Pedoulas (22 953 636). **Open** *Apr-Oct* 9.30am-1pm, 2-6pm daily. *Nov-Mar* 9.30am-1pm, 2-5pm daily. **Admission** free (donations welcome).

Located opposite the small church of the Archangel Michael, the museum contains a number of local religious artifacts and icons from six of the 12 small chapels in the area.

Sulphur Springs

Below Agios Ioannis Lambadistis Monastery, Kalopanagiotis.

These cold mineral springs are famed for their healing properties, making the village of Kalopanagiotis a popular retreat for Cypriots under stress. Crossing the springs are a couple of beautiful old bridges, one of which once served as an aqueduct for watering nearby groves. You can follow the trail that leads along the banks of the Setrachos river, past vineyards and orchards, from the centre of the village to nearby Oikos (a 4km trail).

Throni Shrine

2km west of Kykkos Monastery.

A short drive from Kykkos Monastery lies the sombre stone tomb of Archbishop Makarios III (alias Michael Mouskos). What the sepulchre lacks in grandeur is made up for by the magnificent views – surely a consideration the ethnarch must have had in mind when selecting his place of rest. Climb a little further to the summit, where a shrine to the Virgin Mary and a lone wish tree tied with votive hankies preside over stunning views.

Eating & drinking

Platanos Restaurant

Vasou Hadjiioannou, Pedoulas (22 952 518). **Open** 10am-6pm daily. **€€. Taverna.**

One of the few good dining options around, this restaurant serves a selection of time-honoured Cypriot dishes such as kebabs, grills and village salads. The Cypriot coffee, cooked slowly on hot ashes, is also recommended.

To Vrysi

Pedoulas (22 952 240). **Open** 7am-9.30pm daily. **€€. Taverna.**

Traditional Cypriot cuisine is rustled up at this family restaurant, including tasty mushroom dishes and, if you're lucky, white trout. You can also purchase treats to take away, such as the home-made cherry brandy.

Cedar Valley p140

Cats in Kakoptria

Around Marathasa

Cedar Valley

Reached by unsealed road from Kykkos Monastery or from Pano Panagia if approaching from Pafos.

Thousands of ancient cedar trees make up this natural attraction. The majestic trees are closely related to the famous Lebanese cedars, but are indigenous to the island. Keen walkers can follow the European long-distance walking path (E4) to the peak of Mount Tripylos; alternatively, camp out in the picnic area and enjoy panoramic views of the Pafos forest. The aromatic valley is home to free-ranging moufflon (red-brown wild sheep), but they are usually too elusive for a snapshot. For a closer look at Cyprus's national animal, head for Stavros tis Psokas (see below).

Stavros tis Psokas

Off F733 from Polis (forest station 26 332 144/hostel 26 722 338).

This forest station is one of the highlights of the Tyllirian wilderness – and one of the most frequented spots in this sparsely populated, unspoilt region. Families congregate here for the picnic area and nature trails, but more importantly for the enclosure that pens in a number of the island's shyest species: the endangered moufflon. A number of Dama Dama deer that were at some point imported to the island are also protected here. The hostel at the forest station offers some of the breeziest accommodation around, but it's a popular choice and rooms need to be booked early.

Solea Valley

This sun-drenched valley may catch the day's rays nicely, as its name suggests, but it's by no means dried-out and parched. The Karyotis river runs through it, making this a lush and fertile terrain to explore. It is quickly and easily reached from Nicosia, via a snaking, tree-lined road that's reminiscent of the hills of Tuscany.

Now a haven for holidaymakers, the area's rugged terrain provided an important refuge for the late Byzantines, whose legacy endures to this day; there are a multitude of well-preserved **frescoed**

churches to be found in the valley's villages. Between 1955-59 the natural backdrop again played an important part in national history, setting the stage for the guerilla war fought for Cypriot independence from Britain, as several surviving bunkers and hide-out caves testify.

The remnants of Cyprus's northernmost railway station also lie here, and are being restored to house a brand new railway museum. The picturesque village of **Kakopetria**, with its restored narrow streets full of hanging baskets and lounging cats, is also perfect for a stroll.

Sights & museums

Agios Nikolaos tis Stegis

3km from Kakopetria. Caretaker is Spyroulla Chrissi (99 484 423). **Open** 9am-4pm Tue-Sat; 11am-4pm Sun. **Admission** free (donations welcome).

Of the myriad Byzantine monuments in the Troodos mountains, this 11th-century monastery church boasts the most enchanting setting. It sits in a lush glade, irresistibly conjuring up images of its medieval past as the Karyotis river gurgles by and birds twitter in the trees. Its name, St Nicholas of the Roof, refers to the steep-pitched tiled roof that was added in the 15th century to protect the building from heavy snowfall, setting the distinctive trend for Troodos chapels. The interior is decorated with a rich array of frescoes from the 11th to the 17th centuries. The jewel that clinched the church's place on UNESCO's World Heritage list is a fresco of the Virgin breastfeeding the baby Jesus (the only mural of its kind on the island).

Hani Kalliana

Kalliana, about 2km from Galata.

This restored inn, dating from the 18th century, has been declared an historic building by the Department of Antiquities and is a fine example of popular Cypriot architecture. As the stone-built stables illustrate, the building originally served as a stop-over point for weary travelers and tradesmen on mules and camels. The beautiful arches, which echo those of the adjacent old Agios Heraclidios bridge, now house a coffee shop and the village community council, which uses the building for cultural and recreational events and functions.

Panagia Forviotissa (Asinou)

Nikitari. If the church is locked, the caretaker may need a lift from the village coffee shop (22 852 922). **Open** 9.30am-12.30pm, 2-4pm Mon-Sat; 10am-1pm, 2-4pm Sun. **Admission** free (donations welcome).

A well-preserved and resplendently painted church, this is another gem from UNESCO's list of heritage sights. The wall paintings date from 1105 to the early 1500s and feature hunting hounds, a personified Earth and Sea and a Christ in the narthex dome, designed to lock eyes with you wherever you stand. As with many other Cypriot churches, you will notice that the eyes of most of the saints have been scratched out – reputedly by Muslims, who settled in the region under Ottoman conquest. Saint George, however, was respected as a military personality, and, in this church at least evaded the fate of the other icons. The church overlooks a quiet valley, and could make for a quick detour before heading to the Adelfoi Forest for a picnic.

Panagia tis Podithou & Chapel of Archangelou

Galata. Key kept by Andreas Achilleos, often found at Mrs Maro's coffee shop in the village (99 908 916). **Open** 9.30am-1pm, 2pm-5pm daily **Admission** free (donations welcome).

This pair of beautifully located 16th-century churches comes under UNESCO's protection, and in late 2008 the smaller, timber-roofed chapel of Archangelou (also known as Panagia

Theotokou) was undergoing careful cleaning and restoration of its vivid, cartoon-like panels depicting episodes from the life of Christ. The slightly older church of Panagia tis Podithou, which until the mid-20th century served as a monastery, was built in 1502 in a spot 'by water and under sun', making it a romantic and peaceful place to rest. The Italo-Byzantine interior was never finished, yet is worth a visit for its uncharacteristically expressive rendering of the Crucifixion. There are two more painted churches in the village, the church of Agios Sozomenos and that of Agia Parskevi, which the caretaker can point you towards should you want to see them.

Renovated Railway Station & Museum

NEW *Evrychou, on B9 towards Kakopetria from Nicosia.* **Open** due for completion late summer 2009.

Information on the now defunct Cyprus Government Railway (see box p147) is scarce, so the opening of this new museum dedicated to the British-run locomotive line is an exciting venture. Passenger and freight trains began operating from Famagusta to Nicosia in 1905; the northernmost station in Evrychou was not inaugurated until 1915. This particular station was one of the first to close, as a penalty for anti-colonialist unrest which broke out across the island in 1931. The rich history of the train line will be illustrated inside the old station, while a railroad handcart on the disused tracks outside should keep trainspotters of all ages entertained.

Eating & drinking

Kotsios Café & Restaurant

Archiepiskopou Makariou 61A, Kakopetria (22 923 464). **Open** 11.30am-3pm, 7-11.30pm Tue-Sun. €€. **International**.

For a change from the usual taverna fare, try this spruced up but homely family-run eaterie. You can lounge on the comfy couches with a milkshake, or dine on fresh salads, sesame seed-sprinkled prawns, juicy burgers or beef fillet with noodles. Leave room for dessert though, because the home-made sweets are the real deal. Chocolate mousse, fluffy tiramisu and fresh crêpes, all made by the current owner's daughter, Mrs Agathi, are what make this place a success.

Linos Inn Restaurant & Mesostrato Tavern

Palea Kakopetria 34, Kakopetria (22 923 161/www.linos-inn.com.cy). **Open** *Restaurant* 10am-midnight daily. *Taverna* 10am-10pm Fri, Sat; 10am-1pm Sun. €€€. **International/taverna**.

These affiliated eateries come under the management of Kakopetria's luxury hotel, Linos Inn. The restaurant serves good 'international cuisine', meaning steaks and pastas, on the hotel's garden terrace. The place causing a commotion in the restaurant world, however, is Mesostrato, a tradi-

Moufflon, Stavros tis Psokas p140

tional-style taverna serving home-cooked mezedes (tapas-style dishes comprised of dips, grilled meats and vegetables, halloumi, rice-stuffed vine leaves and the like). Call to book a table in advance and join the feast.

Mill Restaurant

Mylou 8, Kakopetria (22 922 536/www.cymillhotel.com). **Open** 11am-10.30pm daily. **Closed** Nov 20-Dec 20. **€€.** **Taverna.**

This restaurant is part of its namesake hotel, but the food served here is renowned the island over. The 'special trout' comes recommended, while the vegetarian options on the menu are equally tempting. In summer, dining is al fresco on the balcony overlooking a trickling river; during the colder months, enjoy your wine indoors by the crackling log fire. Booking is recommended, because this place gets extremely busy.

Arts & leisure

Mill Hotel

Mylou 8, Kakopetria (22 922 536/www.cymillhotel.com).

If you want to leave the car parked for a while and explore the local landscape on two wheels, the Mill Hotel can supply bikes for €14 a day, or €88 for a week's worth of cycling. The deal includes helmets and a kit comprised of a spare tube, mini pump and padlock. Mountain trail tours are also offered, but need to be pre-booked.

Pitsylia

The area of Pitsylia is one of the least visited in the Troodos massif – and approaching the hair-raising bends that wind through the region, with (on occasion) nothing but precipitous cliffs at the bottom, it's easy to see why.

Having said that, it is a shame more people don't venture here, as the surrounding hills and valleys are gorgeous; adorned with abundant vines, olive trees, wild roses, almond and hazelnut groves.

In contrast to other areas, the late summer months see the mountainside steeped in deep red and honey-hued foliage. The terrain is ideal for keen hikers, and the Cyprus Tourism Organisation (CTO) has set a number of nature trails that pass through forests, orchards and quiet villages, including a section of the cross-European long-distance E4 path.

Sights & museums

Frangoulides Museum

Agros (for information contact the Rodon hotel on 25 521 201 or call L Christodoulou on 99 436 313). **Open** *Aug* 10am-noon, 5-7pm daily, or by appointment. **Admission** free.

Founded in 2004, the museum houses the artwork of Solomos Frangoulides – a Cypriot artist who visited the village in the 1930s and whose hagiographic paintings adorn the church of Panagia Eleousa, next to the museum. The museum itself once served as the local cinema, but now displays rough drafts as well as complete works by the artist. His subject matter varied from the holy to the mundane: among the charcoal sketches of saints mingle watercolour images of the countryside. National politics too, are given voice in a stirring image of Makarios declaring a fight for freedom, and in the portrait of a fresh-faced Glafkos Klerides (former president of Cyprus).

Metamorphosis tou Sotiros

Anastasiou & Konstantinou Leventi, Palaichori. **Open** 10am-1pm Tue, Wed. **Admission** free (donations welcome).

Situated at the summit of a slope in the eastern end of Palaichori, this pleasant church was built somewhere between the 15th and 16th centuries. The anonymous frescoes feature a number of lions: some are intimidating Daniel in their den; one draws near to bury Osia Maria; another has been tamed by Saint

Mamas and now runs with the saint on his back. The iconic image of Saint George and Saint Demetrios riding on horseback together is one of a kind on the island, and perhaps for this reason the church has been included on UNESCO's list of monuments for preservation.

Museum of Byzantine Heritage

Chrysopantanastis 15, Palaichori (99 793 362). **Open** 10am-1pm Tue, Wed. **Admission** free.

Tucked away in the centre of Palaichori village lies this easy to miss museum. Set in a carefully restored old building, it contains a number of important ecclesiastical relics, dating from the Frankish period (1192-1489 AD) to the 20th century.

Old Olive Mill

Next to Ioanni tou Prodromou Church, Agros (99 479 944). **Open** by prior arrangement with the priest, Mr Papastavros. **Admission** free.

A manually-operated mill used for producing olive oil sits in a traditional wood and stone-built room. The heavy grindstone and wicker baskets complete the press, while various other instruments used in rural life are displayed around the room.

Panagia tou Araka

Lagoudera. If the church is not open, the caretaker can be found next door. **Open** 9am-6pm daily. **Admission** free (donations expected).

This 12th-century church is considered one of the finest Byzantine churches on the island. The brushwork is typical of the Comnenian style that's found in the churches of Greece and Russia. The colours are rich and the images sharp, having been cleaned between 1968 and 1973. Note the panel of the Virgin, somberly cradling Christ the child in prescience of his coming suffering, as angels above her hold the instruments for the Crucifixion. The church overlooks a valley, and is set among the wild pea plants that gave the church its name.

Statue of the Cypriot Mother

Eptanison 16, Palaichori.

At the top of 141 steps is a statue in honour of all Cypriot mothers who lost their children in the struggle for independence from 1955 to 1959. The monument itself is disappointing to say the least, but it still affords a fine vantage point over the village. Note that the steps and viewpoint do not have a handrail for support, so it's a climb best left to the sure of foot.

Stavros tou Agiasmati

About 5km north of Platanistassa, where you will need to pick up the caretaker with the key (22 652 562/99 587 292). **Open** *Nov-Mar, June* 10am-3pm Mon-Fri. *Apr, May, Sept, Oct* 10am-3pm Mon-Fri, Sun. *July, Aug* 10am-4pm daily. **Admission** free (donations welcome).

Yet another UNESCO-listed church, Stavros tou Agiasmati holds the most complete cycle of late 15th-century mural paintings on the island, painted in 1494 by the celebrated Philip Goul. The artist, of Syrian background, lends particular interest to the churches he put his signature to as he pioneered a Cypriot School of painting which merged classic Paleologean styles with iconographic elements of Italian art. The whole interior of the church is awash with New Testament imagery and figures, including the beams which support the roof. Some exterior murals also survive on the west and south walls.

Eating & drinking

Bottle House Club

Milouri, look for sign between Palaichori and Agros on E903 (99 469 533). **Open** By appointment 11pm-late Fri, Sat. **Bar**.

This oddity of a bar is made of dusty beer bottles, lying on their sides and set in concrete. The location is baffling yet beautiful; it's built in the bend of a narrow village road, with a huge walnut tree overshadowing the bar and its neighbouring stream. It's become something of a cult joint, and is a unique experience: join the regulars for a beer and listen to the hum of conversation and music, which drifts into the surrounding countryside as night falls.

Dasaki Restaurant

Polystipos (22 652 056). **Open** 7.30am-4.30pm daily. **€€. Taverna.**

This well-known family-run establishment serves traditional grub, including village sausages and meaty stews, at a reasonable price and in a lively, flowery setting. Join the locals and share a carafe of the regional wine.

Giannis Pizza

Palaichori (22 643 212). **Open** 5-9pm Tue-Sun. **€€. Pizzeria.**

If you're in need of a break from the traditional village food served in the mountains, this is the place to pick up a takeaway pizza. Pizza is, of course, served with a Cypriot twist – try it with tangy feta cheese, fresh tomatoes and oregano for a variation on the typical margherita number.

Linari Tavern

Kato Geitonias 35, Agros (25 522 215). **Open** 11am-2pm, 6-11pm Mon-Sat; 11am-2pm Sun. **€€. Café/taverna.**

When this place is open during the daytime it offers frappés and snacks. At night it serves succulent meze, washed down with Cypriot wines.

Rodon Hotel

Agros (25 521 201/www.rodonhotel.com). **Open** 12.30-2.30pm, 7.30-9.30pm daily. **€€€. International.**

The Rodon Hotel also has a reliable restaurant and bar, serving fresh, high-quality lunches and home-made desserts. A la carte is served from Monday to Friday, with a buffet at the weekend. The restaurant is sometimes reserved for private functions, so it's best to call in advance to make sure you can grab a table.

Shopping

Allantika Kafkalias

Kyriakou Apeitou 36, Agros (25 521 426). **Open** *Apr-Sept* 8.30am-5pm Mon-Fri; 9am-6pm Sat. *Oct-Mar* 8.30am-4pm Mon-Fri; 9am-3pm Sat.

Polystipos, Pistylia

Pitsylia is known for the traditional meat goods it produces, and this family-run company has a retail shop near Agros's village square to hawk its wares. The savoury delicacies (mostly pork cuts) are traditionally matured in locally-produced red wine with various spice mixtures, smoked and salt-cured. If you want the really authentic experience, try the tough Cypriot version of jerky: *tsamarella* is sun-dried goat meat, heavily dusted with salt and oregano. The free tasters in the shop are served with a sliver of Cypriot cheese and a shot of fiery *zivania*.

Chris N Tsolakkis

House of Roses, Anapafseos 12, Agros (25 521 893/www.rose-tsolakis.com). **Open** 8am-5pm Mon-Sat; 10am-5pm Sun.

The heavy perfume of roses rises to meet you from this small distillery and earthenware workshop in Agros, overlooking a 'valley of roses'. The products are sometimes gauche, and more often than not dyed a shocking pink colour (including scented floating candles and rose brandy). Nonetheless, it is worth passing by to pick up a bottle of rose-water, as the village is famed not only for its wild roses but also for the mineral water bottled locally.

Niki Agathokleous Traditional Sweets

Anapafseos 5, Agros (25 521 400). **Open** *Summer* 10am-7pm Mon-Fri. *Winter* 10am-5pm Mon-Fri.

This homely shop produces and stocks every kind of sweet you can imagine, including a range of diabetic sweets with no added sugar. Tangerines and aubergines, walnuts and watermelons sit in heavy syrup-filled jars, and there's a whole host of jams and marmalades to choose from too. If you can't decide which goodies to take home, there are usually a few tasters waiting to tempt you. Guided tours are available to explain the process of making traditional Cypriot 'spoon sweets' (so called because a little of the intense sugar hit goes a long way). The treats, which are made locally, are famous in Cyprus and also exported to the UK, France, Australia and Japan.

Arts & leisure

Rodon Hotel

Agros (25 521 201/www.rodonhotel.com).

The Rodon is keen to support local industries and attractions, providing visitors who want to explore the Pitsylia region with home-made yet helpful maps of the amenities in Agros village, as well as walking trails (created by the CTO) to and around the surrounding villages. It is also possible to rent bicycles from the hotel (€6 for two hours).

Around Pistylia

Just east of Nicosia, before you reach the main villages of Pitsylia, sprawls the **Machairas Forest**. Nestled amongst its wild carob trees you will find a seventh-century monastery, and the beautifully-preserved 'museum-village' of **Fikardou**. Meticulously restored by the Department of Antiquities, the village's 18th and 19th-century architecture is in perfect harmony with its rural surroundings; as a result, the entire village is now a UNESCO World Heritage Site. It's around half an hour's drive from Nicosia, yet sits almost 900 metres above sea level.

This is also where Cyprus's endemic cyclamen (the island's national flower) flourishes to wonderful effect between September and January.

Sights & museums

Fikardou Rural Museum

Fikardou (22 634 731). **Open** *Apr-Oct* 9am-5pm daily. *Nov-Mar* 9am-4pm daily. **Admission** €1.70.

Full steam ahead

Firing up the historic CGR.

Cutting a deep groove almost straight across the island, the Cyprus Government Railway (CGR) rumbled with passengers, freight, livestock and mined ores in its heyday, with 74 miles of track. Today, though, even the keenest trainspotter would be hard pressed to find any traces of the once-bustling railway.

The 46-year history of this British venture was all but erased when the railway was declared unprofitable, completely dismantled and auctioned off in 1951. Some pieces were reincarnated: until recenly, two boilers were used for the huge washing machine in Nicosia General Hospital, while a steam-engine furnace became an incinerator for Famagusta council. Old coaches were reborn as chicken coops or garden sheds; one was even used as a bar in the '60s, with drinkers cosying up on the original seats.

One of the last reminders of the railway, the Hunslet engine No.1, now rests on a plinth outside Famagusta Station. The earliest stretch of track was completed in 1905 and connected the burgeoning port with Nicosia. Soon the railway was extended further west, where it picked up fresh goods. The last stop of the CGR, Evrychou Station, has been renovated by the Antiquities Department; a railway museum is set to open here to bring this wonderful steam-powered past to light. See p142.

The Rural Museum comprises two stone-built 16th-century houses, the House of Katsiniourou and the House of Achilleas Dimitri. Meticulous reconstructions, including a weaver's workshop, offer an engaging insight into rural life.

Machairas Monastery

Secondary road a short drive from Fikardou; or junction off E902 through Deftera (22 359 334). **Open** for non-Orthodox visitors, access is restricted to groups only, 9am-noon Mon, Tue, Thur. **Admission** free.

Still an active monastery, whose monks adhere to extremely strict doctrines, this place is a site of reverence for pious and non-religious Cypriots alike. The vestry exhibits valuable manuscripts and relics, while another room is devoted to the most celebrated figure of the national Liberation Struggle, Grigoris Afxentiou. A guerilla fighter, Afxentiou disguised himself as a monk and hid out here, before dying violently at the hands of the British in 1957 (he was burned alive in his hide-out when he refused to surrender). The hide-out, which is a kilometre away from the monastery, is the site of a shrine to Afxentiou, overshadowed by a larger than life statue of the hero.

Eating & drinking

Giannakou's Café & Restaurant

Fikardou (22 633 311). **Open** 9am-5pm daily **€€. Taverna**.

Owned by one of the two permanent residents in this museum-village, Giannakou's restaurant serves good Cypriot coffee throughout the day and traditional village fare at lunchtime, including meze platters and *ofton kleftikon* (slow-cooked lamb). It gets very busy at weekends as coaches of tourists pour into the village, so you will need to book in advance; happily, the service doesn't wane under the pressure of hordes of hungry patrons.

Buffavento Castle p154

North Cyprus

Politics are unavoidable in a divided country such as Cyprus, and nowhere more so than when crossing the border. Internationally, Turkey is still the only country that recognises the areas it occupies in the north as a legitimate state, known as the Turkish Republic of Northern Cyprus (TRNC). Since Cyprus's EU accession, the north is considered EU territory with a disputed foreign military presence. At present, negotiations between the Greek and Turkish Cypriot leaderships are underway, giving rise to hopes of a solution.

Several points along the Green Line, the no-go area also known as the 'dead zone', can now be legally crossed for a day trip or longer stay (see p182 Getting Around).

Two main communities live in North Cyprus: indigenous Turkish Cypriots and mainland Turkish settlers. Life is often taken at a relaxed pace – it's a community that has become used to a slow rate of change and a prolonged sense of limbo, as only a secessionist state that's also a member of the EU can. You may take a few days to adjust, but it will be well worth the wait.

This laid-back attitude translates to details such as opening hours for museums and attractions: they are provided where available, though may not always be strictly adhered to. At other times it's best to take the following as a rule of thumb: May to September: 9am-1.30pm, 4-6.30pm; October to April 9am-1pm, 2.30-4.30pm. Museums are closed on national holidays, and on Sundays outside high season.

North Nicosia (Lefkoșa)

The opening in April 2008 of the Ledra Street checkpoint between north and south Nicosia has raised hopes for the reunification of the last divided capital city in Europe.

The old part of north Nicosia (Lefkoșa in Turkish), mainly inhabited by Turkish settlers, is rather neglected and run down. The recent opening of some quality restaurants in the square by Selimiye Mosque has, however, attracted more locals and visitors to this somewhat derelict part of the city.

Sights & museums

Arabahmet Mosque

Salahi Sevket Sokak. **Map** p150 B4 ❶

The most notable mosque built by the Ottomans in Nicosia was constructed in the 19th century on the site of an old Latin church. A collection of gravestones dating from the 14th century were used as paving stones for its floors.

Arabahmet Quarter

Map p150 B4 ❷

Buildings in this quarter incorporate interesting architectural features, mirroring the area's history, with traces dating back to the Lusignan period. Many of the old houses used to belong to wealthy Armenian families who lived here before the outbreak of intercommunal violence in the 1960s. The ruins of the Armenian Monastery, originally built as the Benedictine Abbey of Our Lady of Tyre, lie close to the Arabahmet Cultural Centre.

Atatürk Square (Saray Square)

Map p150 C3 ❸

The most important square in north Nicosia, this meeting point can be found where Girne Caddesi and Sarayönü Sokak converge. The grey granite pillar in the middle that everyone refers to as the Venetian Column originally came from the temple of Jupiter in the ruins of Ancient Salamis; the Venetians brought it here in 1489.

Bandabuliya Bazaar

Kuyumkular Sokak. **Open** 6am-3pm Mon-Fri, 6am-1pm Sat. **Map** p151 D4 ❹

Arabahmet Quarter, North Nicosia

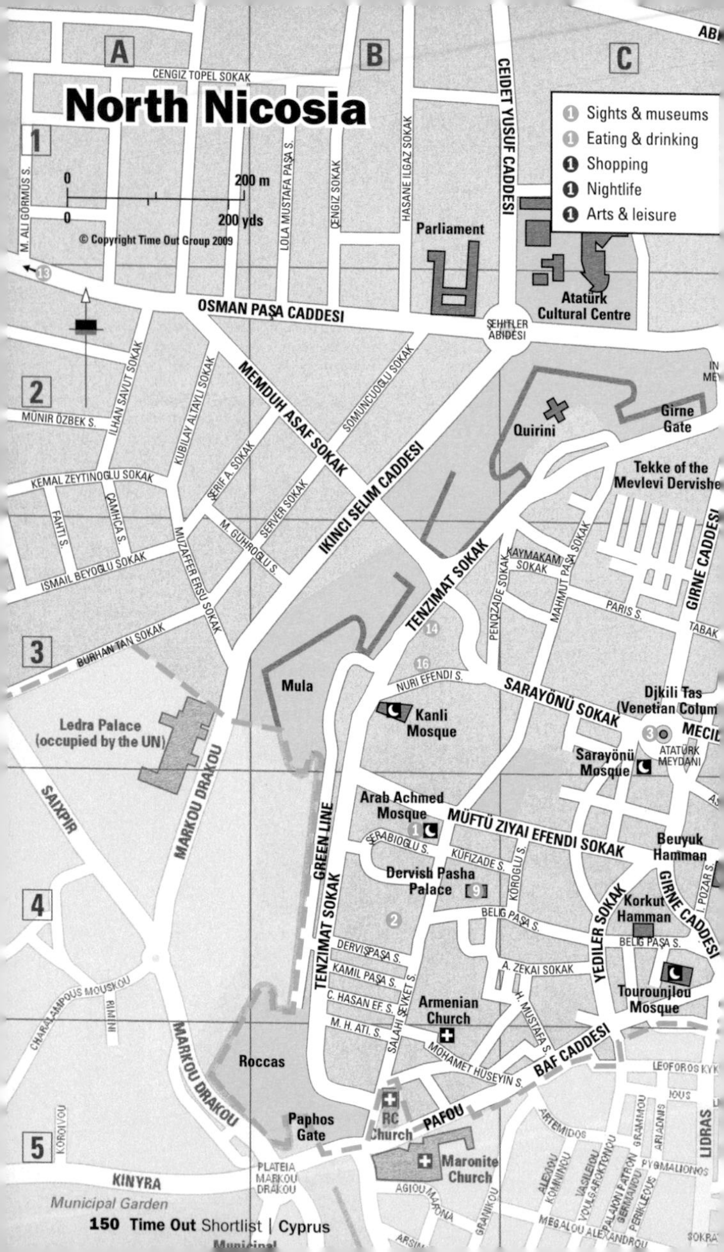
North Nicosia
A
B
C
1
2
3
4
5
0
200 m
0
200 yds
© Copyright Time Out Group 2009
Sights & museums
Eating & drinking
Shopping
Nightlife
Arts & leisure
CENGIZ TOPEL SOKAK
M. ALI GÖRMÜS S.
LOLA MUSTAFA PAŞA S.
CENGIZ SOKAK
HASANE ILGAZ SOKAK
CEIDET YUSUF CADDESI
Parliament
Atatürk Cultural Centre
OSMAN PAŞA CADDESI
ŞEHITLER ABIDESI
MÜNIR ÖZBEK S.
ILHAN SAVUT SOKAK
KUBILAY ALTAYLI SOKAK
MEMDUH ASAF SOKAK
SOMUNCUOGLU SOKAK
IKINCI SELIM CADDESI
Quirini
Girne Gate
Tekke of the Mevlevi Dervishe
KEMAL ZEYTINOGLU SOKAK
FAHTI S.
ÇAMHCA S.
ŞERIF A. SOKAK
SERVER SOKAK
M. GÜHROGLU S.
ISMAIL BEYOGLU SOKAK
MUZAFFER ERSU SOKAK
TENZIMAT SOKAK
KAYMAKAM SOKAK
MAHMUT PAŞA SOKAK
PENÇZADE SOKAK
PARIS S.
GIRNE CADDESI
TABAK
BURHAN TAN SOKAK
Mula
NURI EFENDI S.
SARAYÖNÜ SOKAK
Djkili Tas (Venetian Colum
Kanli Mosque
MECIL
ATATÜRK MEYDANI
Sarayönü Mosque
Ledra Palace (occupied by the UN)
MARKOU DRAKOU
SAIXPIR
GREEN LINE
Arab Achmed Mosque
MÜFTÜ ZIYAI EFENDI SOKAK
SERABIOGLU S.
KÜFIZADE S.
KÖROGLU S.
Beuyuk Hamman
Dervish Pasha Palace
BELIG PAŞA S.
YEDILER SOKAK
Korkut Hamman
I. POZAR S.
TENZIMAT SOKAK
DERVIŞ PAŞA S.
KAMIL PAŞA S.
C. HASAN EF. S.
M. H. ATI. S.
SALAHI ŞEVKET S.
A. ZEKAI SOKAK
H. MUSTAFA S.
Armenian Church
Tourounjlou Mosque
CHARALAMPOUS MOUSKOU
RIMINI
MOHAMET HÜSEYIN S.
BAF CADDESI
LEOFOROS KYK
Roccas
MARKOU DRAKOU
RC Church
PAFOU
Paphos Gate
Maronite Church
ARTEMIDOS
GRAMMOU
ARIADNIS
LIDRAS
KOROIVOU
PLATEIA MARKOU DRAKOU
KINYRA
AGIOU MARONA
GRANIKOU
PYGMALIONOS
Municipal Garden
MEGALOU ALEXANDROU

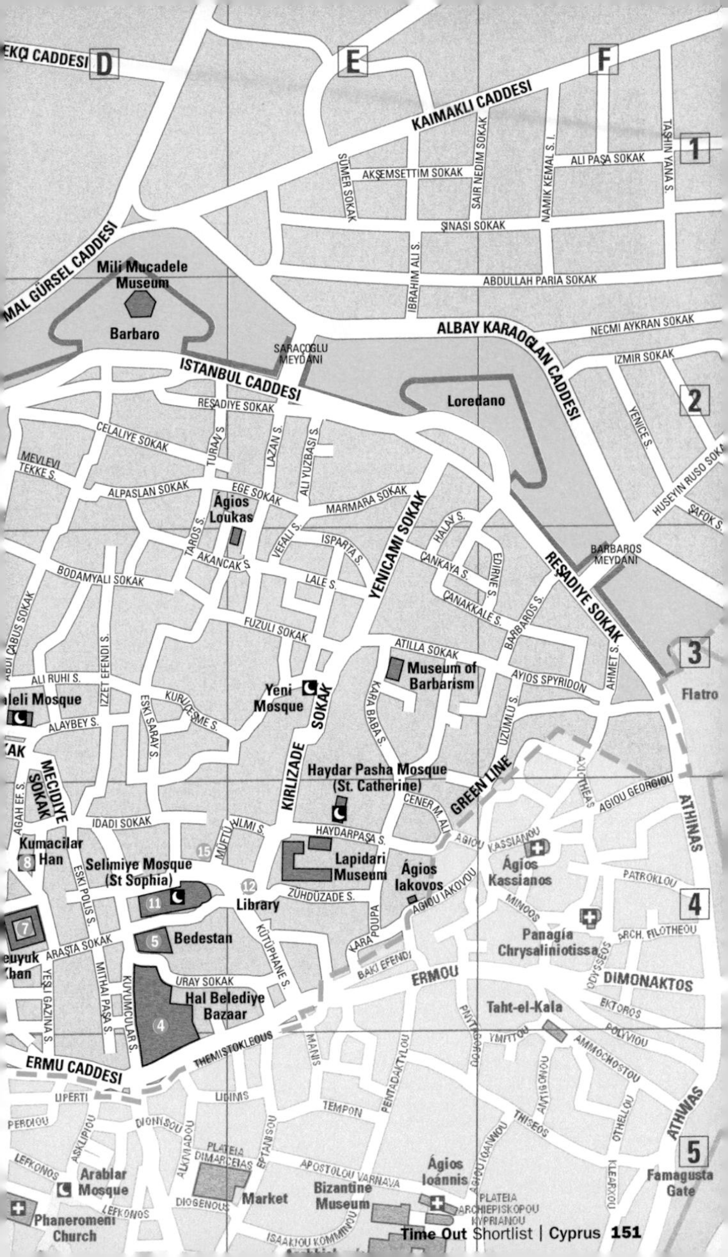
KAIMAKLI CADDESI
Mili Mucadele Museum
Barbaro
ISTANBUL CADDESI
ALBAY KARAOGLAN CADDESI
Loredano
REŞADIYE SOKAK
YENICAMI SOKAK
Ágios Loukas
Museum of Barbarism
Yeni Mosque
Haydar Pasha Mosque (St. Catherine)
GREEN LINE
Lapidari Museum
Ágios Iakovos
Ágios Kassianos
Selimiye Mosque (St Sophia)
Library
Bedestan
Hal Belediye Bazaar
Kumacilar Han
ERMU CADDESI
ERMOU
Panagía Chrysaliniotissa
Taht-el-Kala
ATHINAS
Flatro
Famagusta Gate
Arablar Mosque
Phaneromeni Church
Market
Bizantine Museum
Ágios Ioánnis
PLATEIA ARCHIEPISKOPOU KYPRIANOU
PLATEIA DIMARCEIAS

Just south of Bedesten (see below), this historic covered market (also called the Belediye, meaning municipal market), offers a varied selection of fresh fruit and vegetables, nuts and sweets. If you get hungry there are several good restaurants just down the road.

Bedestan

Uray Sokak. **Map** p151 D4 5

Built in the 12th century as the church of St Nicholas of the English, the Bedestan was further enlarged in the 14th century and modified under the Venetians. Eventually it was given to the Greek Orthodox Church. During the Ottoman period, the building became a depot and market for textile products, before falling into disrepair. At present, the church is being renovated as part of the Nicosia restoration programme of the UN Development Programme.

Büyük Hamam

Irfan Bey Sokak 9 (228 4462). **Open** 7.30am-10.30pm daily. **Map** p150 C4 6

Constructed on the remains of the 14th-century church of St George of the Latins, these are traditional Turkish baths. The hamam still operates, and is mostly frequented by locals.

Büyük Han

Arasta Sokak. **Admission** free. **Map** p151 D4 7

A typical Anatolian *han* (inn house), with two storeys set around a lovely courtyard, the Büyük Han (Great Inn) is a noteworthy monument from both a historical and architectural perspective. It was built in 1572 by the first Ottoman governor of Cyprus, Muzaffer Pasha. Following restoration, it's now home to traditional handicraft shops, a photography gallery and a restaurant serving local cuisine. One of the rooms upstairs is the venue for a popular shadow puppet show held every Saturday at 11am.

Kumarcılar Han

Agah Efendi Sokak. **Map** p151 D4 8

Located next to the Büyük Han, Kumarcılar Han (Gamblers' Inn) was built in the 17th century. The Gothic ornamented arch at the entrance of the *han* differs both in shape and proportions from the arches of the other buildings in the area, and it's thought that the arch may have belonged to another building – possibly an older monastery on the same site. Today, the building is privately owned.

Büyük Han

Mansion of Dervish Pasha

Belig Paşa Sokak. **Open** *June-Sept* 7.30am-2pm daily. *Oct-May* 7.30am-1pm, 2-4.45pm daily. **Admission** 4.50TL. **Map** p150 B4 ⑨

Dervish Pasha, the publisher of *Zaman*, the first Turkish newspaper in Cyprus, was the original occupant of this two-storey mansion. The house, which dates from the 19th century, underwent restoration in the 1980s and is currently home to an ethnographic museum.

Mevlevi Tekke Museum

100m south of Kyrenia Gate. **Open** *May-Oct* 9am-7pm Mon-Fri. *Nov-Apr* 9am-1pm, 2-4.45pm Mon-Fri. **Admission** 4.50TL. **Map** p150 C2 ⑩

Arab Ahmet Pasha, a member of the Mevlevi order (also called the whirling dervishes), constructed this gold-domed building at the end of the 16th century, after the Ottoman conquest of the island. The complex houses the tombs of 16 Mevlevi sheiks; in 1962, it was restored and opened as the Cyprus Turkish Ethnography Museum. Whirling dervishes from Turkey occasionally put on performances here.

Selimiye Mosque (Agia Sophia Cathedral)

Selimiye Meydanı. **Open** Usually daytime in summer. **Admission** free. **Map** p151 D4 ⑪

Originally built as a church and presently operating as one of the chief mosques on the island, this is one of Nicosia's most distinctive landmarks. Built between 1209 and 1228, the Gothic structure bears a close resemblance to French medieval cathedrals. Its interior comprises three aisles, six side sections and several small chapels. Under the Lusignans, coronation ceremonies were hosted here, and the marble gravestones of nobles and kings can still be seen on the floor.

Sultan Mahmut Library

Selimiye Meydanı. **Map** p151 E4 ⑫

Constructed in 1829 at the behest of Sultan Mahmut II, the library is an excellent example of classical Ottoman mosque and *madrasa* (theological school) architecture. Its towering shelves

Selimiye Mosque (Agia Sophia Cathedral)

once housed around 1,700 ancient books, which are currently on loan to the National Archives in Kyrenia.

Eating & drinking

Biyer Restaurant and Café

Mehmet Akif Sokak 61 (228 0143). **Open** noon-1am Mon-Sat. **€€€.** **Café/bar**. **Map** p150 A2 13

Biyer caters predominantly for young, hip north Nicosia locals and students from the Turkish mainland. It has a distinctly Turkish feel, modelling itself on the fashionable street cafés of Istanbul. The establishment is divided into two parts: the formal restaurant serves traditional meze and kebabs, while the more casual café is mostly geared to drinking and partying, although a selection of pasta dishes and snacks is also available. Live Turkish music is a regular attraction.

Cadı Kazanı

Tanzimat Sokak 77, Arabahmet (229 2371). **Open** 3pm-1am Tue-Sat; 6pm-1am Sun. **Bar**. **Map** p150 B3 14

Owned and run by a Turkish-Cypriot artist, Cadi Kazani is quite unlike any other bar in the area. It's a cosy, intimate hideaway with a warm and friendly feel. The owner's paintings adorn the walls and gentle chillout sounds provide the musical atmosphere. The regular clientele is often predominantly female.

Il Sabor Latino

Selimye Meydanı 29 (228 8322). **Open** 11am-midnight Mon-Sat. **€€.** **International**. **Map** p151 D4 15

Located in the centre of old Nicosia, Il Sabor Latino is convenient for sightseers. It's highly popular with locals and tourists alike, serving a large selection of tapas dishes and pastas, along with steaks and fish. It's also a good place to stop for a coffee or a cold beer.

Narnia

NEW *Nuri Efindi Sokak 23, Arabahmet (0533 859 7115).* **Open** 6pm-late daily. **Bar**. **Map** p150 B3 16

With its live blues, rock, jazz and electronic nights, this newly opened bar in the old town is a must for music lovers. Drinks are reasonably priced, and the clientele mostly locals of the 25-plus age group. The bar is set in a converted Ottoman-period building, with a roomy interior and an equally spacious garden to unwind in during the warmer months. There's live music two or three nights a week.

Around North Nicosia

Buffavento Castle

Open Dusk-dawn, days vary. **Admission** free.

Buffavento Castle (its name means 'Insubordinate to the Wind') is one of three castles built along the Kyrenia range to provide defence against the threat of Arab attacks. Set on a hilltop 950m above sea level, it offers magnificent views, stretching as far as the Troodos Mountains. If you're travelling by car, take the Nicosia-Kyrenia motorway heading north. When you reach the Beşparmak pass at the top of the mountains, next to the Five Fingers, you'll see a sign pointing to 'Buffavento Kalesi', and then a track. On the other side of the same road, a charming restaurant serves local food.

St Hilarion Castle

(0533 161 276). **Open** 9am-4.45pm daily. **Admission** 6TL.

The westernmost of the three Crusader castles built on the mountain range, St Hilarion was named after a sixth-century Syrian hermit who spent the last years of his life in hiding in a cave at the Beşparmak pass, having evaded persecution in the Holy Land. Accessible via an approach road that winds up from the Beşparmak pass and through a military zone, the castle was built in the 11th century, on the site of a former monastery and church. Set across two rocky crests, just off the Nicosia-Kyrenia motorway, the castle is an imposing presence on the landscape. Prince John of Antioch sought safety here during the war over the succession of the Lusignan throne in the 14th century;

CYPRUS BY AREA

Kyrenia (Girne)

suspicious of his own Bulgarian bodyguards, the prince ordered their deaths. The tower from which the unfortunate men were thrown still exists, and bears the Prince's name.

Kyrenia (Girne)

Perched on the island's northern coast, with the mountains as a backdrop, this small, picturesque town and its age-old harbour are breathtakingly lovely. A recent construction boom in and around Kyrenia (Girne) may have altered the town's character somewhat, but much of the old charm remains. A mere 19km from Nicosia, the town is a popular weekend destination among Turkish Cypriots living in the north of the capital.

Sights & museums

Folk Art Museum

Kyrenia Harbour. **Admission** 2TL.

Set in an 18th-century building on the harbour front, the museum's permanent exhibits include olive presses, ploughs, weaving looms and jugs. The top floor is devoted to traditional handicrafts, with displays of intricate crochet work, bed covers and tablecloths, wedding dresses and elegantly-carved wooden chests and wardrobes.

Icon Museum

Canbulat Sokak.

Up the steps at the seafront end of Canbulat Street, the Icon Museum is housed inside Archangelos Church, built in 1860. It showcases a collection of centuries-old gilded icons, rescued from abandoned churches in the Kyrenia district.

Kyrenia Castle

Kyrenia Harbour. **Open** *May-Oct* 9am-7pm daily. *Nov-Apr* 9am-1pm, 2-4.45pm daily. **Admission** 9TL.

It's thought that the castle was built by the Byzantines in the seventh century, to protect the town against Arab raids. The Lusignans then made their own additions to the fortress, which played an important defensive role during their reign. Their successors, the Venetians, added their own improvements, but lost the castle to the Ottomans in 1570 without any real resistance. So many changes of hands

have made for a rich architectural legacy: look out for the Byzantine church of St George; the tomb of an Ottoman admiral, Sadik Pasha, who was killed during the 1570 conquest of Cyprus; the Venetian Towers; the guards' room; the great hall and the various dungeons. The entrance is via a bridge, built over a wide moat that was filled with water until the 14th century. The Shipwreck Museum inside exhibits the remains of a fourth century BC cargo ship, raised from the bottom of the sea.

Eating & drinking

Ambiance Restaurant & Beach Club

20 Parasut Sokak, Karaoglanoglu (822 2894/www.ambiancecyprus.com). **Open** noon-4pm, 6.30-11pm daily. €€. **International**.

A small, family-run, beachside establishment, Ambience offers a more upmarket version of the ubiquitous kebab, plus a variety of other dishes: steaks, pizzas, pasta and fish are on the menu for those in need of a break from grilled meats. The best time to visit is on summer evenings, when you can eat under the stars and listen to the Mediterranean lapping gently on the shore.

Café Chimera

Kyrenia Harbour (815 4394). **Open** 10am-midnight daily. €€. **International**.

Of the numerous restaurants and bars around the town's harbour, Café Chimera is one of the best. Set at the castle end of the waterfront, the restaurant specialises in Cypriot kebab and fish dishes, but you'll also find steaks and even curry on the menu. It also serves a decent English breakfast.

Cream Bar & Grill

56 Belediye Otopark (816 0159). €€. **International/bar**.

In what at first glance seems to be a sports bar for British expats, Cream surprises with an atmosphere reminiscent of a house party once it gets going in the late evenings. A good pre-club option, Cream's staff mix both the cocktails and tunes and provide good vibe maintenance. Its child-friendly upstairs terrace serves food during the day and features a separate smoking area. Well worth a look.

Niazi's Restaurant

22 Kordonboyu Sokak (815 2160). **Open** 12.30pm-midnight daily. €€. **Turkish Cypriot**.

Niazi's is probably the most established restaurant in northern Cyprus, having been in business since the 1960s. It is famed for its meze and kebabs of the finest quality, which are cooked on a giant grill in the centre of the restaurant. Situated opposite Kyrenia's Dome Hotel, it is highly popular with both locals and visitors; it's therefore advisable to book ahead.

Roxanne Bar & Grill

Rocks Hotel & Casino, 20 Kordonboyu Sokak (0392 815 2238). **Open** noon-late daily. €€€. **International/bar**.

Linked to the Rocks Hotel & Casino, this is the bar of choice for hip young and not-so-young things who want to let their hair down at weekends (although be warned – Saturday night is the only night to be seen here; on Fridays it's a ghost town). At Roxanne, customers can be confident that what emerges from the cocktail shaker will be exactly what was ordered – which is something of a rarity in north Cyprus. The steaks and pizzas on the daytime menu are a firm favourite among well-to-do locals.

Around Kyrenia

Bellapais Abbey

6km south-east of Kyrenia. **Open** *May-Oct* 9am-7pm daily. *Nov-Apr* 9am-1pm, 2pm-4.45pm daily. **Admission** 6TL.

One of the most beautiful and haunting Gothic monastic ruins in the whole of the Mediterranean, Bellapais Abbey lies at the foot of the Pendadaktylos (Beşparmak) mountains, with a breathtaking, vertiginous view of the sea below. The abbey's name derives from Abbaye de la Paix (Abbey of Peace). It was founded in 1205 by Augustinian monks fleeing Jerusalem and was dedicated to Our Lady of the Hill. The present church was built at the end of the 13th century, while the rest of the buildings were added a century later. The abbey, which also comprises a refectory, dormitory and vaulted cellars, enjoyed power and prosperity until the end of the Venetian era, when its influence declined and its strict rule was increasingly disregarded. When Cyprus was captured by the Ottomans, the monks fled the island, and the abbey was given to the Orthodox Church. Today, it's used as an atmospheric venue for classical music concerts and art exhibitions.

Karmi (Karaman)

5km south-east of Kyrenia.

A quaint village nestled against the mountainside, Karmi is now mainly inhabited by British and German expatriates occupying Greek Cypriot properties. Excavations at an archaeological site near the village, known as the Karmi Necropolis, unearthed the oldest Goddess of Fertility figurine in Cyprus. Karmi is also a good starting point for an adventure on foot

Kyrenia Castle p155

around the countryside, with the villages of Templos (Zeytinlik) to the east and (Ftericha) Ilgaz to the west, both around 5km away.

Lapithos (Lapta)

10km west of Kyrenia.

Once famed for its thriving citrus orchards and fragrant gardens, Lapithos remains one of the most beautiful villages in Cyprus. Located on the northern slopes of the Pentadaktylos mountain range, this used to be a mixed village and is still home to some interesting examples of traditional Cypriot and Ottoman architecture. About 3km outside the village, close to the sea, are the ruins of Lambousa, an ancient settlement raided by the Arabs in the seventh century.

Bellapais

Lawrence Durrell's House

Bellapais.

British author Lawrence Durrell lived in the village of Bellapais in the 1950s. He describes how he came to acquire the house in his book *Bitter Lemons of Cyprus*. The Tree of Idleness café, immortalised in the same book, still survives just across Bellapais Abbey square, as does Durrell's former home, rented out as holiday accommodation by its current owners.

Eating & drinking

Escape Beach Club

Yavuz Cikarma Plaji, Alsancak (821 83 30/www.escapebeachclub.com). **Open** *Restaurant* 9am-11pm daily. *Club* 10pm-late Fri, Sat. **€€. Restaurant/club.**

Five kilometres outside Kyrenia, Escape beach club occupies one of the finest beaches on the northern coast, with its calm waters and golden sands. The expansive club incorporates a restaurant, an enclosed and open-air dance club, sun decks and a scuba school. Child-friendly and with ample car parking, Escape is an inexpensive place to spend a lazy day – a day pass for the beach and facilities goes for around 10TL. Invariably brimming over at weekends, Escape's open-air club frequently hosts big name European DJs and is the club of choice for many in the north.

Archway

Dereboyu Sokak 5, Zeytinlik (816 0353). **Open** 7am-midnight Tue-Sun. **€€€. Turkish Cypriot.**

Tucked away in Templos (Zeytinlik), 15 minutes from Kyrenia, the Archway has managed to remain a well-kept local secret. Opt for the full meze with kebab for a truly extravagant Turkish Cypriot dining experience. The local cognac comes highly recommended too – lighter and smoother than most of its Western counterparts, it's best drunk chilled, accompanying the meal.

Famagusta (Gazi Mağusa)

This seaside town is best known for its historic walled city and characteristic medieval architecture. When Cyprus finally gained its independence from the British Empire in 1960, Famagusta was the island's main port. It comprised two separate parts, divided along ethnic lines. The Turkish Cypriots inhabited the old town within the Venetian walls, known as the Kaleici; the Greek Cypriots lived in Varosia, the New Town outside the walls. In 1974, during the Turkish invasion, Varosia's inhabitants fled the town. Abandoned and uninhabited since then, Varosia has turned into an out-of-bounds ghost town.

Around Famagusta, sights worth seeking out include the impressive archaeological ruins at **Ancient Salamis** and the head-spinning heights of **Kantara Castle**, which rewards the strenuous trek up the Pentadaktylos (Beşparmak) mountains with panoramic views over the surrounding areas.

Sights & museums

City Walls

Famagusta Bay.

At the end of the 15th century, Venetian architect Giovanni Girolamo Sanmichele was commissioned to reconstruct the walls and reinforce the remains of the original Lusignan fortifications, to protect the city from Ottoman aggression. Sanmichele designed an impressive structure, 18m high and 9m thick. The new walls were reinforced by the Diamond Tower, the Citadel (more commonly known as Othello's Tower), and the Djamboulat, Martinengo and Rivettina bastions.

What's in a name?

Navigating the naming minefield.

Names in the north have been systematically changed following the Turkish invasion of Cyprus in 1974. In 1983, nine years after the Turkish invasion of Cyprus, the Turkish Republic of Northern Cyprus (TRNC) was unilaterally proclaimed as an independent state by the Turkish Cypriot administration. Turkey is the only country in the world that has recognised the TRNC as a legitimate state.

Many maps still bear only the official Greek names, and it is difficult to find your way around with just an official map of the Republic of Cyprus. The best map of the north can be bought at Rustem bookshop, next to the Saray Hotel (p180) in the centre of old North Nicosia.

Below is a list of the original and current names of the main towns and villages in the north.

Bellapais	Beylerbeyi
Engomi	Tuzla
Famagusta	Gazi Mağusa
Karmi	Karaman
Karpas	Karpaz
Kormakitis	Koruçam
Kyrenia	Girne
Kythrea	Degirmenlik
Lapithos	Lapta
Lefka	Lefke
Morphou	Güzelyurt
Nicosia	Lefkoşa
Pentadaktylos	Beşparmak
Rizokarpaso	Dipkarpaz
Trikomo	İskele
Vouni	Goghan

Our listings give the official Greek names with the Turkish names in brackets.

CYPRUS BY AREA

Ancient Salamis

CYPRUS BY AREA

Lala Mustafa Pasha Mosque (St Nicholas Cathedral)

Namik Kemal Meydanı. **Open** Dusk-dawn. **Admission** 4TL.

Originally the Cathedral of St Nicholas, this imposing church was subsequently converted into a mosque by the Ottomans. The cathedral was constructed between 1298 and 1326 and designed to emulate Rheims Cathedral in France. One of the finest examples of Lusignan Gothic architecture on the island, it was the town's hub during the peak of the Lusignan era when the cathedral was host to a number of historic events. The last Lusignan Queen of Cyprus, Caterina Cornaro, signed her abdication document here in 1489. Her husband, King Jacques II, and his infant son, Jacques III, were buried at the cathedral.

Othello's Tower

Famagusta Bay. **Open** *May-Oct* 9am-7pm daily. *Nov-Apr* 9am-1pm, 2pm-4.45pm daily. **Admission** 6TL

Though officially named the Citadel, the tower is more commonly known as Othello's Tower; a lieutenant-governor of Cyprus (1506-08) named Christoforo Moro was allegedly the model for Shakespeare's tormented tragic hero. Forming part of Famagusta's medieval fortifications, the structure was built by the Venetians in 1492 on the remains of a smaller 12th-century citadel. A climb up the ramparts affords a stunning view of the harbour and the old town.

Twin Churches of Knights Templar & Knights Hospitaller

Kisala Sokak.

Built in the 14th century, the Twin Churches were once frequented by two rival orders of knights. The smaller of them belonged to the Knights Hospitaller, the larger to the Knights Templar. In 1313, the latter came to a dramatic end and the larger church was then taken over by the Knights Hospitaller. Following a recent restoration, the churches are used as an art gallery and café.

Eating & drinking

Café Ginkgo

Liman 1, Namik Kemal Meydanı (366 6660). **Open** 10.30am-midnight Mon-Sat. **€€. International.**
Built in a restored Ottoman *madrasa* (theological institution) and part of what was once known as St Nicolas Cathedral (since 1571, known as the Lala Pasha Mosque), Ginkgo aims to represent, through its menu, the historical legacies of those who have passed through Cyprus over the centuries. Dishes range from Italian pastas and French crêpes to Ottoman Turkish kebabs.

Petek Pâtisserie

Yiman Yolu 1 (366 7104/www.petekpastahanesi.com). **Open** 8.30am-11pm daily. **€€. International.**
A wonderful array of cakes and rainbow-coloured ice-creams is on show in this popular tea room, which also offers traditional sweet treats like baklava. If you don't fancy something sweet, their burgers and pizzas should satisfy any savoury cravings you might have.

Around Famagusta

Ancient Salamis

8km north of Famagusta on Famagusta-Bogazi highway. **Open** *May-Oct* 9am-7pm daily. *Nov-Apr* 9am-1pm, 2-4.45pm daily. **Admission** 6TL.
One of Cyprus's ten city states, Salamis was first mentioned on an Assyrian *stele* (stone slab) in 709 BC. The extensive and thoroughly impressive site comprises the surrounding city walls, gymnasium, theatre, Roman baths and villa, forum and agora, as well as the Basilica of St Epiphanius and the temple of Zeus Salaminios. Visitors can easily spend half a day exploring Salamis, as there is so much to see on this remarkable site.

Kantara Castle p162

Bogazi

26km north of Famagusta.

Boasting one of the best beaches on the island, the scenic fishing village is popular with both locals and tourists. Offering a selection of seaside cafés and restaurants, Bogazi (or Boğaz) is a convenient stop-off for anyone travelling around the Karpas Peninsula. Despite the recent construction boom in the area, the beach retains its natural beauty.

Kantara Castle

15km north of Bogazi. **Open** *May-Oct* 10am-5pm daily. *Nov-Apr* 9am-1pm, 2-4.45pm daily. **Admission** 5TL.

Built on a steep cliff 700m above sea level, Kantara Castle oversaw the entrances to the Karpas Peninsula and the Mesaoria plain. The best way to access the castle is from Bogazi, which is 45 minutes away by car. The first documented record of the castle dates to 1191, when the impostor emperor Isaac Comnenus took refuge there after losing the island to Richard the Lionheart. It is believed, however, that the castle had been constructed even earlier by the Byzantines as a look-out post against raiding Arabs in the tenth century. It was abandoned by the Venetians in 1525. Dormitories, a cistern, vaulted rooms and a signal tower are still standing, as are many of its defensive walls. Note that it may not always be possible to enter the castle.

Karpas Peninsula

In the the north east of the island, the Karpas Peninsula is one of the island's last areas of natural beauty, largely untouched by commercial development and tourism.

The peninsula offers visitors some spectacular landscapes, ranging from virgin beaches and rolling, pine-clad hills to unspoilt rural villages. A nature-lover's paradise, the Karpas is the last place in Cyprus where wild donkeys roam; in summer, endangered Chelonia Mydas and Caretta Caretta sea turtles nest on its beaches. In spring, meanwhile, cyclists and hikers migrate here.

Due to the remoteness of the region, visitors have to provide their own transport, either by renting a car or taking a taxi. If you're coming from the south on a daytrip, it's advisable to plan a very early start to make the most of your day; otherwise, you'll barely scratch the surface of this unique area.

Sights & museums

Apostolos Andreas Monastery

20km north-east of Rizokarpaso.

Now a UNESCO World Heritage Site, the monastery is built on a rocky promontory just below the north-eastern tip of the island, making for a sublime backdrop. It is dedicated to St Andrew, the first of Christ's apostles to be called to ministry. Legend has it that Andrew, also the patron saint of fishermen and seafarers, restored the sight of his ship's blind captain upon arrival in Cyprus from Palestine. This might explain the monastery's miracle-making reputation, the subject of numerous stories among locals (Christians and Muslims alike). The main church dates back to 1740, although more recent additions have been made to the whole complex. Maintenance and restoration work is long overdue on the building, but it has been postponed due to disagreements on how best to proceed.

Rizokarpaso (Dipkarpaz)

50km north-east of Bogazi.

Rizokarpaso is the easternmost village on the island. Two churches are located here: the former cathedral of Agios Synesios and the church of the Holy Trinity. The Greek Cypriot enclaved community living in the village continues to worship at the churches, while a school for Greek Cypriot children reopened in the village a few years ago.

Essentials

Anassa p176

Hotels

The Cypriot hotel scene continues to suffer from preconceived notions of below-par hotels, bulk-booked by tour operators for package holiday visitors. These places do still exist, but are being steadily challenged by a new wave of image-conscious havens, striving to outdo one another with spas, infinity pools and ultra-luxe add-ons. Chief among these is celebrity favourite **Anassa** (p176), located at a dignified remove from the main town in the Pafos district. **Aphrodite Hills** (p177) is another high-end juggernaut just outside Pafos, a sprawling resort complete with its own golf course.

Establishments responding to ever-growing tourist expectations and renovating their facilities, meanwhile, include the impressively transformed **Napa Mermaid Hotel** (p166).

Self-catering apartments remain hugely popular, thanks to their cost-effectiveness and flexibility. A fridge, kettle and cooking facilities are usually included, and most apartment complexes have their own pool. All self-catering units are rated A, B or C by the Cyprus Tourism Organisation (CTO), according to the facilities offered. An increasing number of villas take self-catering to the next level of comfort (see box p173).

Rather than settling for sometimes lacklustre conventional hotels, a far smarter – and swiftly catching-on – option among visitors is to head inland and go green. Agrotourism – the environmentally conscious restoration of traditional village houses, with a view to encouraging a return to the countryside – is well developed in the area around Larnaka, especially in the villages of Tochni and Kalavasos. For the price of a single hotel room, you can have a beautifully renovated rural house and garden to yourself.

The trend is established across the island, but has really blossomed in the Troodos mountains. Here, you can hunker down in a sweetly charming hideaway with a distinctly personal character, such as **Evghenia's House** (p178). It's a priceless opportunity to experience the hospitality and frequently disarming generosity for which Cypriots are famed, as the intimate setting gives rise to rewarding encounters. Note that you will need your own transport. Visit www.agrotourism.com.cy for a list of properties affiliated to the official CTO scheme.

Accommodation options in the capital are limited, but it will be interesting to see how quickly developers respond to its growing appeal as a tourist destination since the opening of the Nicosia border.

It's usually worth phoning in advance to negotiate prices directly, as there are often good bargains to be had if the hotel has had cancellations. The CTO website (www.visitcyprus.com) is a good place to start your research. It's not the most easily navigable site, but it is up-to-date and exhaustive.

Ayia Napa & Protaras

Grecian Park Hotel

Cape Greco (23 844 000/www.grecian park.com). **€€€.**

Located on a clifftop overlooking Cape Greco, between Agia Napa and Protaras, this five-star bolthole is a small slice of style heaven. The tasteful rooms are characterised by clean lines and neutral tones, while facilities include a gym, hair salon, spa

SHORTLIST

Newly refurbished marvels
- Napa Mermaid (p166)
- So Nice Boutique Suites (p167)

Most fashionable bars
- Cliff Bar at the Grecian Park Hotel (p165)
- Caprice at the Londa (p175)
- Pago-Pago at the Castelli Hotel (p171)

Boutique bolt-holes
- Londa (p175)
- Almyra (p175)
- Thalassa (p178)

Agrotourism gems
- Redblue Door (p171)
- Evghenia's House (p178)
- Spitiko tou Archonta (p179)

Finest dining
- Mavromatis at the Four Seasons Hotel (p175)
- Notios at the Almyra (p175)
- Asiachi at the Amathus Beach Hotel (p176)

Limitless luxury
- Grecian Park Hotel (p165)
- Anassa (p176)
- Columbia Beach Resort (p175)
- Elysium (p177)

Most indulgent spas
- Anagenisis at the Thalassa (p178)
- Le Spa at Le Meridien Limassol Spa & Resort (p175)
- The Retreat at the Intercontinetal Aphrodite Hills (p177)

Best for escaping it all
- Bunch of Grapes Inn (p175)
- Paradisos Hills Hotel (p177)
- Evghenia's House (p178)

Budget bargains
- Aquarius Hotel (p175)
- Stratos House (p171)
- Themis House (p180)
- Onar Village (p180)

and swish sushi bar Umi. The Cliff Bar is a sophisticated spot to sip an evening cocktail, and on-site club Plin 2 (Minus 2) is popular with Cypriots. A short nature trail surrounds the hotel if you fancy a wander, and the natural wonders of the sea caves and relatively uncrowded Konnos Bay are close to hand.

Grecian Sands Hotel

Kryou Nerou 44, Agia Napa (23 721 616/www.graciansands.com). **€€.**

Part of the same group as the Grecian Park (see above), this beautiful hotel backs on to a pretty beach on the fringe of Agia Napa. Recent renovations saw all windows and balconies enlarged to give better sea views, and the addition of wood-clad decor and flooring. Leisure activities on offer include tennis and a sauna, as well as an on-site chapel for picturesque wedding ceremonies.

Limanaki Beach Hotel

Protis Octovriou 18, Agia Napa (23 721 600/www.agianapahotels.net). **€€.**

Wonderfully situated on Agia Napa harbour (the name means 'little harbour'), this quaint, child-friendly hotel is only a few minutes' walk to the centre of town and all the action. Facilities include live entertainment, a sauna, a fitness club and room service. The restaurant serves good food at kind prices.

Napa Mermaid Hotel

Kryou Nerou 45, Agia Napa (23 721 606/www.napamermaidhotel.com.cy). **€€€.**

A complete overhaul has transformed this ugly duckling of a hotel into a graceful swan. Spectacular facilities, impeccably stylish fixtures and fittings, helpful staff and rooms with disabled access have, surprisingly, raised neither the star rating nor the prices; take advantage of this limbo before others catch on and the CTO gets wind of how good it is. This stand-out gem in a sea of so-so accommodation options will wave a wand of pleasurable luxury over your holiday.

Napa Plaza

Archiepiskopou Makariou III 12, Agia Napa (23 816 555/www.napaplaza.com). **€€**.

This chic hotel boasts impressive architecture and is just a short stroll from the beach and nightlife. Features include manicured gardens, a lagoon-like pool and a handful of eating options, including a Tex-Mex restaurant; there's also a comprehensive in-house entertainment programme. Staff will even help you propose in style, providing champagne at just the right moment and a celebratory breakfast in bed the next morning.

Olympic Lagoon Resort

Xylofagou-Agia Napa road, Agia Napa (23 722 500/www.kanika-group.com/olympic). **€€**.

It's difficult to work out why this recently refurbished resort doesn't have a fifth star, as its extensive facilities and beautiful grounds – complete with expansive, ancient Greek-themed pools – are as aesthetically pleasing as they are practical. Service is also top notch.

Grecian Sands Hotel

So Nice Boutique Suites

Nissi, Agia Napa (23 723 010/www.sonice.com.cy). **€€**.

Set on the western outskirts of Agia Napa, this apartment complex is slightly removed from clubbing central and therefore an ideal spot for families. Attractive gardens and children's play areas add to its appeal to families, while the friendly atmosphere makes it a good choice for anyone who is after a quiet break. A sprucing up in late 2008 saw rooms made over in brilliant white, offset by flashes of tropical colour, and filled with designer details such as Philippe Starck furniture and LCD TVs. Tellingly, the complex has a high rate of repeat visitors, which is likely to increase following the revamp.

Sunrise Beach Hotel

Xenodohion, Protaras (23 831 501/www.sunrise.com.cy). **€€€**.

A classic spot for Cypriots, who flock to the beach in front of this hotel to see and be seen. Residents can survey the scene from the comfort of their more generously spaced sunbeds on the lawn between the beach and hotel. After a renovation in spring 2008, rooms are sleek and understated; facilities include a buzzy beach bar in a prime location, tennis and squash courts and a whirlpool.

Vrissiana Beach Hotel

Xenodohion, Protaras (23 831 216/www.vrissiana.com). **€€€€**.

This ship-shaped building is a landmark on the Protaras strip, and is yet another establishment which has recently called the decorators in to spruce the place up. Luxury abounds, from vast expanses of polished white marble to piles of fluffy white towels. Junior travellers are well catered to with thoughtful touches such as a freshwater children's swiming pool.

LONDA
REDEFINING STYLE

So Nice Boutique Suites p167

Larnaka

Aldiana Hotel

Georgiou Mouski, Alaminos (24 849 000/www.aldiana.com). €€€.

Built on the seafront near the quiet village of Mazotos (which doe make a hire car or taxi necessary if you intend to visit Larnaka), the Aldiana is a comfortable, modern four-star property that caters mostly for German visitors. Most of the staff speak excellent English and are always helpful.

Golden Bay Beach Hotel

Larnaka-Dhekelia road (24 645 444/ www.lordos.com.cy). €€€€.

Larnaka's only five-star hotel is located on the beachfront, close to the tourist area's myriad pubs, bars and restaurants. All the expected amenities – beauty salon, gym, indoor and outdoor pools, childminders – are present and correct, but the rooms are tending to look a little dated these days.

Lysithea Beach Hotel Apartments

Larnaka-Dhekelia road (24 646 009/ www.lysitheahotel.com). €.

These family-run holiday apartments are a short drive from the centre of town, within easy reach of a blue-flag beach. The complex has an inviting swimming pool, surrounded by palm trees, plus a smaller pool for children. Visit the website for seasonal deals on room rates.

Palm Beach Hotel & Bungalows

Larnaka-Dhekelia road (24 846 600/ www.palmbeachhotel.com). €€€.

The self-contained bungalows are the most appealing part of this recently refurbished complex. The decor is designed to evoke an Indonesian aesthetic, with shades of beige and brown. The hotel rooms are old-fashioned in comparison, but the extensive facilities include a squash court, table tennis, a solarium and a children's pool.

DISCOVER yourself in Cyprus
Now Open!!!
Enjoy the perfect day with family or friends in an exciting and picturesque environment.
The Santa Marina Retreat offers activities guaranteeing you lifetime memories and exciting moments. The activities on offer cater for all age groups. Children can meet the animals at the petting zoo and explore the Castle of Troy, whilst the adrenaline junkies can have a go at climbing our challenging wall. If your not that adventurous, you can enjoy a quiet snack or a coffee at our Terrace café.
The Santa Marina Retreat offers 100 acres of adventure and fun for everyone!
Activities
• Olympos Challenge - wall climbing
• Odysseus Challenge - target archery
• Manghaleni Copper Mine • Nature Trails
• Golf Driving Range - range & putting green
• Kentavros Ride - horse riding hack
• Pegasus Ride - junior riding experience
• Castle of Troy - childrens' fun
• An Encounter with Horses
• Horse Visitors' Centre
• The Wise Old Olive Tree • The Terrace Café
• Proteas Fish Feeding Point
• Minotaur's Labyrinth
• Horse Riding Arena
• Noah's Petting Zoo
• Santa Marina Chapel
• Mountain Bike Trails
Open Tuesday – Sunday
Entrance €3.00 - Under 16's go free
Santa Marina Retreat
Incentives - Leisure - Sports
Parekklisia - Limassol
Tel: +357 99 54 54 54, +357 99 53 50 00, Fax: +357 25 63 45 99
e-mail: info@santamarinaretreat.com www.santamarinaretreat.com

Redblue Door

Redblue Door

Lefkara (99 420 984/99 488 272/ www.redbluedoor.com). €€.

Set in a rustic village, a short drive away from Larnaka and Nicosia, this pair of boutique holiday homes glams up the agrotourism formula. The blue door leads to a family-friendly house with connected bedrooms and shared bathroom; the red opens on to a luxury pad with its own 'health room' (think steam bath and spa). Fireplaces and fully-equipped kitchens complete the home comforts, and the internal courtyard that connects the two restored buildings contains a pool. A stunning property.

Stratos House

Protis Apriliou 16, Kalavasos (24 332 293/www.stratoshousecyprus.com). €.

Kalavasos (and the neighbouring village of Tochni) has embraced agrotourism, and this is one of the most charming retreats in the area. Double arches frame the 300-year-old building as you enter, and three apartment-houses lead off from the courtyard. Each house has self-catering facilities, and you can enjoy the fruits of your labour on the vine-clad veranda. You can also swim in the private pool, set on a hill some 300m away.

Sun Hall Hotel & Apartments

Athinon 6 (24 653 341/www.aquasol hotels.com). €.

One of the best known hotels in Larnaka, Sun Hall is ideal for those who want easy access to the beach and Larnaka town centre for shopping. The cafés and bars of the Phinikoudes promenade are also close to hand, and there's a restaurant, bar and live music venue on the premises. A jacuzzi and sauna are also available.

Lefkosia (Nicosia)

Castelli Hotel

Ouzounian 38 (22 712 812/www. castellihotelcy.com). €€.

This three-star hotel is perfectly adequate, and features rooms equipped with an internet connection and satellite TV. The hotel is well known locally for its Polynesian restaurant and bar, Pago-Pago, where many a happy hour can be spent sipping cocktails. It's conveniently placed for exploring the Old Town.

Centrum Hotel

Pasikratous 15 (22 456 444/www.centrumhotel.net). **€**.

As the name suggests, this hotel's strongest selling point is its central location, just off Eleftheria square in the bustling Laiki Geitonia area of the old town. Its recently refurbed facilities are pretty standard (20-inch TVs, safe-deposit boxes, air-conditioning and heating in all rooms), but free wireless internet access is a bonus. A very pleasant budget option.

Hilton Cyprus

Archiepiskopou Makariou III (22 377 777/www.hilton.com). **€€€**.

The only five-star hotel in Nicosia, the Hilton is about ten minutes' walk from the main shopping area. Everything you need is on-site, including a cosy bar, an excellent restaurant, a beauty salon, a bank, shops, a gym, a playground, a heated indoor pool, an outdoor pool and squash and tennis courts.

Hilton Park Nicosia

Griva Digheni (22 695 111/www.hilton.com). **€€€**.

Another hotel in the Hilton stable, on the other side of town to its sister establishment (see above). It's slightly cheaper and offers a similar but smaller range of the usual corporate facilties – pools, spa, hairdresser and in-room internet access.

Holiday Inn

Rigainis 70 (22 712 712/www.holidayinn.com). **€€**.

Set in the Old Town, this outpost of the international chain features an indoor pool and Roman-style baths. The hotel houses three of the capital's top restaurants, which attract plenty of non-residents: Bonzai offers authentic Japanese dishes, Vivere provides Italian classics and Marco Polo serves an international menu, accompanied by great rooftop views.

Londa Hotel p175

Villa vacations

Self-contained luxury for groups or families.

Aquamarine

The areas around the island's coastal towns, particularly Pafos, are filling with a mushrooming crop of holiday villas. Usually found some distance from the urban centres, villas offer a desirable combination of peaceful remove from and convenient access to the nearest town.

Autonomous accommodation is a convenient option for families or groups of friends, who can share communal areas without feeling crowded. They can also work out to be a more economical choice than booking several hotel rooms, especially if you factor in communal cooking over eating out for some meals. A touch of luxury is part of the package with most villas. You can usually count on a private pool and spacious living room with tasteful furniture, while added extras could include a jacuzzi, built-in barbecue, DVD player and satellite TV.

Tempting as it is, it would be criminal to get so ensconced in your abode that you neglect to venture out to explore the island's natural beauty. Happily, most villas are a decidedly undemanding distance from the sea.

Near Larnaka, and a mere 15 minutes' drive from the beach in the agrotousrism hotspot of Tochni, villa **Myrto** (www.cyprus villages.com.cy) is a traditional stone-built house, surrounded by fruit trees and bougainvillea. Cycling and horse-riding trails lead off from here and from the neighbouring village of Kalavasos.

One notable villa in the Pafos region is the architecturally striking **Aquamarine** (www.zandx group.com). The key material employed, glass, lends light and panoramic sea views to the open-plan lounge (complete with glass fireplace), while a mini gym and vertiginous horizon pool help justify the 'deluxe' label.

At the **Whiteley** villa (www.holidaylettings.co.uk) in Pegeia, location is everything. It's four kilometres from the lovely Coral Beach and three kilometres from Lara Bay, in the wilderness of the Akamas area. Pomos and Latsi are other great places to start your search for an escapist property.

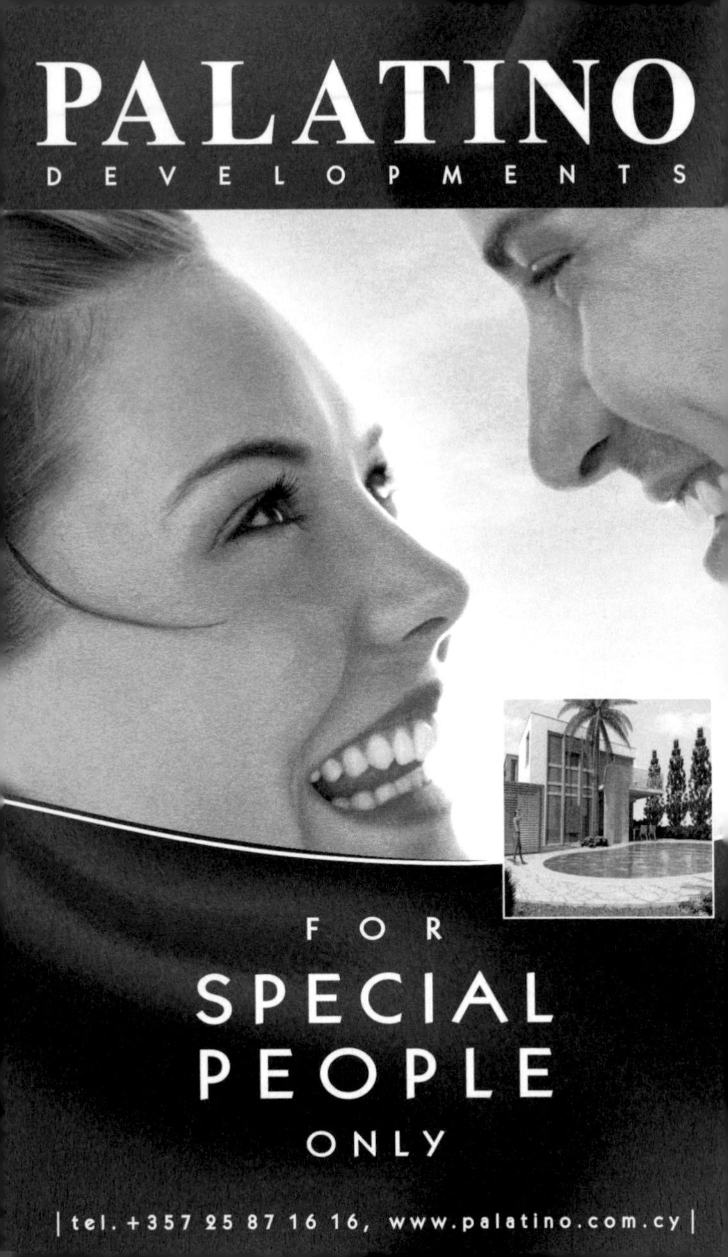
PALATINO
DEVELOPMENTS
FOR
SPECIAL
PEOPLE
ONLY
| tel. +357 25 87 16 16, www.palatino.com.cy |

Lemesos (Limassol)

Aquarius Hotel

Amathus 11 (25 326 666/www.aquarius-cy.com). **€**.

Virtually rebuilt in 2006, this two-but-nearly-three-star hotel is almost too good to be true for its rating. The fabulous stone façade fronts a series of rooms, each with its own balcony and modern comforts such as LCD TVs. A heated indoor pool, sauna and gym are the icing on this budget-priced cake.

Atlantica Oasis Hotel

Stymfalidon 11 (25 883 500/www.atlanticahotels.com). **€€**.

Having upgraded from a three to a four-star rating, the Atlantica offers self-catering apartments as well as an inviting all-inclusive option. Its attractions include an impressive events programme, beautifully manicured gardens and a convenient location, minutes from the beach and tourist centre. It gets the family vote with a great in-house animation team and round-the-clock kids' club to keep little people occupied.

Bunch of Grapes Inn

Ioannou Erotokritou 9, Pissouri (25 221 275). **€**. **Closed** Nov-Feb.

As far as atmosphere goes, this enchanting inn deserves a constellation rather than the single star awarded by the CTO. Set in a 19th-century building, its clean, simply furnished rooms cluster round a picturesque courtyard. Each comes with a toilet, shower, heating and ceiling fan. The inn is located in the delightful surrounds of Pissouri Bay, with only the twittering of birds to interrupt the tranquility.

Columbia Beach Resort

Pissouri Bay, Pissouri (25 833 333/www.columbia-hotels.com). **€€€**.

Stunning architecture in the local style sets the mood in this ultra-luxurious resort at tranquil Pissouri Bay. Plus points include faultless service, a renowned spa facility, magnificent views over the Mediterranean and the chance to sample innovative molecular gastronomy. An all-round five-star experience.

Four Seasons Hotel

Amathus (25 858 000/www.fourseasons.com.cy). **€€€**.

Synonymous worldwide with luxury, the Four Seasons upholds its reputation with beautiful decor, extensive facilities, superb restaurants, jacuzzis in all double rooms and an enviable location on one of Lemesos's nicest beaches. Recent additions include a cigar bar, on-site chapel, Shiseido spa and beach bar.

Londa Hotel

Georgiou I 72 (25 865 555/www.londahotel.com). **€€€**.

This boutique hotel is unique in the area and boasts a style-conscious decor in neutral tones with shots of primary colour. Added extras include a spa, trendy Nespresso machines in the suites and an air of contemporary cool that sets it apart from the local competition. The famous Caprice Restaurant of Mykonos and its Scandinavian chef have staked a claim here, serving a delectable selection of dishes with an unmistakably Italian influence.

Le Meridien Limassol Spa & Resort

Old Limassol-Nicosia road (25 86 2000/www.cyprus.lemeridien.com). **€€€**.

The island's sole residents-only hotel, Le Meridien is a famous name locally and lauded by returning visitors for its superb thalassotherapy spa facilities, saltwater swimming pools and well equipped children's play area. Spacious rooms are decorated in warm shades of amber and rust, while a legion of dining options includes an elegant, alfresco Japanese restaurant.

Pafos

Almyra

Poseidonos (26 888 700/www.thanoshotels.com). **€€€**.

A family-friendly hotel by the sea, with a modern, minimalist look. Perhaps unusually for a design-conscious establishment, children are not only welcome here but very well looked after, with a reliable crèche and activities for older children. Parents can pre-order all the necessary gear, including buggies and cots, then relax and enjoy superb food, eight acres of gardens and beautiful views on to the historic fort and harbour.

Amathus Beach Hotel

Poseidonos (26 883 300/www.amathus-hotels.com). **€€€**.

One of the best hotels in town, the Amathus has been around for a long time and knows how to indulge its guests. It possesses lovely gardens, a great outdoor Italian bistro, airy, light interiors and a full activity programme for kids and adults. This is the sort of place guests are reluctant to leave after two weeks of professional pampering.

Anassa

Loutra tis Aphrodites, Latsi (26 888 000/www.thanoshotels.com). **€€€€**.

A celebrity-magnet of a hotel (the Beckhams are among the starry guests who have stayed here), with prices to match the level of luxury. Anassa boasts a fabulous beachside location, pared-down classical architecture and excellent restaurants, making it all too easy to lose yourself in this rarefied world. The glamour continues with an infinity pool, swim-up bar and swoon-worthy treatments in the Thalassa Spa, from Organic Pharmacy facials to couples' massages. Getting away from it all doesn't get much more luxurious than this.

Aquamare

Poseidonos (26 966 000/www.aquamare hotel.com). **€€**.

The hotel's relaxing atmosphere, state-of-the-art fitness centre, sublime spa treatments and indoor and outdoor pools create the perfect combination of ingredients for a family holiday – and at reasonable prices too. It's also conveniently located for easy access to the attractions of Kato Pafos.

Ascos Coral Beach Hotel

Coral Bay (26 621 801/www.tsokkos.com). **€€**.

Situated in Coral Bay, Ascos is reserved for adults only from May to October. It's near some good swimming areas, if a little removed from central Pafos. The hotel has its own private shingle beach and there are plenty of activities and entertainment laid on to keep you occupied for the duration of your stay.

Dionysos Central Hotel

Dionysou 1 (26 933 41/www.dionysoshotelpaphos.com). €€.

Right in the heart of town and only a few minutes' walk from the harbour, this family hotel is perfect for visitors who want everything on their doorstep. Clubs, restaurants, bars and shops are just a few minutes' walk away. Set in lovely gardens, away from the hustle and bustle of the street, the Dionysos offers some very good open-air restaurants, a private pool and comfortable accommodation well above its current star rating.

Elia Latchi Holiday Village

Latsi, Polis Chrysochous (26 321 011/www.eliavillage.com). €.

Located on a small hill, in 63 acres of grounds, all Elia Latsi units offer great views of the sea and sunset over Chrysochou Bay. The complex is ideal for families, with extensive lawns, three swimming pools, a playground, a children's club and plenty of sporting facilities. There's a taverna and bar and a recently renovated health club on-site. The municipal beach and the fish taverns and shops of Latsi harbour are just 200m away.

Elysium

Vasilissis Verenikis (26 844 444/www.elysium-hotel.com). €€€€.

Complete with drawbridge and countless arches, Elysium is straight from the pages of a medieval fairytale – with 21st-century levels of comfort. Luxuries include fabulous food, a world-class spa and unsurpassable pool service. The atmosphere is best described as tranquil and classy, but if you crave a bit of bustle the centre of town is barely ten minutes' walk away.

InterContinental Aphrodite Hills

Off the A6 highway (26 829 000/www.aphroditehills.com). €€€€.

Set in a marvellous location overlooking the sea, with a bird's eye view of Aphrodite's rock, this resort is located a 15-minute drive from Pafos. It's first class all the way, from the room decor to the food; guests also have a heavenly spa and top-notch golf course right on their doorstep.

Louis Imperial Beach Hotel

Poseidonos (26 965 415/www.louishotels.com). €€.

Boasting a long, clean and safe beach area, the Louis is ideal for children and adults alike. Surrounded by lush gardens of cascading bougainvillea and sweet-scented shrubs, this hotel is so child friendly you'll have a hard time convincing the youngsters to return home.

Paradisos Hills Hotel

Lysos (26 322 287/www.paradisoshills.com). €.

Anassa p176

Forty minutes' drive from Pafos, in the village of Lysos, this small, family-run hotel was built in the traditional style using locally sourced materials. It offers stunning sea views from its cliff-top vantage point, great home cooking, and plenty of peace and tranquility. It's ideal as a base for exploring the surrounding region.

Thalassa

Coral Bay (26 881 500/www.thalassa.com.cy). **€€€**.
A child-free zone in the Coral Bay area, Thalassa offers a peaceful, intimate, boutique-style getaway. Myriad little luxuries join forces to leave visitors rested and rejuvenated: holistic spa treatments in the Anagenisis spa, fine cuisine served with panoramic views of the bay and, of course, highly professional service.

Troodos Mountains

Evghenia's House

Gregori Afxentiou 77, Askas, Pitsylia (22 642 644). **€**.
Overlooking the narrow, stone-paved streets of quiet Askas village, this house has been spruced up and meticulously decorated to take you back to the 1800s, with an old-fashioned loom, woven carpets, millstones, bread racks and other curiosities. The building exudes character even without these details, as the exposed beams and thatched ceilings lend charm enough. Bear in mind there are no self-catering facilities, although the nearest taverna is only a short drive away.

Linos Inn

Palea Kakopetria 34, Kakopetria, Solea Valley (22 923 161/www.linos-inn.com.cy). **€€**.
Proving that luxury accommodation can be found outside the familiar seaside resorts formula, this hotel consists of a cluster of lovingly restored old houses. Rooms and suites have been kitted out with all mod-cons, including satellite TV; some have jacuzzis. Antique furniture such as four-poster beds keep the ambience traditional yet cool, and if you book the villa suite you can enjoy a dip in the adjoining pool.

Mill Hotel

Mylou 8, Kakopetria, Solea Valley (22 922 536/www.cymillhotel.com). **€**.
Idyllically nestled into the mountainside, this hotel is built on the site of

a renovated 17th-century mill; hence the name. Despite being a grand, three-storey affair, the hotel doesn't upset the quaint atmosphere of the village. Its traditional feel extends inside, where period details such as exposed beams and stone-flagged flooring add antiquated flair to a modern affair. To top it all off (quite literally), the third floor balcony is home to an excellent restaurant manned by affable staff.

Okella

Moniatis/Saittas, Central Troodos (25 432 521). €.

A fully-restored *hani*, which centuries ago served as a stables and inn for merchants traveling through the mountains, Okella has a distinctive un-Hellenic ring to it, as the area was once home to a small Turkish-Cypriot community. The simply furnished, stone-built rooms catch the pine-scented air up on the second floor, while the restaurant below serves village specialties.

Olgas Katoi

Kalopanagiotis, Marathasa Valley (22 350 283/www.olgaskatoi.com). €.

The main house of this agrotourism bed and breakfast retreat dates back over 300 years, and is decked out in traditional village furniture and handmade lace doilies. Each of the ten attached guest rooms opens on to a sunny balcony that overlooks the Marathasa wilderness, from which the freshest ingredients are plucked for the landlady's taverna. Try the aromatic stuffed pumpkin flowers (*anthous*), a tasty village classic.

Rodon Hotel

Agros, Pitsylia (25 521 201/www.rodonhotel.com). €.

Recently revamped, the three-star Rodon Hotel sits grandly at the top of a steep hill, overlooking the fragrant valley below. Soak up the view from the shaded balcony, where you can sip a traditional Cypriot coffee, and don't miss out on the faithfully prepared local cuisine. The hotel offers outdoor swimming pools and sports courts (tennis, basketball), also encouraging visitors to explore the surrounding sites by providing maps of nearby nature trails and a bike rental service.

Spitiko tou Archonta

Treis Elies, Central Troodos (25 462 120/www.spitiko3elies.com). €.

Amid groves of cherry blossoms, this agrotourism lodge sits conveniently close to the central Troodos villages for day trips, yet is a cut above the rundown tourist traps that dot the region. The old house has been retouched with

Spitiko tou Archonta

an authentic and unpretentious air – after all, a simple table and chairs are all you need to appreciate the fresh air under the shady grape vines. Generous home-cooked meals can be arranged, but the apartments also have self-catering facilities. You can even book yourself on to a traditional cookery class for an introduction to Mediterranean cooking techniques.

Themis House

Lemithou, Central Troodos (25 462 525/www.themishouse.com). **€**.

Though these ten restored apartments don't ooze agrotouristic authenticity, they have been refurbished to a good standard for a comfortable, self-catered stay. Some rooms have a jacuzzi, but it would be madness to sit soaking indoors when you could get some serious tanning sessions in beside the small swimming pool.

North Cyprus

British Hotel

Kyrenia Harbour, Kyrenia (0392 815 2240/www.britishhotelcyprus.com). **€€**.

A family-run hotel that caters best for older customers, the British Hotel is close to Kyrenia's picturesque marina. Rooms are clean and well-appointed, and the roof terrace offers panoramic views of the surrounding area. The downstairs lounge and bar area is a soothing spot in which to while away the evening hours.

City Royal Hotel

19 Kemal Asik Caddesi, North Nicosia (0392 228 7621-11-30/www.city-royal.com). **€**.

Situated outside the walls of old Nicosia, the City Royal Hotel is a 20-minute stroll from the old town and the Green Line. A marbled frontage gives way to an elegant reception hall, which in summer is an oasis from the dry heat of Nicosia. Staff are efficient and friendly and the array of amenities on offer should suit those in town on business. There's also a casino – that ubiquitous entertainment form of the north.

Dome Hotel

Kordonboyu Sokak, Kyrenia (0393 815 2453/www.domehotelcyprus.com). **€€**.

This recently renovated, 70-year-old four-star hotel has the advantage of being located both in the centre of town and on the waterfront. As one the oldest hotels in town, it is also seen as more established and classy than the newer establishments in Kyrenia. Facilities include a casino, a fitness centre, wireless internet and an outdoor swimming pool.

Merit Hotel

Lefkosa Merkez, North Nicosia (0392 228 2571/72). **€€€**.

North Nicosia's newest hotel opened in late 2008, and offers five-star accommodation close to the heart of the city. While single rooms are available at mid-range prices, VIP suites can also be booked at more extravagant rates. The hotel has a casino, swimming pools, sports facilities and hairdressers.

Onar Village

Off the Kyrenia-Nicosia highway (0392 815 5850/www.onarvillage.com). **€**.

This small, family-run bungalow and hotel complex is set in the Five Finger mountain range overlooking Kyrenia, and affords spectacular views of Cyprus's northern coastline. Onar also offers fitness facilities, a sauna, Turkish bath and massages.

Saray Hotel

Ataturk Meydani, North Nicosia (0392 228 3115/saray.hotel@superonline.com). **€€**.

The Saray was the first Turkish Cypriot-owned hotel in Nicosia, and for many years the loftiest structure in the northern part of the town. Today, it is neither the finest nor the tallest building but, being the only hotel in the northern part of the walled city, it does offer the most central location. The hotel may have seen better days, but has been partially renovated in recent years and features a casino, club and restaurants.

Getting Around

Arriving & leaving

Most visitors to Cyprus will arrive into the Republic of Cyprus, whose legal entry points are Larnaka and Pafos airports and Larnaka, Lemesos, Latsi or Pafos ports. There is an airport in the Turkish-occupied north of the island, Tymbou (Ercan) but there are currently no direct flights here, as the region is not recognised by the international community; flights must arrive via Turkey. If you are planning to arrive into the north, check in advance with the Cypriot embassy in your home country whether or not you will be allowed to cross to the south.

By air

Note that the airports are still often referred to internationally as Larnaca and Paphos, respectively.

Larnaka International Airport

77 778 833/www.larnaca-airport.info. 5km from Larnaka (45km from Agia Napa, 50km from Nicosia, 70km from Lemesos, 140km from Pafos).

If your holiday package doesn't include transfers from the airport, taxis are available 24 hours a day outside the terminal building.

A bus service to all major towns exists, but is infrequent and somewhat unreliable. Kapnos Airport Shuttle (77 771 477, www.kapnosairportshuttle.com) runs regular services to the Filoxenia Hotel in Nicosia, from where you can hop into a taxi to your final destination. The service costs €7 and runs 5.30am-11pm (from Larnaka) and 5.30am-midnight (from Nicosia).

Pafos International Airport

77 778 833/www.pafos-airport.info. 15km from Pafos (180km from Agia Napa, 130km from Larnaka, 145km from Nicosia, 65km from Lemesos).

Taxis are available 24 hours a day outside the terminal building, and there is a regular bus service into Pafos.

By boat

Most passenger cruise liners arrive at Lemesos Port, the main port on the island. It is also is linked by ferries to Greece, Israel, Egypt and Lebanon. It serves a large number of cruise liners which use the port as a base or stopover. Note that the ports of Kyrenia and Famagusta in the Turkish-occupied north of the island are officially designated as illegal points of entry.

Car hire

Renting a car is a good idea if you want to travel independently around the island. All the main international firms are represented in Cyprus, with offices in all towns. EasyCar (www.easycar.com) operates online.

Astra Self Drive Cars

77 777 800/www.astracarrentals.com.

Budget

24 643 293/www.budgetcyprus.com.

Europcar

24 643 085/www.europcar.com.cy.

Hertz

24 643 388/www.hertz.com.cy.

Petsas Rent a Car

22 456 450/www.petsas.com.cy.

Public transport

Public transport in Cyprus is unreliable and inefficient. Very few people (bar pensioners or visitors) use public transport on the island. The only mode of public transport on offer is the bus network, but the service is poorly run, unreliable and with limited routes. Plans are in the works for the development of an improved urban public transport system, starting with Nicosia and Lemesos.

Nevertheless, do enquire about bus services to the mountain villages, which start from Nicosia's central bus station at Plateia Solomou (22 665 814). PEAL Troodos (25 552 220) has recently introduced a service to Troodos via Platres and other scenic villages, leaving from the CTO office on Germasogeia and from behind the central bus station.

Taxis

All taxis are legally obliged to have a meter. There are taxi ranks in all towns and they may also be flagged down on the street, but booking over the telephone is the easiest and most efficient way (www.cytayellowpages.com.cy). Be aware that fares are slightly more expensive after 8.30pm and on certain public holidays.

Taxis are relatively costly and therefore not recommended for travelling between towns. The best way to get from one town to another in Cyprus, if you're not driving yourself, is to take a Travel Express service taxi. The shared taxis pick you up and drop you off precisely where you want to go, and are much cheaper than normal taxis. They do take longer, however, as they collect passengers from various addresses around town and deliver them to their specific destinations. Taxis operate every half hour between all the main towns, with the last one leaving at 6pm. Routes served are Nicosia-Lemesos, Larnaka-Nicosia, Nicosia-Larnaka Airport, Larnaka-Lemesos, Lemesos-Larnaka Airport, Lemesos-Pafos and Lemesos-Pafos Airport.

Travel Express

77 777 474/www.travelexpress.com.cy.

How to cross to the north

On foot

There are several crossing points along the north–south border, of which the most commonly used by visitors are the two in Nicosia (Lefkosia). EU and US citizens are allowed into the north without visas at time of writing, though check in advance of a visit. Do not try and cross between the north and south other than at a designated checkpoint.

The opening of Nicosia's Ledra Street checkpoint in the wake of Cyprus's accession to the EU has eased the movement of locals and visitors across the border. Ledra Street is a mostly pedestrianised commercial road through the heart of old Nicosia; the crossing is for foot and bicycle traffic only. The wall that used to divide Ledra Street (or Lidras) in two was torn down in April 2008 and, for the first time since 1964, people can move freely back and forth. Passports or EU IDs still need to be presented at the Greek Cypriot and then Turkish Cypriot checkpoints. Once across, you will be within a few strides of most major sights.

If going through Ledra Palace, take the Pafos Gate roundabout and from there walk west along and from there walk west along the Venetian Walls. After a two-minute walk you will see the Greek Cypriot checkpoint. Just past that, you will enter the UN-controlled buffer zone. On your left is the famed Ledra Palace Hotel. Just in front of the hotel, you will see a small grey pavilion with a display of photographs and drawings documenting the Nicosia Master Plan, a project that focuses on the restoration of old buildings on both sides of Nicosia, funded by USAID and the EU. Ask inside for a free guide to Nicosia's historical and cultural sights and a map of the city.

When you reach the Turkish Cypriot checkpoint, you will be asked to show your passport. There is a taxi stand just beyond the checkpoint, but if your plan is simply to visit the old town, you won't need one; it's only five minutes away (go straight on from the checkpoint and turn right at the first traffic lights). Several currency exchange points are located on the same street. Almost all shops in the north accept Euros and pound sterling as well as Turkish lira.

By car

Crossing to the north by car requires additional insurance, as the insurance issued in the south is not valid in the occupied north. Insurance can be obtained either when you cross – several Turkish Cypriot insurance companies have their stands at each crossing point – or in advance, at the Ledra Palace checkpoint, where a friendly insurance man called Dervis will help you. (The Ledra Palace crossing itself is for pedestrians only.) On average, a three-day insurance package costs €17 and a month's €26, depending on the terms and conditions. Prices are the same for private and rental cars.

The Agios Dometios crossing point in Nicosia is about ten minutes' drive north-west from the city centre. Visitors should carry their passport and driving licence. Usually it will take five to ten minutes to cross, providing it is not a public holiday, when the queues are always longer (especially just before lunchtime). Then follow the signs for the motorway to Kyrenia (Girne), Famagusta (Gazi Mağusa) and Morphou (Güzelyurt).

The other checkpoints are useful if you are staying in Pafos or one of the Troodos mountain resorts (try Zodhia) or Agia Napa, Protaras or Paralimni (the Strovilia and Pergamos checkpoints are much closer than Agios Dometios).

Getting around north Cyprus

Taxis are a convenient way of getting around if you do not have your own car. There are two types of taxis, private ones and local service taxis. A one-way trip by private taxi from Nicosia to Kyrenia costs about €21, to Famagusta €43 and to Morphou €35. The service taxi company that goes to Kyrenia is Kombos, located at Elim Sokak 29, close to Kyrenia (Girne) Gate in north Nicosia. A one-way trip costs about €2.60. The service to Famagusta is run by Itimat (Yolu Sokak, just outside the walls) which charges €3.50 for a one-way journey. If you want to travel to Morphou, you should use Cimen (Yolu Sokak). The trip costs about €2.60 and taxis leave every 15 minutes.

There are also buses from north Nicosia to all main towns and villages. The bus station is located in Gazeteci Kemal Asik Caddessi, about 15 minutes' walk from the Ledra Palace crossing.

Resources A-Z

Accident & emergency

Below are listed the main district hospitals with 24-hour Accident & Emergency departments. Operators at all of them can be expected to speak English. For private doctors on call (during weekends and public holidays), call 90 901 432.

Cyprus uses 112, the EU-wide emergency number for police, fire and ambulance.

Agia Napa & Protaras
23 200 000.

Larnaka
24 800 500.

Lemesos
25 801 100.

Nicosia
22 603 000.

Pafos
26 803 100.

Credit card loss

JCC, the main credit card transaction processing company, operates a 24-hour service for lost or stolen cards.

JCC Payment Systems *22 868 100.*

Customs

For details of customs allowances, see www.visitcyprus.com.

Dental emergency

You will need to see a private dentist. Private doctors and dentists are available in every town. All hotels can make recommendations, and doctors and dentists will provide receipts for insurance purposes. They are also listed in the Yellow Pages, available online at www.cytayellowpages.com.cy.

Disabled travellers

Both Larnaka and Pafos airports are accessible for disabled travellers. Hotels with special facilities can be found in the Cyprus Tourism Organisation's (CTO) annual 'Guide to Hotels and other Tourist Establishments' publication. Transport around the island for wheelchair users, via bus and taxi, can be arranged with prior notice; the CTO can provide information.

GC Paraquip is a firm which hires out wheelchairs, scooters and other equipment for disabled visitors.

GC Paraquip *Megalou Alexandrou 3, Polis Chrysochous, Pafos (99 647 669/ www.paraquip.com.cy).*

Electricity

The standard current in Cyprus is 230V, 50 Hz. Three-pin rectangular plugs are used, as in the UK. Adaptors are widely available.

Embassies & consulates

Most embassies or consulates are headquartered in Nicosia.

American Embassy *Corner Metochiou & Ploutarchou (22 393 939).*

Australian High Commission *Annis Komninis 4, 2nd Floor (22 753001).*

British High Commission *Alexandrou Palli (22 861100).*

Irish Embassy *Aiantas 7 (22 818 183).*

Internet

Internet cafés can be found in all town centres.

Agia Napa *Backstage Internet Centre Ari Velouchioti 7 (23 816 097).*

Larnaka *Replay, Leoforos Athinon (24 621 588).*

Lemesos *Speednet, Georgiou I, Galaxy Court (25 320 404).*
Nicosia *Travelex Money Centre, Rigainis, next to Holiday Inn (22 451 020/22 818 766).*
Pafos *Intencity, Agias Napas 12 (77 772 055).*

Money

Cyprus adopted the euro on January 1 2008, when the currency replaced the Cyprus pound.

In the Turkish-occupied area, the Turkish lira is the 'official' currency, but most shops, restaurants and taxis accept US dollars and euros. Major credit cards are accepted almost everywhere in Cyprus.

Opening hours

Banks *Sept-Apr* 8.30am-1pm, 3.15-4.45pm Mon; 8.30am-1pm Tue-Fri. *May-Aug* 8.30am-1pm Mon-Fri. Centrally located banks provide an 'afternoon tourist service' by opening their foreign exchange counters.
Businesses *Mid Sept-May* 8am-1pm, 3-6pm Mon-Fri. *June-mid Sept* 8am-1pm, 4-7pm Mon-Fri.
Public services *Sept-June* 7.30am-2.30pm Mon-Wed, Fri; 7.30am-2.30pm, 3-6pm Thur. *June-Aug* 7.30am-2.30pm Mon-Fri.
Shops Shops open from 7am and 9am until the following times: *Nov-Mar* until 7.30pm Mon, Tue, Thur, Fri; 3pm Wed; 7pm Sat. *Apr-Oct* until 8pm Mon, Tue, Thur, Fri; 3pm Wed; 7.30pm Sat.

During the period June 15-Aug 31 there is an optional afternoon break between 3pm and 5pm.

Special shopping hours apply for Christmas and Easter. In December, shops may remain open until 8pm throughout the week, but must close by 6pm on Christmas Eve and New Year's Eve. Shops can also remain open until 8pm for ten days before Easter Sunday, but must close by 6pm on Good Friday. Post-Christmas, bigger shops and supermarkets reopen on Dec 26, but a lot of smaller shops take a longer break.

Pharmacies

Pharmacies are subject to the same opening hours as other shops. However, they take it in turns to stay open late at night on Sundays and public holidays. The names and addresses of late-night and emergency pharmacies are published in all daily newspapers, including the English-language *Cyprus Mail* and *Sunday Mail*, as well as in *The Cyprus Weekly* (published on Fridays).

Alternatively, this information is available by phone on the following numbers:
Agia Napa *90 901 413.*
Larnaka *90 901 414.*
Lemesos *90 901 415.*
Nicosia *90 901 412.*
Pafos *90 901 416.*

Police

Telephone numbers for police headquarters in each town are given below.
Agia Napa *23 803 200.*
Larnaka *24 630 200.*
Lemesos *25 805 050.*
Nicosia *22 802 020.*
Pafos *26 806 060.*

Post

Post offices in Cyprus offer airmail service, international money orders and Intelpost fax services worldwide, and Datapost courier services to 116 countries. All items, from the smallest letter to the heaviest parcel, must have a 2 cent Refugee Fund stamp affixed. Post Restante services, for those planning to spend an extended time on the island, are are offered by the central post offices listed below (except Agia Napa).

Main post offices

Agia Napa *Dimitri Liperti 3 (23 922 265).*
Larnaka *Plateia Vasileos Pavlou (24 802 406).*
Lemesos *Gladstonos 3 (25 802 259).*
Nicosia *Plateia Eleftherias (22 303 219).*
Pafos *Nicodemou Mylona (26 940 220).*

Opening hours

Opening hours for the main post offices (in Larnaka, Nicosia, Lemesos and Pafos town centres), are listed below and other post offices (including Agia Napa) are as follows:
Main post offices *Sept-June* 7.30am-1.30pm; 3-6pm Mon, Tue, Thur, Fri; 7.30am-1.30pm Wed; 8.30-10.30am Sat. *Jul, Aug* 7.30am-1.30pm, 4-7pm Mon, Tue, Thur, Fri; 7.30am-1.30pm Wed; 8.30-10.30am Sat.
Other post offices *Sept-June* 7.30am-1.30pm Mon, Tue, Wed, Fri; 3-6pm Thur. *July, Aug* 7.30am-1.30pm Mon-Fri.

Public holidays

The following are public holidays in the Republic of Cyprus. All public services, private enterprises, banks and shops are closed on public holidays, though many shops and certain services remain open in resorts and coastal areas. Banks are closed on Easter Tuesday but not Christmas Eve. Note that the two weeks around August 15 are the most popular time for Cypriots to take their holidays, so coastal resorts are extremely busy during this time.

Jan 1
New Year's Day
Jan 6
Epiphany
Feb/March
Green Monday (50 days before Greek Orthodox Easter)
March 25
Greek National Day
April 1
National Anniversary Day
April/May
Good Friday & Easter Monday (Greek Orthodox Church)
May 1
Labour Day
May/June
Pentecost (Kataklysmos)
Aug 15
Assumption of the Virgin Mary
Oct 1
Cyprus Independence Day
Oct 28
Greek National Anniversary Day
Dec 24
Christmas Eve
Dec 25
Christmas Day
Dec 26
Boxing Day

Smoking

Smoking is permitted in most areas. Certain venues such as airports have non-smoking areas, but these are rare. An outdoor table is your best bet for enjoying your meal without being surrounded by a fug of cigarette smoke.

Telephones

Cyprus phone numbers have eight digits, the first two of which are the area codes: 22 (Nicosia), 23 (Agia Napa, Protaras), 24 (Larnaka), 25 (Lemesos) and 26 (Pafos). Mobile numbers start with 99 or 96. Some new business numbers are prefixed 77.

To call Cyprus from abroad, dial 00 357 followed by the 8-digit number. For directory enquiries call 118 92, or 118 94 for international directory enquiries.

To call North Cyprus, dial 0090 for a mobile number, or 392 for a landline, followed by the area code and the number. At present it is impossible to send an SMS message from a Greek Cypriot mobile phone to a Turkish Cypriot one.

To dial abroad from Cyprus, first dial 00, then the relevant country code (Australia 61; Canada 1; New Zealand 64; Republic of Ireland 353; South Africa 27; UK 44; USA 1).

Public phones

Public phone booths take telecards or coins, and many now accept both. Telecards in €5 and €10 denominations are available from banks, post offices, souvenir shops, kiosks and Cyta (Cyprus Telecommunications Authority) shops in all towns. Coin-operated phones take 2 cent, 5 cent, 10 cent and 20 cent coins.

Tickets

Tickets can be purchased from the box offices of individual cultural institutions.

Time

Cyprus operates on Eastern European Time (EET), which is two hours ahead of Greenwich Mean Time. In spring, clocks are put forward one hour to Eastern European Summer Time, and in autumn they go back to EET.

Tipping

Tip in restauants, taxis, hotels and hairdressers. A 10 per cent service charge is often included in the bill at restaurants. It is customary to leave a further tip of 10 per cent. For taxis it is generally fine to round up the fare.

Tourist information

The **Cyprus Tourism Organisation** (CTO) (www.visitcyprus.com) is the country's official visitor information service, with branches in all towns, as well as at Larnaka and Pafos airports and Lemesos port.

Agia Napa *Kryou Nerou 12 (23 721 796).* **Open** 8.15am-1.30pm, 3-6pm Mon, Tue, Thur, Fri; 8.15am-1.30pm Wed, Sat.

Protaras *Cavo Greco 356 (23 832 865).* **Open** 9am-3pm Mon-Fri; 9am-2pm Sat.

Larnaka *Plateia Vassileos Pavlou (24 654 322).* **Open** 10am-1pm, 4-7pm Mon, Tue, Thur, Fri; 10am-1pm Sat.

Lemesos Town centre *Spyrou Araouzou 115A (25 362 756).* **Open** *Sept-June* 8.15am-2.30pm, 3-6.15pm Mon, Tue, Thur, Fri; 8.15am-2.30pm Wed; 8.15am-1.30pm Sat. *July, Aug* 8.15am-2.30pm, 4-6.30pm Mon, Tue, Thur, Fri; 8.15am-2.30pm Wed.

Lemesos Germasogeia *Georgiou I 22 (25 323 211).* **Open** *Sept-June* 8.15am-2.30pm, 3-6.15pm Mon, Tue, Thur, Fri; 8.15am-2.30pm Wed. *July, Aug* 8.15am-2.30pm, 4-6.30pm Mon, Tue, Thur, Fri; 8.15am-2.30pm Wed.

Nicosia *Aristokyprou 11 (22 674 264).* **Open** 8.30am-4pm Mon-Fri; 8.30am-2pm Sat.

Pafos Kato Pafos *Poseidonos 63A (26 930 521).* **Open** 10am-1pm, 4-7pm Mon, Tue, Thur, Fri; 10am-1pm Wed, Sat.

Pafos Ktima *Gladstonos 3 (26 932 841).* **Open** *Sept-June* 8.15am-2.30pm, 3-6.15pm Mon, Tue, Thur, Fri; 8.15am-2.30pm Wed. *July, Aug* 8.15am-2.30pm, 4-6.30pm Mon, Tue, Thur, Fri; 8.15am-2.30pm Wed.

What's on

English-language newspapers the *Cyprus Mail*, published Tuesday to Sunday, and *The Cyprus Weekly*, published on Fridays, carry events listings. *Time Out Cyprus* is published monthly in Greek.

Visas

Citizens from the EU, United States, Canada, Australia and many other countries do not require a visa to enter Cyprus for periods of up to 90 days. Check current status on www.mfa.gov.cy well before you travel.

Menu Glossary

The island's geographic position and its long succession of conquerors make for a menu that encompasses culinary influences from sources including Greece, Turkey and the Middle East. Dishes marked (GC) indicate a Greek Cypriot speciality.

Meze (plural *mezedes*) are a selection of either hot or cold appetisers and main dishes.

Drinks

Commandaria (GC) *a sweet, robust red dessert wine.*
zivania (GC) *a clear alcohol, distilled from the skins and stalks of local grape varieties; similar to Italian grappa.*

Starters, side dishes & meze

gigantes or **gigandes** *white butter beans baked in tomato sauce; pronounced 'yigandes'.*
horiatiki salata *Greek 'village' salad of tomato, cucumber, onion, feta and sometimes green pepper, dressed with ladolemono (oil and lemon).*
horta *side dish of cooked wild greens.*
houmous or **hummus** *a dip of puréed chickpeas, tahini, lemon juice and garlic, garnished with paprika. Originally an Arabic dish.*
skordalia *a garlic and breadcrumb or potato-based dip, used as a side dish.*
koukia *broad beans.*
koupepia *young vine leaves stuffed with rice, spices and (usually) minced lamb. Known as dolmades in Greece.*
melitzanosalata *purée of chargrilled aubergines.*
spanakopitta *small pastries, traditionally triangular, stuffed with spinach, dill and often feta or some other crumbly, tart cheese.*
taboulleh *generic Middle Eastern starter of bulghur wheat, chopped parsley, cucumber chunks, tomatoes and spring onions.*
tahini *A dip made with sesame seed paste, garlic, lemon and olive oil.*
taramas, properly **taramosalata** *fish roe pâté, originally made of dried, salted grey mullet roe, but now more often smoked cod roe, plus olive oil, lemon juice and breadcrumbs.*
trahanas *a mixture of cracked wheat and milk, sun-dried and used to make a soup incorporating pieces of halloumi and sometimes chicken.*
tsakistes (GC) *split green olives marinated in lemon, garlic, coriander seeds and other optional flavourings.*
tzatziki or **talatouri** (GC) *a dip of shredded cucumber, yoghurt, garlic, lemon juice and mint.*

Main meals

afelia (GC) *pork cubes, ideally from filleted leg or shoulder, stewed in wine with coriander and other herbs.*
avgolemono *a sauce made of lemon, egg yolks and chicken stock. Also a soup made with rice, chicken stock, lemon and whole eggs.*
gemista *vegetables (often tomatoes and peppers) stuffed with mince meat, rice, onion and herbs.*
keftedes *herby meatballs made with minced pork or lamb (rarely beef), egg, breadcrumbs and sometimes grated potato.*

kleftiko (GC) *slow-roasted lamb on the bone (often shoulder), stewed in wine with coriander and other herbs.*
koupes or **koubes** *croquettes made with a mixture of minced beef and pork, onions and parsley, coated in bulghur wheat and fried.*
moussaka *a baked dish of mince (usually lamb), aubergine and potato slices and herbs, topped with béchamel sauce.*
pourgouri or **bourgouri** (GC) *a pilaf of cracked bulghur wheat, often prepared with stock, onions, crumbled vermicelli and spices.*
sheftalia (GC) *little sausages stuffed with minced pork and lamb, onion, parsley, breadcrumbs and spices, then grilled. Usually served with souvlaki.*
souvla *large cuts of lamb or pork, slow-roasted on a rotary spit.*
souvlaki *chunks of meat quick-grilled on a skewer (known in takeaways abroad as shish kebab).*
tavas (GC) *lamb, onion, tomato and cumin, cooked in an earthenware casserole.*
stifado *a rich meat stew (often beef or rabbit) with onions, red wine, tomatoes, cinnamon and bay.*

Meat

hiromeri (GC) *smoked pork leg matured in wine.*
loukanika or **lukanika** *spicy coarse-ground sausages, usually pork and heavily herbed.*
lountza (GC) *smoked pork loin.*
pastourmas *dense, dark-tinted garlic sausage, usually made from beef.*

Fish & seafood

garides *prawns, fried or grilled.*
kalamari, **kalamarakia** or **calamari** *small squid, usually sliced into rings, battered and fried.*
marides *picarel, often mistranslated as (or substituted by) 'whitebait' – small fish coated in flour and flash-fried.*
psarosoupa *fish soup.*

Cheese

anari (GC) *a cheese made from goat or sheep's milk which can be hard or soft. The fresh, soft version is often drizzled with honey as a dessert. When salt is added and it matures, it is grating over savoury dishes.*
feta *a crumbly, sharp cheese made either from sheep's milk or a mixture of sheep and goat's milk.*
flaouna (GC) *a traditional sweet-and-savoury Easter pastry filled with cheese, eggs and often raisins.*
halloumi (GC) *a rubbery-textured cheese traditionally made from sheep or goat's milk, but increasingly from cow's milk. Best served fried or grilled.*
saganaki *fried cheese, usually kefalotyri; also means anything (mussels, spinach) made in a cheese-based red sauce.*
tyropitta *general name for a variety of cheese pies, some of which may be similar to spanakopitta but without spinach.*

Desserts & sweets

baklava *a pan-Middle Eastern sweet made from sheets of filo layered with nuts.*
galatoboureko or **galaktoboureko** *sweet egg custard in filo pastry.*
glyko *literally 'sweet' – preserved fruits in syrup, served with a spoon.*
kataifi or **kateifi** *syrup-soaked 'shredded-wheat' rolls.*
loukoumades or **lokmades** *tiny, spongy dough fritters, dipped in honey.*
loukoumi *or* **lukumi** *'Turkish delight' made with syrup, rosewater and pectin, often studded with nuts.*

Index

Sights & Areas

ESSENTIALS